Undertones of War

EDMUND BLUNDEN (1896–1974) was raised in Kent and educated at Christ's Hospital and at Queen's College, Oxford. His first two collections of poetry were published in 1914, the year before he volunteered with the Royal Sussex Regiment. During World War I Blunden won the Military Cross for his actions at the battles of Ypres and Sommes.

Winner of the Hawthornden Prize for Poetry in 1922, Blunden went on to hold academic posts in Tokyo and Hong Kong. He was a Fellow of Merton College, Oxford, from 1931 to 1944, and was elected Professor of Poetry there in 1966, succeeding Robert Graves. Blunden published several volumes of poetry, as well as studies of Charles Lamb, Leigh Hunt, Percy Bysshe Shelley, and Thomas Hardy. He also edited collections of poetry by Wilfred Owen and Ivor Gurney.

EDMUND BLUNDEN

Undertones of War

THE UNIVERSITY OF CHICAGO PRESS

The University of Chicago Press, Chicago, 60637
Copyright © Edmund Blunden, 1928
All rights reserved.
First published November 1928
University of Chicago Press edition 2007
Printed in the United States of America
16 15 14 13 12 11 10   2 3 4 5

ISBN-13: 978-0-226-06176-4 (paper)
ISBN-10: 0-226-06176-0 (paper)

Library of Congress Cataloging-in-Publication Data
Blunden, Edmund, 1896–1974.
    Undertones of war / Edmund Blunden.
          p. cm.
    Originally published: London : R. Cobden-Sanderson. 1928.
    ISBN-13: 978-0-226-06176-4 (pbk. : alk. paper)
    ISBN-10: 0-226-06176-0 (pbk. : alk. paper)
    1. Blunden, Edmund, 1896–1974.   2. World War, 1914–1918—Personal narratives, British.   3. World
War, 1914–1918—Poetry.   4. Great Britain. Army—Biography.   5. War poetry, English.   6. Soldiers—
Great Britain—Biography.   I. Title.
    D640.B5833 2007
    940.4'1241092—dc22
    [B]

                                                                                        2007022665

♾ The paper used in this publication meets the minimum requirements of the American National
Standard for Information Sciences—Permanence of Paper for Printed Library Materials,
ANSI Z39.48-1992.

A Harmless Young Shepherd: Edmund Blunden

An extended pastoral elegy in prose is what Blunden's *Undertones of War* (1928) may be called. Whatever it is, (G. S. Fraser once called it "the best war *poem*" and printed some of it as free verse in the *London Magazine*), no one disagrees that together with Sassoon's and Graves's "memoirs" it is one of the permanent works engendered by memories of the war. Its distinction derives in large part from the delicacy with which it deploys the properties of traditional English literary pastoral in the service of the gentlest (though not always the gentlest) kind of irony. If Spenser or Milton or Gray or Collins or Clare or the author of *Thyrsis* had fought in the Great War, any one of them could have used Blunden's final image to end a memoir of it. With a due sense of theatrical costume and an awareness of a young subaltern's loving responsibility for the flock under his care, Blunden brings *Undertones of War* to a close by calling himself "a harmless young shepherd in a soldier's coat." That characterization is English to a fault, and beautiful.

He was eighteen when the war began. Early in 1915 he joined the Royal Sussex Regiment as one of its youngest, most innocent lieutenants. He was nicknamed "Rabbit" and later, "Bunny." In May, 1916, he was in the trenches. Guy Chapman remembers: "On our third evening in Hedge Street we welcomed a very young, very fair and very shy subaltern from Royal Sussex, who were to relieve us the next day. . . . I showed our incoming tenant from the Sussex over his noxious habitation. As we bade him good-bye, he shyly put a small paper-covered book into my hand. *The Harbingers,* ran the title, 'Poems by E. C. Blunden.'" After two years at the front, during which he was gassed and won the Military Cross (typically, he withholds mention of either event in *Undertones of War*), he was invalided home to a training camp in March, 1918.

When all is said, it is the sheer literary quality of *Undertones of War* that remains with a reader. One does not forget its rhythms ("Musically sounded the summer wind in the trees of Festubert) nor its shrewd, witty reliance on etymology: "The officer and I, having nothing to do but wait, sat in a trench . . . considering the stars in their courses." Blunden's weakness, on the other hand, is a calculation so precise, even niggling, that on occasion it leads to the archness of the confirmed schoolmaster. . . . The constant allusion and quotation reveal a mind playing over a past felt to be not at all military or political but only literary. The style is busy with rhetorical questions and exclamations, with half-serious apostrophes evocative of Sterne. A pleasant room in a farm cottage behind the line is thus addressed: "Peaceful little one, standest thou yet? cool nook, earthly paradisal cupboard with leaf-green light to see poetry by, I fear much that 1918 was the ruin of thee." And the archaism points back even earlier than to Sterne, back to Sir Thomas Browne and Robert Burton and Isaak Walton, who might lament of the peasantry very much the way Blunden ironically does of the infantry: "There is no pleasing your ancient infantryman. Attack him, or cause him to attack, he seems equally disobliging."

But archaism is more than an overeducated tic in Blunden. It is directly implicated in his meaning. With language as with landscape, his attention is constantly on pre-industrial England, the only repository of criteria for measuring fully the otherwise unspeakable grossness of the war. In a world where literary quality of Blunden's sort is conspicuously an antique, every word of *Undertones of War*, every rhythm, allusion, and droll personification, can be recognized as an assault on the war and on the world which chose to conduct and continue it. Blunden's style is his critique. It suggests what the modern world would look like to a sensibility that was genuinely civilized.

Is Blunden "escaping" into the past? If he is, let him. But I don't think he is. He is, rather, engaging the war by selecting from the armory of the past weapons against it which seem to have the greatest chance of withstanding time. In his own shy way, he is hurling himself totally and emotionally into opposition. This is what H. M. Tomlinson seems to recognize when he says of *Undertones of War,* "Something in Blunden's story is more than queer. . . . This poet's eye is not in a fine frenzy rolling. There is a steely glitter in it." We can now begin to understand what Blunden is getting at when in his "Preliminary" he says that he's afraid "no one will read it. . . . No one? Some, I am sure; but not many. *Neither will they understand . . .*"

From 254–69 of *The Great War and Modern Memory* by Paul Fussell

© Oxford University Press

Dedicated to Philip Tomlinson
Wishing him a lasting peace and myself his companionship in Peace or War

It is lawful for Christian men, at the commandment of the Magistrate, to wear weapons, and serve in the wars.

Articles of the Church of England
No. xxxvii

Yea, how they set themselves in battle-array
I shall remember to my dying day.

John Bunyan

Contents

Preliminary xv
Preface to the Second Edition xvii

i The Path without Primroses 3

ii Trench Education 7

iii The Cherry Orchard 20

iv The Sudden Depths 25

v Contrasts 34

vi Specimen of the War of Attrition 42

vii Steel Helmets for All 48

viii The Calm 53

ix The Storm 61

x A Home from Home 74

xi Very Secret 83

xii Cæsar Went into Winter Quarters 95

xiii The Impossible Happens 105

xiv An Ypres Christmas 109

xv Theatre of War 117

xvi A German Performance 125

Contents

xvii Departures   128

xviii Domesticities   137

xix The Spring Passes   143

xx Like Samson in his Wrath   149

xxi The Crash of Pillars   154

xxii Backwaters   161

xxiii The Cataract   167

xxiv 1917 in Fading Light   172

xxv Coming of Age   178

xxvi School, not at Wittenberg   182

xxvii My Luck   185

A Supplement of Poetical Interpretations and Variations

A House in Festubert   195

The Guard's Mistake   196

Two Voices   197

Illusions   197

Escape   198

Preparations for Victory   199

Come On, My Lucky Lads   200

At Senlis Once   201

The Zonnebeke Road   201

Trench Raid near Hooge   203

Concert Party: Busseboom   204

Rural Economy   205

E.W.T.: On the Death of his Betty   206

Battalion in Rest   207

Vlamertinghe: Passing the Chatêau, July, 1917   208

Third Ypres   209

Pillbox   212

The Welcome   213

Gouzeaucourt: The Deceitful Calm   214

The Prophet   215

II Peter ii, 22   217

Recognition   218

La Quinque Rue   219

The Ancre at Hamel: Afterwards   220

'Trench Nomenclature'   221

A.G.A.V.   222

Their Very Memory   223

*On Reading that the Rebuilding of Ypres approached
   Completion*   224

Another Journey from Béthune to Cuinchy   227

Flanders Now   231

Return of the Native   232

The Watchers   233

Preliminary

Why should I not write it?

I know that the experience to be sketched in it is very local, limited, incoherent; that it is almost useless, in the sense that no one will read it who is not already aware of all the intimations and discoveries in it, and many more, by reason of having gone the same journey. No one? Some, I am sure; but not many. *Neither will they understand* – that will not be all my fault.

I know that memory has her little ways, and by now she has concealed precisely that look, that word, that coincidence of nature without and nature within which I long to remember. Within the space of even one year, this divinity seems to me to take a perverse pleasure in playing with her votaries; 'you'd like to see this, my friend' (she shows for the second time the veiled but seemingly perfect novocreation of some heart-throbbing scene – she slides it into secrecy) 'wouldn't you?' But I am inclined to think that her playfulness has been growing rather more trying latterly: and perhaps I am gradually becoming colder in my enthusiasm to win a few games. If these things are so, it is now or never for the rendering, however discoloured and lacunary, which I propose.

I tried once before. True, when the events were not yet ended, and I was drifted into a backwater. But what I then wrote, and little enough I completed, although in its details not much affected by the perplexities of distancing memory, was noisy with a depressing forced gaiety then very much the rage. To call a fellow creature 'old bean' may be well and good; but to approach in the beanish style such mysteries as Mr Hardy forthshadowed in *The Dynasts* is to have misunderstood, and to pull Truth's nose.

And I have been attempting 'the image and horror of it,' with some other personations, in poetry. Even so, when the main sheaves appeared fine enough to my flattering eye, it was impossible not to look again, and to descry the ground, how thickly and innumerably yet it was strewn with the facts or notions of war experience.

I must go over the ground again.

A voice, perhaps not my own, answers within me. You will be going over the ground again, it says, until that hour when agony's clawed face softens into the smilingness of a young spring day; when you, like Hamlet, your prince of peaceful war-makers, give the ghost a '*Hic et ubique?* then we'll change our ground,' and not that time in vain; when it shall be the simplest thing to take in your hands and hands of companions like E. W. T., and W. J. C., and A. G. V., in whose recaptured gentleness no sign of death's astonishment or time's separation shall be imaginable.

Tokyo, 1924.
E. B.

Among the poems now printed, only one, 'Third Ypres,' is taken from the author's book of verse called *The Shepherd*, it being one of his most comprehensive and particular attempts to render war experience poetically. Through *The Shepherd* and *The Waggoner* are scattered other war poems, which the author has taken the liberty of indicating to those interested, as a genuine supplement to the present work, although to reprint them now was considered to be too much like bookmaking in view of their being already easily accessible.

Preface to the Second Edition

It has been read and understood by many, this attempt on the oracular archives of the War; and now I fear that in making some corrections of phrase or letter, and rescuing an occasional significance that had been omitted, I may be blamed by some who liked the original statement. That was written in Japan with no other assistance than the old maps Hazebrouck 5A and Lens 11 and one of the Cemeteries in Ypres Salient. Hence some confusions and telescopings. I am now in reach of authorities and papers which could perhaps direct me towards blue-book precision. However, there is no heavy reconstruction anywhere; and even some uncertainties of time and situation, about which I have been notified, are left, because their character was genuine. Among the lucky issues of the book, I count conspicuously the return into my little world of Sergeant Worley; without him I should have seen War and Peace in other hues; I speak of this because several readers wished that my question (I leave it as it was at p. 45) might be favourably answered. Many other names have come back as living friends; but indeed there is a future where the roll-call will be read with a full answer.

Despite some protests, I retain the poems; if they are of no other quality, they supply details and happenings which would have strengthened the prose had I not already been impelled to express them, and are among such keys as I can provide to the fuller memory.

No book could have been honoured with more generous readers, and I should be at fault if I did not thank here both the critics (at home and abroad) and the wider audience who, mindful of the front-line meaning of the late war, welcomed these 'Undertones.'

E. B.

xvii

Third Edition

Some slight corrections and additional observations are made on re-reading, in September 1930.

Undertones of War

i

The Path without Primroses

I was not anxious to go. An uncertain but unceasing disquiet had been upon me, and when, returning to the officers' mess at Shoreham Camp one Sunday evening, I read the notice that I was under orders for France, I did not hide my feelings. Berry, a subaltern of my set, who was also named for the draft, might pipe to me, 'Hi, Blunden, we're going out: have a drink'; I could not dance. There was something about France in those days which looked to me, despite all journalistic enchanters, to be dangerous. For a fortnight or so I had been in charge of a squad of men nominally recovered from wounds and awaiting their next transmigration. It had been my happiness to march them out to a place at once as sequestered and sunny as I could find, overlooking the lazy Adur, and there to let them bask on the grass, and tell their tales, and be peaceful. How contentedly they had rested in the lucky sun! Nor was much said among them – their thoughts were their conversation. In that brief fortnight I began to love these convalescent soldiers, and their distinguishing demeanour sank into me. They hid what daily grew plain enough – the knowledge that the war had released them only for a few moments, that the war would reclaim them, that the war was a jealous war and long-lasting. 1914, 1915, 1916 ... Occasionally I would ask the silly questions of non-realization; they in their tolerance pardoned, smiled and hinted, knowing that I was learning, and should not escape the full lesson.

Such formalities as were attached to a temporary second lieutenant's departure for the front no doubt took place on Monday morning, but I have forgotten them. The adjutant, warranted by expert observers to have been previously a commercial traveller, though I did not think his heavy gleamless manner supported that theory, smiled sourly, and inwardly congratulated himself on having four fewer unnecessary officers. (There were still about 150 to dispose of.) The commanding officer, a timid fragile man, gave me (as his way was) a pocket Testament bound in green suède, with coloured pictures. It went with me always, mainly unconsulted; it survives. I took myself off to Framfield, home, and all too soon it came out why. Walks and depredations round the glebelands, and stolen fishing at Heaver's Mill, and Sunday service with its acceptable display of amusing human peculiarity – all faded from my head, and my brothers and sisters allowed a melancholy hue to steal upon their mood. The builder's daughter too showed signs of emotion, under the evening star.

My mother went to the station with me, between pride and revolt – but the war must be attended to. Next, let us remark the platforms of Victoria, on this occasion perceptibly more remarkable to me than hitherto. That evening, a lugubriously merry Highlander and a sturdy Engineer, to whom I had democratically appealed for help on some matter, who were themselves returning to the British Expeditionary Force next morning, asked me my age. I replied; and, discipline failing, the Scotchman murmured to himself 'Only a boy – only a boy,' and shed tears, while his mate grunted an angry sympathy. Then, 'But you'll be all right, son – excuse me, won't you? – you'll be all right!' They were discussing the diminished prospect of a bombardment of Lille when I withdrew.

Light does not gleam upon the immediately following journey; surely I shall recall, from that crisis of my life above all, the evanescence of England beyond the grey waves, and the imminence of France. Surely the usual submarine excitement, and avoidance of the captain selecting victims for duties, marked the crossing. Something about an hotel, and manful drinks, and going down to the saloon for a plate of ham, and meeting a school-fellow pensively returning to the line, and then the cloak-room at Boulogne Station, flutters dimly for elucidation; there was a train journey between verdurous banks and silvering poplars, ending drearily at Etaples, known as Eatapples or Heeltaps. The Base! dismal tents, huge wooden warehouses, glum roadways, prisoning wire. I took my share of a tent, trying to remember the way to freedom, and laid on my valise the ebony walking-stick which had been my grandfather's, and was to be my pilgrim's staff. It went. I was away from it only a few minutes – it went. But this was before the war was officially certified to be making the world safe for democracy.

Was it on this visit to Etaples that some of us explored the church – a fishing-village church – and took tea comfortably in an inn? Those tendernesses ought not to come, however dimly, in my notions of Etaples. I associate it, as millions do, with 'The Bull-Ring,' that thirsty, savage, interminable training-ground. Marching up to it, in the tail of a long column, I was surprised by shouts from another long column dustily marching the other way: and there, sad-smiling, waving hands and welcoming, were two or three of the convalescent squad who had been so briefly mine on the April slopes opposite Lancing. I never saw them again; they were hurried once more, fast as corks on a mill-stream, without complaint into the bondservice of destruction. Thinking of them, and the pleasant chance of their calling to me, and the evil quickness with which their wounds had been made no defence against a new immolation, I found myself on the sandy, tented training-ground. The machine-guns there thudded at their targets, for the benefit of those who had advanced through wire entanglements against such furies equally with beginners like myself. And then the sunny morning was darkly interrupted. Rifle-grenade instruction began. A Highland sergeant-major stood magnificently before us, with the brass brutality called a Hales rifle-grenade in his hand. He explained the piece, fingering the wind-vane with easy assurance; then stooping to the fixed rifle, he prepared to shoot the grenade by way of demonstration. According to my unsoldierlike habit, I had let the other students press near the instructor, and was listlessly standing on the skirts of the meeting, thinking of something else, when the sergeant-major having just said 'I've been down here since 1914, and never had an accident,' there was a strange hideous clang. Several voices cried out; I found myself stretched on the floor, looking upwards in the delusion that the grenade had been fired straight above and was about to fall among us. It had indeed been fired, but by some error had burst at the muzzle of the rifle: the instructor was lying with mangled head, dead, and others lay near him, also blood-masked, dead and alive. So ended that morning's work on the Bull-Ring.

This particular shock, together with the general dreariness of the great camp, produced in me (in spite of the fear with which I had come into France) a wish to be sent quickly to the line. The wish was answered the next afternoon or thereabouts. I hear now the tink-tink-tink of the signal bell, the thin insistent cry Abbéville, Abbéville, through the dark; but many train journeys made later in that curious country have with their rumbling wheels and jerking, banging trucks drowned the self-story of that first one. At last we were unloaded at Béthune, many young officers and bulging valises; it was morning, a staff officer or two walked and illumined the platform. That sinister war was not far off, and air seemed to communicate without noise or any definite instance; but I looked along the railway track going on eastwards, and saw how high the grass and weeds had grown between certain of the metals. Orders were given me: with my excellent companion Doogan, a plump, ironical, unscareable Irishman, and others, I was to travel by light railway to Locon, a place of which the newspapers had not spoken. Meanwhile, Doogan decided that we must have coffee before setting out again, and he had led the way into a shop outside the station, and with little or no French caused two cheerful cups to appear, when there was shouting outside, and across the cobbled square the little street-train for Locon was on the instant of departing.

Locon is a few miles north of Béthune. Many times afterwards did the blush come to my cheeks as I recalled my asking a sapper, on this first approach, whether things were very noisy at Locon. In truth it was not a long way behind the trenches, but those trenches were a 'rest sector,' and peace prevailed much nearer their barbed wire and rusty tins than Locon. The steam-car rattled on. 'Are we anywhere near Manchester?' shouted a Tommy to a peasant on the track. We presently alighted in a muddy country road, alongside a green ditch and a row of short willow-stubs, looked for our valises in the heap, and then were haled to a kind of loft, the Brigade office, to be told our further proceeding. 'Report at le Touret.' The battalion mess-cart was coming to carry us.

ii

Trench Education

Although May had come, the day was dull and the clouds trailed sadly. In the hooded cart, we sat listening to the strong Sussex of the driver and looking out on the cultivated fields and the colonnades of trim trees. Here, explained the transport man, turning a corner, a night or two before, the Germans had dropped several very large shells almost on top of the quartermaster and his horse. Blew his horse one-sided. This information sat heavily on me. The roar of a heavy battery, soon following, also troubled me, for as yet I did not know that sound from the crash of arriving shells. ' 'Tis only some 'eavies our party brought up yesterday.' The heavy battery was firing at the German area over the farmhouse, chickens, children and all, which ended this stage of our progress. Rustic le Touret was apparently making no such heavy weather of the war. In the farm we found the Quartermaster, Swain, and the Padre. It was a cool, shady, swept and garnished interior in which Swain first came into our view, a man whose warmth of heart often cheers me in these later times, a plain, brave, affectionate man. Swain had come from Canada to the battalion, his hair already gone grey, his cheeks bright, and his eyes gleaming purpose. I well remember him crossing the flagged floor of the farmer's parlour to welcome and accustom two boys. He did it well, for he had a boyish readiness about him, such as gave confidence – and he knew what danger was and what duty was. Fear he respected, and he exemplified self-conquest.

Swain told us that the Colonel wished us to go up to the battalion in the front line that evening 'with the rations.' He gave us tea. He gave us anecdotes, even rallying the Padre on a visit to a boot-shop in Béthune. The howitzer occasionally loosing off outside punctuated these amenities. The Padre, a Catholic, selected Doogan as his affinity, Doogan also being a Catholic, and I felt that he repulsed me. Speak, any relic of honesty that may be in Blunden – was it not this slight and natural inequality, at this time, which caused you afterwards to spread satirical parodies of the Padre's voice, remarks and habits? Walking up and down the road after tea, the new-comers fell in with friends who had been until lately in training with them. One of these, who came into view at the entrance to a YMCA canteen, was a doubtful blessing; he was noted for hairy raggedness and the desire to borrow a little money; he now appeared stumping along as though with a millstone about his neck, and, questioned, did not comfort us. The line was hell, he said, and flung his arms heavenwards as some explosions dully shook the silence. It was a likely description with him. In the huts at Shoreham, months before, he had been wont to quote soulfully the wild-west verses of Robert Service, then read by thousands, cantering rhetoric about huskies and hoboes on icy trails; at length he had said, with the modest yet authoritative tone suitable to such a disclosure, 'I AM – Robert Service.' Some believed. He never retreated from the claim; we heard it again in France; and the poor fellow was at last killed at Richebourg on June 30th in a hell more sardonic and sunnily devilish than ten thousand Robert Services could evolve, or wolves and grizzlies inhabit.

The other acquaintance was F. Prior, whose reputation was that of dryness and common sense. He, too, objected to the line. It was not a line at all, he said. I put in something about 'trenches?' 'Trenches be damned,' he said, 'look here, I went up the *road* to the front line two nights ago and had to lie in the ditch every two minutes. There's only one road and Fritz puts machine-guns on it through the night. Same on the duckboard track. Lend us your notebook.' He drew a sketch something like this (see page 9). So the scattered breastwork posts called the Islands were our front line: no communication trench sheltered the approach to them. What, at this stage of the war? Yes, shamelessly. But, the newspaper correspondents? F. Prior told us to expect nothing, and went his ways.

In the shallow ditch outside that le Touret farm, among the black mud now nearly dry, were to be seen a variety of old grenades brown with rust, tumbled in with tin cans and broken harness. I looked at them with suspicion; and later on, returning on some errand, I saw them again. Why did no one see to it that these relics were duly destroyed? For that same summer they brought death to some sauntering Tommy whose curiosity led him to disturb the heap, seeming safe because of its antiquity. This was a characteristic of the war – that long talon reaching for its victim at its pleasure.

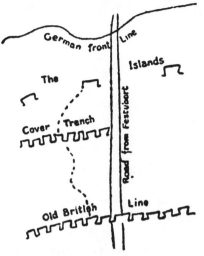

When dark had fallen, 'the rations' went up, a jolting, clattering series of waggons and limbers; Doogan and myself crept along somewhere in the middle, with the mules behind us nosing forward in a kindly manner, as if wishing to impart some experience to the novices. It seemed a great way, but it cannot have been so, before this column, passing cellars from which lights yellowed through chinks hung with canvas or blankets, halted. The rations were unloaded and packed in trolleys waiting at the edge of a field by several soldiers who had met the transport there with a bantering exchange of family remarks and criticism. With this ration-party Doogan and I went awkwardly up the tram-lines, often helping to push the trolleys, which fell off their wooden railway now and then.

It was both profoundly dark and still. In the afternoon, looking eastward from le Touret, I had seen nothing but green fields and plumy grey-green trees and intervening tall roofs; it was as though in this part the line could only be a trifling interruption of a happy landscape. I thought, the Vicarage must lie among those sheltering

9

boughs. Now at night, following a trolley along a track which needed watching, I as yet made out little more about the fighting man's zone, except the occasional lights flying on a curve and sinking away on the horizon. When at last the trolleys were at their terminus, and Doogan and myself went with a guide to report to battalion headquarters, several furious insect-like zips went past my ear, and slowly enough I connected these noises with loud hollow popping of rifles ahead, and knew that the fear of my infancy, to be among flying bullets, was now realized. The sense of being exposed suddenly predominated. We crossed a narrow wooden bridge, and came under the shelter of a sandbank rampart, which to eyes striving through the darkness appeared vast and safe.

Battalion headquarters was in this rampart, the Old British Line. It was a simple little cave, with a plain table and candlelight, and earth walls concealed with canvas. In it sat the commanding officer, H. J. Grisewood, dark-eyed and thoughtful, his brother, F. Grisewood, and his adjutant, T. Wallace. A somewhat severe air prevailed and not much was said, except that the Colonel was glad to see us, remarking that we were the first officer reinforcements to reach the 11th Royal Sussex. Of Colonel Grisewood, I cannot add much, for I seldom rose to the eminence of conversation with him. Once, presently, as we marched back to billets, he corrected me for carrying an untrimmed and sizeable stick which I had found in the line, ordering me to respect society and 'get an ash plant.' He was very grave and conscientious; there is an admiring view of him in Neville Lytton's *The Press and the General Staff.*

Doogan was sent to A Company, I believe, then in the front trench; and luckier I, as I felt, to C Company in the Old British Line, along which on a greasy wooden track a guide soon led me past solemn sentries and strings of men with shovels and other burdens. The dugout in which C Company officers were was smaller and blacker and much more humane than that where the dark-eyed Grisewoods and austere Wallace sat. I had, of course, more introductions at once. In charge of C Company was the boyish Captain Penruddock, perhaps one-and-twenty years old, rosy-faced, slender, argumentative. Second in command, Edmond Xavier Kapp appeared, ready with scribbles and charcoal drawings not unworthy of his reputation as a satirical artist. Charlwood, inclined to stammer, who as I soon found out had played cricket for Sussex, and Limbery-Buse, the 'Lumbering Bus,' who did stammer, made up the headquarters. These I saw in the dugout. A call, 'Mess,' produced a young soldier like Mr Pickwick's Fat Boy in khaki, who went away (humming 'Everybody calls me Teddy') with his orders, and soon I was given a large enamel plate full of meat and vegetable rations; not long after, Penruddock told me to 'get down to it.' At this early stage unused to going without sleep, I felt very weary, and gladly crawled into a kind of low recess in the dugout, where with sandbags below, above, around, and my British warm-coat, it was easy to sleep and sleep deeply, too.

I am ashamed to remember that I was accused of sleeping ten hours. The morning when I emerged was high and blue and inspiriting, but the landscape somewhat tattered and dingy. I washed ungrudgingly in a biscuit-tin, and Limbery-Buse took me for a walk along the reserve line, explaining as we went the system of sentries and trench duty. At some points in the trench, bones pierced through their shallow burial, and skulls appeared like mushrooms. The men with whom I was now consorted instantly appeared good men, shy, quiet, humorous and neat. The sandbag walls did not look so mighty as the night before, but still I thought that they must be able to withstand a great deal. Limbery-Buse thought not. As I look back on those breastworks, very often single walls, with no protection at all against the back-blast of shells, with their wooden fire-steps, their roofings of corrugated iron or old doors, I am of his opinion; and even that first morning I might have known; for the howling and whooping of shells suddenly began, and a small brick outbuilding between our trench and Festubert village behind began to jump away in explosions of dusty yellow smoke. The sight was attractive, until Limbery-Buse mentioned that Fritz might drop a shell or two short of his ruin, and in that event we were standing in the probable point of impact.

One of the first things that I was asked in C Company dugout was, 'Got any peace talk?' It was a rhetorical question. One of the first ideas that established themselves in my inquiring mind was the prevailing sense of the endlessness of the war. No one here appeared to conceive any end to it. I soon knew that

> Day succeeded unto day,
>> Night to pensive night.

Such as it was, the Old British Line at Festubert had the appearance of great age and perpetuity; its weather-beaten sandbag wall was already venerable. It shared the past with the defences of Troy. The skulls which spades disturbed about it were in a manner coeval with those of the most distant wars; there is an obstinate remoteness about a skull. And, as for the future, one of the first hints that came home to me was implied in a machine-gun emplacement stubbornly built in brick and cement, as one might build a house.

We were well off in this reserve trench, though my blood ran high in the excitement of novelty. In the evenings, while some of the men were amusing themselves in digging out a colony of rats, for which sport they had enlisted a stray terrier, there would suddenly begin a tremendous upheaval two or three miles to the south. The officers not on definite duty would leave their dinner to stand and terrify their eyes with this violence. On the blue and lulling mist of evening, proper to the nightingale, the sheepbell and falling waters, the strangest phenomena of fire inflicted themselves. The red sparks of German trench mortars described their seeming-slow arcs, shrapnel shells clanged in crimson, burning, momentary cloudlets, smoke billowed into a tidal wave, and the powdery glare of many a signal-light showed the rolling folds. The roarings and cracklings of the contest between artilleries and small-arms sometimes seemed to lessen as one gigantic burst was heard. We watched, with murmured astonishment; and often Charlwood would say, 'Hope to God we don't go south of the Canal.' The canal was that which runs from Béthune to La Bassée, and south of it festered that shattered and shattering length of battlefield of which Loos was the centre. Need I note that Charlwood's sensible petition was to be rejected?

My trench education advanced, and I learned of sentry groups and trench stores, dispositions and defence schemes. I attached the requisite importance to the Vermoral Sprayers for counteracting gas

– simple machines such as were used in Kent to wash cherry-trees with insect-killer – and to the clearance of match-sticks illegally thrown into the gutters under the duckboards. Above all the needs of the fighting man, except his pay-book, a rifle-rack now appeared to be paramount. There was a wonderful tidiness in trench housekeeping at that period. One night, something a little more adventurous in suggestion befell me. Penruddock went up to the front line by the 'overland route,' and he thought it would be for my good if I went with him. The moon was high and clear. We worked our way over old farmlands, and crossed the Old German Line, attacked and passed by the British a year before in that typically wasteful experiment or audacity, the Aubers Ridge battle. The old trench lay silent and formidable, a broad gully, like a rough sunk lane rather than a firing-trench. It was strewn with remains and pitiful evidences. The whole region of Festubert, being marshy and undrainable, smelt ill enough, but this trench was peculiar in that way. I cared little to stop in the soft drying mud at the bottom of it; I saw old uniforms, and a great many bones, like broken bird-cages. One uniform identified a German officer; the skeleton seemed less coherent than most, and an unexploded shell lay on the edge of the fragments. What an age since 1914! Meanwhile, so many bullets cracked with whip-like loudness just over our heads that it seemed we were being actually aimed at, though it was night and the enemy at half a mile's distance. We went on, through straggling wire and wet grass, and then by a wooden track, until the lee of Cover Trench rose in view: we entered it by an opening known in that time and district as a 'sally port,' a term readily connecting us with Marlborough's wars.

In Cover Trench night life was much more vigorous than where I had been so far. The Islands, each with its small contingent of infantry, lay yet ahead: but Cover Trench was the real front line. Doogan, my old companion, was here in the narrow hole which was company headquarters, talkative and cheerful, looking as if he liked it. Another officer who had been trained with me, Vorley by name, showed me where the sentries were posted, and how to fire a flare. This was very simple: he had with him a cumbrous brass gun, called a duck-gun; from this, going round a corner into an unused bay and mounting the fire-step, he fired a Very cartridge. Sergeant Williams encouraged me to sustain this event. But the effect was one of ejaculation rather than illumination; two or three deafening cartridges provided a thin whirl of sparks that died on their early way into the sightless sky; meanwhile the Germans were sending up fine confident lights, which soared and sank in beautiful curves, or, suspended on parachutes, delayed their spiral fall and sought out all nooks and corners. The superiority of their flares was mortifying, and may have been the original reason why British trench practice was to put up Very lights at the rarest moments. The abstention came to be defined as 'a point of honour,' and it certainly was no disadvantage in the long run, for the Germans mostly supplied an excellent profusion of illuminants. It was the dream of our rank and file that the capture of one of their signal-light cartridges would be rewarded with ten days' leave. Several bold optimists went into danger pursuing this dream. And, on the other side of fate, there were tales of what happened to a man lying in No Man's Land when a burning flare shot down on his back.

I was put in charge of No. 11 Platoon, but in the trenches a subaltern's business was rather general than particular. He took his turns of trench watch with the others, which meant responsibility for the company's whole front at those times. The courtesy of Sergeant Unsted, who continued to father No. 11 Platoon, was charming at every point. Chivalry was certainly not dead. Soon enough we relieved the forward company, and new excitements came my way. The nights were certainly a strange experience, which in retrospect largely defines itself as the mystery of finding where people and places were. The Cover Trench lay at the head of a salient, and darkness emphasizes the precariousness of such places; puzzling flares, evidently the enemy's, would soar up as it were behind one's back, and not only would these mislead one's strained polarity, but bullets would smack into our parapet from the wrong side – a dismal thing to do. One night while Doogan was sitting in the headquarters dugout with *La Vie Parisienne* as a *memento vivere*, a shot arrived in the earth wall just above him by way of *memento mori*. The Islands in front were lonely places, and at first, as I followed a guide through the blackness, much like a hen, among old tins and holes and diggings and wreckage, it seemed to me likely that one would miss them altogether and end up in the German line. They were short butts of sandbag-work, without dugouts. Some were regularly manned by us, others not; and the circuit of them always hinted the fancy that a German ambush *might* be encountered in the derelicts. Our men were very quiet, but very watchful and fearless in these outposts. A strong group looked out on Canadian Orchard, with its naked historic trees: it was their habit to annoy the Germans opposite with a Lewis gun, and at their invitation I also caused the weapon to speak. The answers were bullets, that flayed the sandbags in awkward nearness to one's head, and brought from our good Sergeant-Major Lee as he leaned there most violent phrases of contempt, as if he were being worried by street arabs.

Two German machine-guns were famous, 'almost legendary monsters' here. Blighty Albert and Quinque Jimmy fired across a road called Kinky-Roo, which our ration parties and others used: and I have dropped with the rest in its insufficient gutter while the sprays of bullets rushed as though endlessly just above, or sometimes struck fire from the cobbles, and while the long pallor and malice of the flares whitened the broken trees, the masses of brickwork, and the hummocks of old defences. Their subtle whiteness sometimes contoured the enemy's parapet in staring proximity; then they fell, and darkness rushed up to meet the weary sky.

Want of sleep soon impressed me. There was always some interruption when one lay down. In the day time, Cover Trench was not to be reached from the Old British Line; but what with domestic details, reporting and mapping, the censoring of the letters scrawled in copying pencil by our home-yearning stalwarts, the inspection of stores and rifles and localities, one was busy. At night, higher ranks appeared in our midst, and, chief of all, one whose approach caused the bravest to quail – the Brigadier-General. I was reading in the headquarters shelter when the great man suddenly drew aside the sacking of the entrance, and gleamed stupendously in our candlelight, followed by an almost equally menacing Staff Captain. What was my name? I had not been round the company's wire? Why not? I was to go. Authority was at this time persistent that all officers should take their nightly constitutional in No Man's Land, and it was ungainsayable that such as myself should so exercise ourselves; but the rule did not except company commanders. They could only murmur and go forth. Shortly afterwards a valued captain in another battalion, generally known because he had played cricket for Surrey, was obeying the expensive mandate, when he was hit and killed.

Many harsh and even maledictory notes on the General passed among us. We still remember that brooding discontent. The wild look in his eye at this period used to accompany wild orders. Where the line was being held with some degree of contentment, mutual contact and pride, he was liable to set people off on cross purposes. He rejoiced in inventing new Army Forms, which he called 'pro forma's.' There were 'pro forma's' for everything; had they been good 'pro forma's' criticism would be foolish, but some of them were such that one's best information could not find a heading in them. A patrol went out, returned, and its officer had then to struggle in the candle's flickering light with the composition of a report under such heads as 'Enemy Activity,' 'Enemy Dispositions,' 'Our Activity,' and so on, the result being strained and parcelled out of all value. One night, Kapp went out to study a suspected sniper's post in a ruin. He stayed out too long, and when at last he scrambled back from the hurrying light of day to the Island where I awaited him, one of his men had been badly wounded. Poor Corporal Mills was carried down, and died later. But (at this cost) Kapp's patrol had been remarkable, and he sent back a long precise report, full of suggestive information. The Olympian comment was, 'Too flowery for a military report.' Our chieftain could not encourage anything that bore the semblance of the mental method of a world before the war. That temperaments vary was a conception which he doggedly cancelled. But I shall have much more to say of this singular man, whom we all found difficult, and whom we honour.

As yet my notion of modern war was infinitesimal. Of the possibilities of artillery there was no example at Festubert; the spectacular outbursts round Givenchy seemed to be the extreme of mechanized fury, while for ourselves in the front trench the guns were quiet. A few rounds might occasionally go whizzing over our heads, and I was alarmed by the report that one had burst almost exactly over the doorway of battalion headquarters, a thousand yards behind! Was there no safety anywhere? The shortened, quietened cough of anti-aircraft shells often came down from the blue morning sky, and it was fashionable to stand watching these pretty explosions, and counting up the waste of public money on the part of our 'Archies' shell by shell, the rumoured cost of these shells being then half a guinea each. Sometimes this cynical mathematics was brought to an end as the air round us began to buzz and drone with falling fragments; large and jagged shards of steel would plunge murderously into the sandbags, and one discreetly got into the dugout.

Let me take you back now from the imbecile, narrow, bullet-beaten, but tranquil front line into the stand-to billets in Festubert village. And let me say here that, whereas to my mind the order of our humble events may be confused, no doubt reference to the battalion records would right it; yet does it matter greatly? or are not pictures and evocations better than horology? What says Tristram? – 'It was some time in the summer of that year.'

Festubert village was an interesting contortion of whimsically balanced bricks and beams, and on the whole friendly to the fighting man. The Brewery was shelled, being prominent and used as an observation post; if any other place received a salvo, the local public preferred to think that some mistake had been made. In ancient days, perhaps in 1914, the village had been bombarded with serious intention by guns of horrid weight, and one gazed wonderingly into several enormous holes. Our company headquarters in the hulk of a once pretty house could show two or three magnificent examples at its threshold, round the marble steps, and in one of these pits lay a monstrous rusty shell, which, it was said, our Engineers would not attempt to explode. (That remark shows the innocence and serenity of the period.) Apart from this, our garden was lovely, with flowering shrubs, streaked and painted blooms, gooseberry bushes, convenient new gaps and paths, and walks between evergreen hedges – 'unsafe by day,' as the notice-boards said. Not far down the road was a wooden bathhouse, where one splashed in cold water agreeably, yet with a listening ear. Not far, again, was a red brick wall, to which fruit-trees reached their covert; this red wall was an instance of man's duplicity, for part of it, being but painted wood, presently swung open, and a field battery glaring brutally out would 'poop off.' The contrivance was universally admired; was it not the work of our own Divisional Artillery? Yet at this time I was more afraid of our own guns than of the enemy's. Here and there, stretched from tree to tree, one saw wire netting, intended, we heard, to interrupt the roar of firing and so to hinder the Germans' sound-ranging.

C Company officers were very amicable, though Penruddock was reckoned rather too young for the command; and, as I see him in the pool of time gone by, he appears as a boy, fair-haired, fine-eyed and independent of experience. Our lodging was an 'elephant dugout,' an arched iron framework, built into the house which I mentioned, and called advanced brigade headquarters. Here we were amused by the skill of Kapp, who made charcoal drawings, no doubt scarcely proper, but as clever as anything he has done; nor was he artist alone; he also tried to popularize rounds and catches, as 'Great Tom is cast,' 'A Southerly Wind and a Cloudy Sky,' 'Go to Joan Glover.' The intellects of the others scarcely rose to his magazines from home, among which was *The Gypsy*, a frolic in decadent irreverences published in Dublin; it was a most unexpected visitor to a table meant for Army notebooks, compasses, fuse-caps, aluminium mugs of lime-juice and plates of variegated bully beef. Kapp was a lively hand to have in a dugout; his probably imaginary autobiography, peeping out at intervals, and enriched by other versions, was also a diversion; but one day he was called away to an interview with the Colonel, and soon he disappeared into the irrelevant air of GHQ, far beyond the stars. He was a shrewd critic, and on the spot demonstrated the weakness of some verses which I wrote on a beautiful seventeenth-century shrine in Festubert, still peeping out its innocent but shrapnel-scarred assurance between its sycamore trees. Musically sounded the summer wind in the trees of Festubert.

Our men lived in the 'keeps' which guarded the village line. East Keep in particular was a murky sandbagged cellar and emplacement smelling of wet socks and boots. To go from keep to keep alone in the hour before dawn, by way of supervising the 'stand to arms,' was an eccentric journey. Then, the white mist (with the wafting perfume of cankering funeral wreaths) was moving with slow, cold currents above the pale grass; the frogs in their fens were uttering their long-drawn *co-aash, co-aash*; and from the line the popping of rifles grew more and more threatening, and more and more bullets flew past the white summer path. Festubert was a great place for bullets. They made a peculiar anthem, some swinging past with a full cry, some cracking loudly like a child's burst bag, some in ricochet from the wire or the edge of ruins groaning as in agony or whizzing like gnats. Giving such things their full value, I took my road with no little pride of fear; one morning I feared very sharply, as I saw what looked like a rising shroud over a wooden cross in the clustering mist. Horror! but on a closer study I realized that the apparition was only a flannel gas helmet spread out over the memorial.

The quiet life here yet had its casualties, for we were sent up as working-parties in the night-time, to dig a new communication trench. The procession groped dispassionately past the church with its toppling crucifix, and the Brewery's sentinel in the shadow ('That you, Dick?' ''Ow's business, Dick?' 'Wind favourable for whizz-bangs?') along the Old British Line, and so to the place of work. All trenches hereabouts were merely cast-up ridges of earth held in places by stakes, wire, hurdles and wooden framework. Underneath their floors of planks and slats, water welled and stagnated, and an inde-scribable nocturnal smell, mortal, greenweedy, ratty, accompanied the tramp of our boots to and fro. The process of thickening the trench walls meant working in the open, and the enemy laid his machine-guns accurately enough on the new job which could not be concealed from him, letting drive when he chose. So we lost men. The company worked well, though not in very good temper: the continued want of rest was naturally resented; but they were men who knew how to use spades, and I was ashamed of my puny hasty efforts in comparison with their long and easy stroke. After work, there was a glow of satisfaction among us. The nights being cold as yet, a soup-kitchen was still kept open in Festubert, and we were glad of it. There I first saw F. Worley, a glorious fellow whose real connection with my story begins somewhat later.

Over all our night activities the various German lights tossed their wild incoherence. Three blue lights, it was half-humorously said, were the signal for peace; as time went on the definition was revised – four black lights. But superstition could not be altogether thrust back in this district of miasma and mist, and when one evening a wisp of vapour was seen by my working party to glide over the whole sky from west to east, preserving all the time a strange luminous whiteness and an obvious shape, as some said, that of a cross, as others antipathetically held, of a sword, then there was a subdued conversation about it, which spread from man to man. My batman Shearing, whose characteristic attitude was 'It is the Lord: let Him do what seemeth Him good,' told me that he read coming disaster in this sword.

iii

The Cherry Orchard

We returned to the front line, and after some nights there Penruddock told me that we were going out to rest billets: I was to go ahead with some non-commissioned officers to take over the accommodation. Other representatives from the other companies would join me next morning early in the Old British Line opposite our former headquarters. I therefore took my party there that night, and gave them word about reappearing at the proper hour; then, entering our little dugout now held by another company's officers, I asked someone's leave to sleep on a bench there. My warm-coat was not adequate, and I was irritably awake in the early day when from his more comfortable lair in the recess the company commander, yawning and stretching, looked over to me and charitably asked, 'What's that thing?' I sat up quickly and told him; he stayed with the battalion long enough for me to be equally uncharitable to him, but at that luxurious period there was a wonderful superiority about some of the original officers of the battalion. It made life difficult. When the billeting party was assembled, this haughtiness was again discernible. Man is a splendid animal, wherever possible.

The joyful path away from the line, on that glittering summer morning, was full of pictures for my infant war-mind. History and nature were beginning to harmonize in the quiet of that sector. In the orchard through which we passed immediately, waggons had been dragged together once with casks and farm gear to form barricades; I felt that they should never be disturbed again, and the memorial raised near them to the dead of 1915 implied a closed chapter. The empty farmhouses behind were not yet effigies of agony or mounds of punished, atomized materials; they could still shelter, and they did. Their hearths could still boil the pot. Acres of self-sown wheat glistened and sighed as we wound our way between, where rough scattered pits recorded a hurried firing-line of long ago. Life, life abundant sang here and smiled; the lizard ran warless in the warm dust; and the ditches were trembling quick with odd tiny fish, in world as remote as Saturn.

Presently we came to a shrine on a paved road, and near by the houses were still confidently held by their usual families. Their front windows, between the blue shutters, one and all exhibited silk postcards, with excessively loving messages and flags ('The Flags of Civilization') and flowers on them, neighboured by 'Venus' pencils, red herrings in tumblers, and chocolate bouchées in silver paper. Innocency of life! how it carried one back, so that the long hot walk to Hinges, our due resting-place, was like the flight of a bird. And yet, when war seemed for the time being left behind, belts of barbed wire again appeared, crossing the beet-fields, and wicker-lined trenches curved along waterways and embankments. And yet – so I thought! not having cleared up the point that the defence of a country must be miles in depth.

Had our leaders cleared it up? This may be lightly touched upon as I proceed.

Hinges was a village on the canal from Béthune to Aire, a place of orchards 'hidden from day's garish eye,' of mud barns, of columned pollards and level flourishing fields. That part of it which we were to inhabit was called Hingette, and adjoined the canal. I found the company commander from whom I was to take over sitting pleasantly in the tall open parlour window of a big farmhouse, just as Shelley would have been sitting; he received me as a sort of fellow-collegian, and my business was made easy for me. Such characters and occasions were the charm of the BEF. There was a grace that war never overcast. If you except the great refuse reservoir in the middle of the farmyard, this place was in itself one of the happiest to which my lamented battalion ever went. But the men had hardly exchanged nods with sleep, next morning, when a training programme was put into force. One of the few advantages which I had fancied we should have in coming to France was a relaxation from the artificial party of army life – 'eyewash,' in the term then universal. But here, after two or three weeks in the line, was a battalion undergoing the same old treatment, which uselessly reduced its chances of rest. Uselessly? I believe so: these men were volunteers of the first months of the war, most willing but most intelligent, and the only effect that petty militarism and worrying restlessness had on them was to set them grumbling. About now, the signallers revealed the general feeling by sending in to the Colonel a round robin protesting against field punishment awarded one of them. This beautiful but unregimental act was the cause of a parade, when the Colonel spoke with surprise and anger; yet I believe he knew what was really annoying his subjects, without being able to change the orders from above.

The training programme did not last long, nor did I visit our farmhouse billets with the gossip of the moment many evenings. About five one afternoon, when the greener light began to cool the senses, and many a letter was being written and many a pack of cards starting to run, all officers were called to battalion headquarters. Mystery: theory: premonition. 'I told you so, Limbery,' muttered Charlwood, with a doleful smile. 'I knew we should be tooling up the road again in a couple of nights.' What exactly was amiss at the line the adjutant, speaking in his dry, deliberate way, did not announce: there was something in the air, he admitted, and the battalion was to take over trenches south of the canal. Another doleful smile from Charlwood to Limbery-Buse. The conference scattered to the various billets with no delay, and the companies prepared for the new French tour. Floors were swept clean, stores of bully beef and bombs examined and found correct, and all else attended to. But I, to my surprise, was not to go up at once to the trenches; an elementary gas course, lasting three days, was prescribed for me. I nevertheless watched the company depart down the muddy by-road past the ovens and tents in a depressed mood, nor was I alone in regret. The smelly little farmyard dog, who had been taken off his chain in the night by our humanitarians, and walked out into a liberty which he could scarcely remember since his puppy days, also gazed, and hung a mournful head.

It must have been during this brief encampment at Hinges that Kapp ceased to philosophize, scandalize, harmonize and anatomize among us, and departed for that mysterious Press Bureau where it was supposed his remarkable faculty for languages would be needed; and while we lost him, we gained another artist of quality. This was Neville Lytton. Tall, of a fine carriage, his outward and physical appearance expressing an intellect rather than a body, he at once attracted me. He was outspoken in his loathing of war, he did not rely on his rank to cover all points of argument or action, and his gallantry in going through the dirtiness, the abnegations of service, the attack upon all his refinement, was great. It naturally remained unrecognized by the crasser part of the officers and men. He commanded the company with thoroughness and caution, and sat at our mess, piously endeavouring to keep up his vegetarian habits (apart from an occasional ration of bacon) and to keep alive a spirit of artistic insight without refusing military method.

So the company has gone down the road, and doesn't know quite where it is bound for; and here, with my batman Shearing, lately a gardener, I am free for an hour to play *Il Penseroso* round the cherry orchard and between the orderly thrifty root-crops. I will stay in this farmhouse while the gas course lasts – the school is only a few miles away, at Essars – and get the old peasant in the evenings to recite more *La Fontaine* to me, in the Béthune dialect, and walk out to see the neighbouring inns and shrines, and read – Bless me, Kapp has gone away with my *John Clare*!

He has the book yet, for all I know; has he the memory of Hinges?

On the next morning, that had risen in calm glories as though there were no war, I took my way along the wide canal towards Essars, swinging my stick, and noticing the 'twined flowers,' the yellowhammer and the wagtail. The water was clear, glittering roach buoyed themselves in the light, young jack shooting into deeper water as I passed flicked up the mud in the shallows. A Red Cross barge steamed in state along the channel. Presently I turned across the fields, and the spire of Essars and the contrasting stream of cars and lorries came in view among the rich mantles of trees, which canopied the road from Béthune to Neuve Chapelle. The gas school was a little cluster of huts in this busily traversed yet unruined village; and here a number of us went through gas chambers and took spasmodic notes of lectures. It was all very leisurely, alarming and useful. A slight asthma caused me to be exempt from running with the flannel bag over my head. The flannel mask was respected, for (as I had already noticed in the line) it kept your ears warm! It smelt odd and breathing in it became sugary, while the goggles seemed to be inevitably veiled with moisture, highly beneficial in a crisis to one's opponent.

At lunch-time I vanished into the fields and, under one knotty willow by a dyke, ate my rations, still, as an angler of sorts, studying the waters. But one of my constant instinctive terrors in early life had been the sudden sight of great fish lurking; and I feel to-day the start with which I became aware, in this little dyke, under a thick hanging branch, of a ponderous and ugly carp. He set eyes on me almost as soon, and dived. I mention this, to show what tenacity the fancy had in days of 'grim reality,' and actual monsters. One lunch hour I spent less irrationally with two officers of the Gloucester Pioneer Battalion, which had an enviable reputation with us as a gathering of good fellows altogether; my friends were Hillier and Crockford, whom I see yet in the *al fresco* spirit of that leafy corner. There was poetry about these two, nor was I afraid to speak of poetry to them; and so long as the war allowed a country-rectory quietude and lawny coolness three kilometres from the line, and summer had even greater liberty than usual to multiply his convolvulus, his linnets and butterflies, while life was nevertheless threatened continually with the last sharp turnings into the unknown, an inestimable sweetness of feeling beyond Corot or Marvell made itself felt through all routine and enforcement; an unexampled simplicity of desire awoke in the imagination and rejoiced like Ariel in a cowslip-bell. It was for a short time, but even that decree heightened the measure.

24

iv

The Sudden Depths

The brief gas course being ended, I set out to rejoin the battalion, who had disappeared in an easterly direction, somewhere south of the ominous canal. We therefore strapped up our packs and stepped off in the bright weather along the towing-path, passing through Béthune without the chance to explore that popular town, or see why the Padre's visit to the boot-shop was interesting. I heard that the battalion had been at le Quesnoy for a night, but where le Quesnoy was I did not know, and when I asked a Frenchman he assured me indignantly that it was in the hands of the Germans. He meant a large town, I meant some small group of cottages; and continuing our waterside walk, at last we discovered that hamlet. The battalion had left, and was in the trenches. By now we were sweating and thirsty, and the evidence of a war began to gnarl the scenery. We passed the last melancholy estaminet on the eastward track, with shell-holes round the door, and we tried (at the suggestion of my batman) its coloured syrups: no more Rhum Fantaisie for me, I decided; then on again past battery pits and excavations. Here telegraph wires no longer ran aloft in the air, but lay festooned thickly along the torn-up railway bank, their poles and teeth-like rows of insulators leaning this way and that, the several rails here and there curved up like hurt reptiles into the air. The day was sultry, and the brooding presence of war made one's whole being sultry; yet things were generally quiet. The red-brick hollow ruin of a station marked 'Cuinchy' told us that we were almost at our journey's end; other ruins of industrial buildings and machinery hovered through the throbbing haze; the path became corrupt, and the canal dead and stagnant. Over it stood a steel bridge, with a deep deformity in the middle, where no doubt some huge shell had landed. This was Pont Fixe. Here silence, heat and blind terror shared the dominion. One did not wish to loiter. I forget who gave us the instruction to turn southward into 'Harley Street'; battalion headquarters was in one of the best of the tottering anatomies of houses here, which no specialist could have cured. So, reporting, dusty, mystified and cowardly, at barricaded and padded 'Kingsclere,' a tall villa with mattresses stuffed into the upper windows, I was sent with Hunt the runner (like a young Athenian torch-bearer he was) to my company, now installed beyond any question south of the infamous canal.

The way had grown long that day as the sun climbed high; and the final passage through cuttings in chalky ground, zig-zagging and wire-entangled, was weary going. But fortune allowed me this – C Company was in support. The officers' mess, dormitory and council-chamber was a fair-sized cellar under a once capacious farmhouse. Thence, it was not far to Cuinchy Keep, where I was finally due. At first sight the keep appeared as a group of irregular, low, brick walls enclosing a dust-heap. 'You've timed it well,' said Charlwood, meeting me outside. 'Fritz put 600 shells on this keep in an hour this morning.' 'Has he finished?' 'I doubt it.' I detachedly looked round for the dugout, and made for it.

That dugout was a deep one, with a steep mud-slide of an entrance; it was the smallest deep dugout that I ever saw, and yet it was friendly to us. So much could not be said for the area in which we were; it was one of violent surprises. Esperanto Terrace, our principal holding, was a tidy trench, but sudden shrapnel bursting over it destroyed several of our men, two brothers among them. Some of us were just in time, when next the enemy gunners whizzbanged here, to jump down from the fire-step into a dugout stairway; waiting there, I felt the air rush in hot tongues on us as shell after shell burst just at the exit. One could never feel at ease in the Cuinchy sector, though perhaps I imagined all was well one afternoon as I went down through a trench dark and cool with tall grass and arched branches above it – there was also an iron railway overhead, a contrivance for carrying stretchers – to battalion headquarters in Kingsclere.

Kingsclere's shuttered windows, and masses of sandbags, looked better than C Company's cellar. Kingsclere had a cellar, too, a delicate retreat from the glaring heat-wave outside, and a piano in it, and marguerites and roses in jars on the table. But there was an air of anxiety and uncertainty about the headquarters staff as they came and went. Had I lived longer in the line I could have interpreted this particular muteness and inquietude in regard to the job which I had been fetched to do. That was to produce an enlargement of the trench map showing our front line and the German front line at a chosen point. The cause, of which I remained innocent, was that the Colonel had been ordered to make a raid at once on that point. The word 'raid' may be defined as the one in the whole vocabulary of the war which most instantly caused a sinking feeling in the stomach of ordinary mortals. Colonel Grisewood was confronted with the command to attack some part of the enemy's line, here fortified with the keenest intelligence, the thickest wire and emplacements, in the dark and without any preparation. Not unnaturally, he was worried. What came of this is told by Neville Lytton in his war memoirs: Grisewood demurred, was disposed of, and another battalion was forced to lose the lives which ignorance and arrogance cost. But of such perturbations I felt no tremor as I finished my map, in colours, and enjoyed my tea, and the genteel conditions.

There was enough to occupy a commanding officer in the Cuinchy trenches, without lightning raids. It was as dirty, bloodthirsty and wearisome a place as could well be found in ordinary warfare; many mines had been exploded there, and tunnelling was still going on. We had scarcely found out the names of the many trenches, boyaux and saps when midnight was suddenly maddened with the thump and roar of a new mine blown under our front companies. The shock was like a blow on the heart; our dugout swayed, there were startled eyes and voices. I was sent up, as soon as it appeared that this disaster was on our front, with some stretcher-bearers, and as we hurried along the puzzling communication trenches I began to understand the drift of the war; for a deluge of heavy shells was rushing into the ground all round, baffling any choice of movement, and the blackness billowed with blasts of crashing sound and flame. Rain (for Nature came to join the dance) glistened in the shocks of dizzy light on the trench bags and woodwork, and bewilderment was upon my small party, who stoopingly hurried onward; we endured a barrage, but we were not wanted after all.

Brothers should not join the same battalion. When we were at the place where some of the wounded had been collected under the best shelter to be found, I was struck deep by the misery of a boy, whom I knew and liked well; he was half-crying, half-exhorting over a stretcher whence came the clear but weakened voice of his brother, wounded almost to death, waiting his turn to be carried down. Not much can be said at such times; but a known voice perhaps conveyed some comfort in the inhuman night which covered us. In this battalion, brothers had frequently enlisted together; the effect was too surely a culmination of suffering; I shall hint at this again.

The casualties caused by the mine were nearly sixty. Cuinchy (which the battalion was proud to hold, believing it a sector hitherto allotted solely to Regular troops) was a slaughter-yard. My ignorance carried me through it with less ado than I can now understand. The front line, which C Company in a few nights occupied, was in all ways singular. It ran through an extensive brickfield, with many massive foursquare brickstacks, fused into solidity; of these historic strange monuments about a dozen lay in our lines, and about the same number in the German lines. The brickstacks, such of them as were occupied, were approached by insecure, narrow windings through a wicked clay; our domestic arrangements naturally grouped themselves on the home side of them, and no less naturally the Germans at their discretion belaboured them and their precincts with high explosive. The deep dugouts behind them were not quite deep enough, but to any one arriving there the sight of a smoky black stairway down, with equipments suspended like trophies at the entrance, was better than what Moses saw from Pisgah. From the gap in the sandbags above, a bulky benevolent figure, reminiscent of the police force, emerges with a frying-pan, or a canvas bucket, and grins respectfully. 'Corporal Head, dare you laugh at my huge stick? Isn't it helping me through this filth to a couple of hours' rest?' – 'Well, I *hope* you'll get your rest, sir. Here they come again.' – Just in time; the most malevolent flattening crash follows one down the steps: one's body tingles: the candles are out. This is the first line of a long monotonous poem, but we are inside, and can wait for the end. The roof-beam may be cracked, but that need not be one's only thought. Who's got the matches?

I have heard it ruled that the minenwerfer was unimportant, and its effect principally (to use the obtuse English of this subject) moral. But in stationary war it seemed to me to make large holes not only in the nervous but also in the trench system. My first glimpse of what I likened to a small black cask wabbling over and over in the air at a great height above us produced from me the remark: What a large rifle-grenade! The cask pounced down with speed and a corner of the brickstack flew into a violence of dust and smoke; but meanwhile other 'airy devils hovered,' and Corporal Rowland, who had smilingly corrected my error about rifle-grenades, watched with as keen an eye as ever faced fast bowler, and scuttled one way or the other. There was nothing for it but to copy experience, and experience was nothing but a casual protection, for one of our soundest officers was killed at the entrance to the brickstacks. I still hear the voices of his friends, sharing this news, shocked and sad. A problem also recurs to me, which became for a time a bad dream; in the narrow slit, already knocked nearly shapeless, and sloppy with rain, which led from our company headquarters towards the rear, a large 'minny' fell but did not explode. Something must be done about it, quickly – for traffic must pass, day and night. I suppose that this dud was presently set off by an electrical charge, but it had an awkward effect on a person expecting to pass that way – the only way.

Meanwhile, our trench protection was most meagre. The front trench, then marked at intervals with large location-boards reading (from our side) somehow thus: 1. d.   7 was shallow and uncommanding. I could not understand its connections, one part with another. Probably nobody else could. Saps ran out, like thin arms reaching towards the enemy, but whether they or the fragmentary fire-step from which they emerged formed our chief bulwark, I did not know. We held Jerusalem Crater, an enormous hole in brown exploded soil with a pool in the bottom of it; we held it, but our post was at the bottom of it too. The sentry had to lie down behind a few sacks of clay and glare with intensity into his periscope. One reached him through a burrow under our parapet, a sort of culvert, a heroic ingenuity; if one lay long beside him, one of the periodical releases of stick-bombs from the overhanging German side of the crater would reward such patience. At night our patrols inquired perilously into the farther side of this crater; I went; there was nothing to be discovered but fractured earth, old iron and anxiety. We even dragged ourselves to the possible lair of our opponents; but found no person nor prepared position. Clearly the German habit was to crawl out in the day and throw the bombs from 'no fixed abode.' Sometimes the bomber would show himself, head and shoulders, in an unexpected position, out of contempt or daredevilry. He was always reported to be of gigantic stature – no mere Saxon youth. It was here that one of our officers sent back a note to Lytton, 'Germans have thrown six bombs into Jerusalem Crater. Shall we throw any back?'

Now this was the tendency of our brigade; one's mind was more filled with one's relation to superior beings behind us than to those who were not losing the war in front of us. Such questions as these, 'Have your men had Porridge this morning?' 'Have you your Gas Message in your pocket?' and 'What is the number of Loan Boots in your company?' were never far away from the young officer, even as a German bomb burst beside him; they impeded, shall I say, his 'offensive spirit.' This awkwardness pervaded trench war. Even when our headquarters were wildly calling for information and co-operation on the stormy occasion of our mine, an urgent message came in demanding an immediate return of the number of picks and shovels on our sector, or something still wider – the usual 'Please expedite.'

Who that had been there for but a few hours could ever forget the sullen sorcery and mad lineaments of Cuinchy? A mining sector, as this was, never wholly lost the sense of hovering horror. That day I arrived in it the shimmering arising heat blurred the scene, but a trouble was at once discernible, if indescribable, also rising from the ground. Over Coldstream Lane, the chief communication trench, deep red poppies, blue and white cornflowers and darnel thronged the way to destruction; the yellow cabbage-flowers thickened here and there in sickening brilliance. Giant teazels made a thicket beyond. Then the ground became torn and vile, the poisonous breath of fresh explosions skulked all about, and the mud which choked the narrow passages stank as one pulled through it, and through the twisted, disused wires running mysteriously onward, in such festooning complexity that we even suspected some of them ran into the Germans' line and were used to betray us. Much lime was wanted at Cuinchy, and that had its ill savour, and often its horrible meaning. There were many spots mouldering on, like those legendary blood-stains in castle floors which will not be washed away.

In our front line under the fire-step, and indeed now chiefly propping it up, were numerous cylinders of gas, installed for the Loos battle, but undischarged. These could not easily be dug out, and promised additional inconvenience or murder at all hours of shelling. I had been talking on this and similar matters one evening with Corporal Rowland, when, he having gone away to some minor job, I heard a dozen bombs burst very loud. What to do I did not know: I was in a disused bay alone; I was hurrying to find someone else when he came running along, saying that they were German bombs. We both waited on the parapet, with our own bombs ready, but after a few more abrupt thunderings the episode ceased. It turned out that some Germans had tried to raid our right company. In such a dark night it was not easy to be sure of that wandering front line.

At four o'clock one afternoon our tunnellers, suddenly locating German mining near their own, put up a defensive mine between the two lines. All had been drowsy till some pale-faced engineers with lengths of fuse in their hands came past, flinging their brief news over their shoulders at us. Now for it: a big drum-tap underground, and the earth heaved up to a great height in solid crags and clods, with devolving clouds of dust; there was the flame and roar, then this dark pillar in the sunlight, then a twittering, a hissing and thudding as it collapsed. At once the new crater was raked with machine-gun fire and blasted with trench mortars and rifle grenades; neither side wanted it, but neither would let the other set foot in it. Several of us, highly excited, regardless of machine-gun bullets, stood up on the fire-step staring into the confusion and trying our longest throws with Mills bombs; the smoke and dust hung long and swallowed up hundreds of such missiles. At length the affair died out; dixies of tea went round at the usual hour and easily became more important than the blowing of a mine.

The strain of this sector made everyone exceedingly tired. I tremble at one particular memory of this. I had taken trench duty at the dawn 'stand to,' it had been quiet enough, and now the sun was warming and gilding the grey dawn on the sandbags; having dragged myself up and down the trench many times, and used up all my store of intended jokes and encouragements at each group of sentries, I sat down on a convenient sandbag emplacement. Like a fool; the occasional bullets sounded more and more peaceful to my ears, and ceased; I woke up some minutes after, thanking heaven it had not been the General's morning, and that no one had come to the little outlet in which I was nodding. But I was an officer, and fortunate: when my hours of trench watch were over, I could plough my way back to the black hole under the brickstack, and there imitate sleep with no greater defect than that of rats running over me, or explosion somewhere. The men must hunch and huddle on the fire-step, their legs pushed aside every two minutes by passers, the sky above perhaps drizzling or pouring, and nothing but hope and a mackintosh sheet between them and the descent of minenwerfer shells or 'rum jars.' And yet they were in general alert and proud – the first Kitchener battalion, they said, to hold the sector. While we were here, the news came that Kitchener had been drowned. I believe the Germans hoisted a blackboard with this information on it above their parapet.

If these British trenches were not a masterpiece of fortification, at least they were well equipped with notice-boards. Some fine examples of sign-writing adorned the least desirable localities. The brickstacks proclaimed in graceful characters that persons who, speaking over the field telephones, gave away any information at all, which the enemy with his listening sets would undoubtedly pick up, would be court-martialled. And high up inside these mausoleums of much labour, another notice, worthy of an expert monumental mason, played on the imagination. It set forth instructions to the machine-gunners sitting there for throwing open with a pole their secret loophole and coming into action on the day of attack. Clear as these orders were, I felt nevertheless that I would rather not be the executant of them in that odd casemate at the top of the ingenious cemented staircase. Another noticeboard, which I must not be so squeamish as to ignore, led to a familiar place far enough from the brickstack which we held to receive the 'overs'; it is the case that a trench latrine and a trench mortar emplacement mapped from the air look alike, and one's visits were always the worse for that knowledge and occasionally for directed or misdirected shells.

Our work in the Cuinchy trenches was pleasantly relieved by a night or two in a village a short march westward – first through long trenches across the Tourbières or swamp (hence of course 'Tubular Trenches'), and then down the Béthune road; Annequin, where holes made in roofs by enemy guns were speedily repaired by the imperturbable inhabitants. The village was friendly, and near it lay the marshy land full of tall and whispering reeds, over which evening looked her last with an unusual sad beauty, well suiting one's mood. But gloomy we were not. I remember how Limbery-Buse and myself chirped and rarefied over some crayfish and a great cake, in a little side room of a miner's cottage, with vine leaves peeping in, and a flower-bed in front. The miner told me that he was one of some forty who daily inspected the state of the coal-mines from the pit-heads close by so far as those in the German area. Over Annequin towered its slag-heap with a trolley-tip on its pyramidal apex, looking like a big gun; the gunners observed from this eminence, and one heard thereabouts at night the huge crash of German shells intended to spoil their chances. Brief as our stay in Annequin was, we nevertheless went up to the trenches as working-parties from there; and so generally at this period whenever there was a prospect of genuine recuperation, it had to be ruined with long trampings up and down communication trenches for digging or carrying. Many of us would say that it was the better part to stay in the line.

At last, the wonderful news came that we were to be withdrawn from the Cuinchy system, and march back to rest billets. A tired and bemired platoon it was that, after the painful delays usual to night reliefs, I presently led down in the oily black night. How they hated, how I hated the innocent Lytton, riding up and down beside the strung-out company on the charger brought to the foot of the trenches for him. He was gentle, indeed, but the suspicion of 'march discipline' rankled along that canal bank. The chief business was to avoid staggering into the canal. Somewhere near the village of Gorre we had a long halt by the towpath, almost all falling asleep at once on their packs; daylight was waterily spreading as we passed the cemetery and timber-yards of Béthune; too silently we bowed along to Hinges, our former haunt. But if we were so profoundly tired then, how must the battalion have been almost mad for sleep when two years later it had stood before the master offensive of Germany? I cannot speak as those could who were there before me, and who were there after me – some of whom survived and truly came out of great tribulation. Imagine their message; they will never open their mouths, unless perhaps one hour, when the hooded shape comes to call them away, they lift from the lips of their extremest age a terrible complaint and courage, in phrases sounding to the bystanders like 'the drums and tramplings' of a mad dream.

V

Contrasts

The battalion at Hinges was promptly subjected to the harassing training programme in vogue. We all growled, but the military efficiency of headquarters was not troubled. One day when I was 'for' orderly officer, the adjutant, Wallace, twice sent back the guard of our best men whom I paraded before him, telling them to clean their equipment, to my eye clean already; I still hear him saying, when at last he gloomily approved, 'Never bring me a guard like that for inspection again.' What a war! This I reported to my company mess, and received sympathy. In truth, I trembled at any prospect of my having to appear at battalion headquarters, and blessed my fate when one evening I was ordered away to take charge of the equipment of a bombing school near a little place called Paradis. On the way there, feeling like a free man again, I had an estaminet meal 'with the family,' who were unwilling to let me depart; it got very dark, and I could not afterwards find the house intended in the map reference given me. The quartermaster of the Warwickshires gave me a night's lodging;

next morning early I traced the bombing school which had been shut. And now a tender and charming life shone before me. The school had been held in the outbuildings of a château; its stock of stationery, explosives and supplies of other kinds was still there; I saw myself beginning a holiday in the château, the owner of which still lived in it. A courteous and conversational man he was, who, when he saw me up to bed in the top storey, would come in, and stand looking from his window, with occasional remarks to me, at the incessant phantasm of flares red and white and green ascending and descending a few kilometres off in the eastward darkness. That line of lights was now almost two years old, and he had known it from the first. In the garden with its knolls and bowers he told of hand-to-hand fighting in the earliest weeks, and was evidently proud of the occurrence, inconvenient as it might have been. Evenings were spent in the drawing-room, where the widower's two daughters would sing and talk sweetly; the younger of them, pale with an illness, was in love with another officer who on some business like mine was billeted in the house. I did not think he was in love with her; but I will not go into that aspect. She sang and on a sudden she was singing to him; her dark and enchanting and piteous eyes would seek him in the silences. It was another of the Salon pictures to be seen in these parts.

This melodious existence, attained out of the black dreariness of trench warfare, should have lasted longer; but you have already foreseen that after two or three days I was visited by a runner from my battalion, with a message recalling me. So engaged had I become in my walks abroad down the pollarded lanes, piecing out the local life and turning my map into realities, with the big sheepdog whom my host let me take as company, that I scarcely reckoned on so quick a recondemnation. Regretfully I went round my stores, one being a considerable way off; rescued a couple of tents, a hundred grenades and a case or two of rations from a too thrifty peasant; handed over to my successor, and shouldered my pack to Hinges.

The battalion moved at once into the area of the Richebourgs, two tattered villages south-west of Neuve Chapelle. We marched up through Lacouture, with its stately church used as a dressing-station, and, what puzzled us somewhat, its numerous brick-built redoubts in the orchards, and work still being pressed on there. It was surmised that a German attack was feared, but why Lacouture particularly should be turned into a fort did not emerge. There were tales of wealthy landowners, permitted by the French Government to fortify at their own expense. C Company halted after many turnings at a large farmhouse two miles behind the front line, almost unspoiled by war, yet not unaffected by it; though our guard at the gate seemed superfluous. Not far down the road was 'the famous Red Barn' – but no Maria Marten. Everyone was well lodged. The officers had a cottage with no window-glass, but with the best wire-netting bunks that I had yet seen (and I was a close observer of such furniture); our sleep thereon was erratically broken by messages, working-parties and gas alarms. To hear the thin beating of the gas tom-toms for many an acre, when the night mist lay heavily in the moonlight, traversing a silence and solitude beyond ordinary life, was fantastic enough. It was all a ghost story. In the day anti-aircraft guns battered away at heaven, just in front of our billets. They fired without concealment from the farm track which led from our house to battalion headquarters, and I prayed earnestly that these furious ironmongers might not open up at the identical moment of my passing that way.

For as yet, you must know, I was in a sense more afraid of our own guns than I was of the enemy's. I feared, wherever I went, that I might be in front of some cleverly hidden muzzles, which would at any moment make my scalp and brain tingle. It was a physical trouble. As we went up to reconnoitre the trenches, I hurried past our gunpits at Croix Barbée, then opening fire, but on the Rue du Bois, where German snipers were understood to be dangerous, I stupidly stood up with no apprehension, and surveyed at leisure. The Richebourg secondary defences consisted of keeps, or detached strong-points, mediævally constructed in and about ruined buildings, and very numerous. It was a district of shrines and keeps. St Vaast had resplendent examples of both; a white marble shrine, if I remember, looked eastward there, its saints gleaming like Byron's Assyrians. Then the keep was inside a great farmhouse, and its sandbags were beautified if not strengthened with some splendid expensive woodwork, detached from the ruin. Richebourg St Vaast was a prosperous-looking (but deserted) village, with aspiring poplar colonnades; nailed to the most satisfactory trees for the purpose were the tall ladders of artillery observers. The windows of the houses were mostly heavily sand-bagged, and the walls loopholed, as though there had been or was to have been street fighting in the old days. The large church, and the almost rococo churchyard, astonished everybody: they had been bombarded into that state of demi-ruin which discovers the strongest fascination. At the foot of the monolith-like steeple stood a fine and great bell, and against that, a rusty shell of almost the same size; the body and blood of Christ, in effigy of ochred wood, remained on the wall of the church. Men went to contemplate that group, but more to stare into the very popular tombs all round, whose vaults gaped unroofed, nor could protect their charges any longer from the eye of life. Greenish water stood in some of these pits; bones and skulls and decayed cerements there attracted frequent soldiers past the 'No Loitering' notice-board. Why should these mortalities lure those who ought to be trying to forget mortality, ever threatening them? Nearly corpses ourselves, by the mere fact of standing near Richebourg Church, how should we find the strange and the remote in these corpses? I remember these remarks: 'How long till dinner, Alf?' 'Half an hour, chum.' 'Well, I'll go and 'ave a squint at the churchyard.'

In *Waiting for Daylight*, Mr H. M. Tomlinson has perpetuated in his true-born imaginative English the library which he found in Richebourg St Vaast, a year before my time there. I wish I could tell half as intricately and spiritually the spell which made us haunt there; the cajoling ghostliness of the many printed papers and manuscript sermons which littered the floor of the priest's house and drifted into his garden; the sunny terror which dwelt in every dust-grain on the road, in every leaf on the currant bushes near that churchyard; the clatter of guns, the co-existent extraordinary silence, the summer ripeness, the futility of it, the absence of farmyard and cottage-doorway voices which yet you could hear.

Our stay at Croix Barbée was long enough to produce one good thing: and that was a spontaneous concert by the company signallers, who, sitting in the twilight under a cherry-tree, sang such rude old masterpieces as 'The Ram of Derby' with irresistible spirit. Lytton, looking up from a heap of official papers, laughed till he cried; and the war faded far away. It soon returned to us with what may be called an additional presence; for it began to be known that the Brigade was to be used for an attack. With some, unbelief, and with me, ignorance, made a shelter 'against eating cares' for the time being, and at all events some busy weeks must pass before the attack was made.

We were soon holding the line again – breastworks, one simple sandbag wall, with scraps of dugouts like toolhouses leaning against it, and a useful but naked duckboard walk running along behind them past graves, shell-holes and ditches. The weather grew foul and everything was mud and moisture. Lytton went round his front assiduously (though the breastwork was mostly not so tall as himself), asking, 'Well, have you seen anything of the Hun this morning?' but the men did not respond much. They looked after their own business, and expected the Hun to look after his. But there was more in their mood. We had previously helped to dig in bullet-ridden moonlight 'close support lines,' which perhaps had seemed perilous to those who knew; now more serious and immediate omens of ordeal appeared in the mounds of trench mortar bombs – 'plum puddings' or 'footballs,' steely and shining – and other new dumps along the front line. The guns began to wrangle. Where the La Bassée road cut our front line stood an old-fashioned sandbag barricade, behind the actual breastwork; one afternoon this was fired upon by some heavy howitzer whose shells, for the most part being duds, hit the stone highway and were seen to rebound monstrously thence – sensation the first. Sensation the second was provided at the same place, where, as I stood talking with some sterling independent – 'Jerry can come over if he likes,' 'Anybody'd think the boys had had to be *fetched*' – suddenly with horrible spinning clang a layer of the sandbags was knocked over us, and similar clangs and displacements followed, while we cowered and shook the earth off. The gun soon became known as the 'parapet-bruiser,' and whether it was a revolver-gun or a field-gun I do not know, but it seemed to fire from the German front line. Lytton commented: 'Just what I've been trying to suggest all along – high explosive and flat trajectory. If we had a Staff—' Now, too, over our heads would roar the volcanic 'woolly bears,' or 'black crumps,' perhaps a hundred feet in the air, uncoiling downwards as they burst great swift whorls of sooty smoke; and (one of many incidents) as Limbery-Buse and myself sat in a dugout about as large but hardly as strong as a cabin trunk, amusing ourselves with very light literature and local satire, salvoes of whizzbangs gouged up the ground and splintered the duckboards two or three steps from our 'door.' This went on much too long. It was no use looking at the roof. Any attempt to thicken it would have promptly evoked a deliberate knock-out.

No Man's Land was corrupt and dangerous here. An old digging ran out of our line, forked like a fish's tail; Sergeant Bodle, Sergeant May and myself crawled along it towards a supposed German post, pausing every few yards. It smelt badly, even for a disused sap; and we were pretty certain that German topographers were crawling from their end in like fashion. A rashness suddenly entered my head, and I moved impulsively round an angle; there was something or somebody in the sap not twenty paces along. Bodle crept up, looked, pulled me. He was an elderly soldier, and his graver manner now caused my inflation to disappear as suddenly. We returned. The next night, we went out with bomb and cudgel in hand to report on a little round prominence which the periscope easily showed near some pollards. A rose-bush in flower could also be seen by it. It was a long way there, but we fancied that we took it quietly and quickly. To our surprise at last (but countrymen should have known) the pollards lined a wide dyke, and the mound, covered with stirring sword-grass, was on the far side of deep water, unmanned. That unnoticed dyke might have suggested an unpleasant peculiarity of the coming attack. We had now been out in the open long enough for our sentries to forget us; and as we came back to our wire one did forget us, firing excitedly. Splinters of wire tinged into my cheek, lights went up, I had to bawl out my name, and we scrambled in as the German machine-guns took up the story.

Before long 'secret' attack orders came, which everyone had to know. The phrase was that 'The following officers and men have been carefully selected to participate,' or some such honorific proscription; however, our battalion was supplying only various detached parties, the real assault falling to the share of the other three in the Brigade.

My name was not among the selected, and in that moment, so absurdly dominant is the desire to be particularized, disappointment was among my feelings. But what was the attack? This. The German line ran out in a small sharp cape here, called the Boar's Head. (The line had several such – The Pope's Nose, Cæsar's Nose, Duck's Bill.) This was to be 'bitten off,' no doubt to render the maps in the châteaux of the mighty more symmetrical. The other battalions were being hurriedly exercised a mile or two behind through wheatfields, where the Pioneers had run up a canvas model of the enemy lines, and instead of some weeks, some days only were left; the day of decision came swooping upon the Brigade. Over the way the Bois du Biez, with many trees still black and scowling amid the greenness of June, and empty houses along its verges, stood in our common gaze; the legend that, when Neuve Chapelle (also close at hand, in sight) was assaulted, battalions went into the wood to be heard of never again, was not separable from its gaunt omnipresence. I explored some of the derelict trenches prepared for the concentration of unhappy infantry during the offensive of a year before, and found them terribly punished and shapeless, grassless, full of warnings, sown with jagged iron.

And yet, these strong, cheerful, clean, determined men? these accumulations of trench mortar bombs, hand grenades, bright blue long-barbed wire, small arms ammunition? these cruelly gleaming machine-guns in hitherto unrevealed emplacements, neat as office safes, of our trenches? On the afternoon before the attack, Penruddock (now away from us on some special duty) came up to give our selected ones the latest instructions, and also lanyards wherewith to bind numbers of prisoners. On that same afternoon, our heavy artillery thundered away for hours at the German line: no answer came. How could we lose?

June 30th, 1916. At the moment of the attack my platoon was in a familiar strong-point on the La Bassée Road, called Port Arthur, two hundred yards in rear of our foremost breastwork. Sergeant Garton and myself obliged the men to withdraw into the cellars, and waited ourselves on the fire-step in the failing darkness. Mad ideas of British supremacy flared in me as the quiet sky behind us awoke in a crescent of baying flashes, a half-moon of avenging fires; but those ideas sank instantly for the eastward sky before us awoke in like fashion, and another equal half-moon of punishing lightnings burst, with the innumerable high voices of machine-guns like the spirits of madness in alarm shrilling above the clashing tides of explosion. A minute more, and a torrent of shells was screeching into Port Arthur; we had been in no doubt about receiving this attention, for the place was an obvious 'immediate reserve'; we (it was our good fortune) went below. The brickwork of the cellar cracked under one or two direct hits, but stood. Presently the German gunners switched away, and we went out again into the summer morning, with an aeroplane or two arriving on bright wings.

There was not much shelling now, but machine-guns continued to fire in a ragged way, which in fact meant a particular and sharp-eyed opportunism elsewhere; no news came. My expectation was that we should be called up to reinforce, but no news came. At last (time seemed without any measurement or reference that day) a small straggling group of those unfortunate selected soldiers blundered dazedly round the trench corner into Port Arthur, and lay down in the first shelter available, among them Sergeant Compton, a brave and brilliant young fellow. All too eagerly I asked him, as I brought out to the sweating and twitching wretches whatever refreshment my dugout held, 'what things were like'; in a great and angry groan he broke out, 'Don't ask me – it's terrible, O God—' Then, after a moment, talking loud and fast, 'We were in the third line. I came to a traverse, got out of the trench and peeped; there was a Fritz crawling round the next traverse. I threw a bomb in, it hit the trench side and rolled just under his head: he looked down to see what it was—' He presently said that the attack had failed. Of his party, none had returned without bullet-holes in their caps, uniforms or equipment; one Single was already exhibiting his twice perforated mess-tin with his usual wit of dejection. In No Man's Land a deep wide dyke had been met with, not previously observed or considered as an obstacle, which had given the German machine-guns hideously simple targets; of those who crossed, most died against the uncut wire, including our Colonel's brother. Meanwhile a trench had been partly dug across No

Man's Land at heavy cost. So the attack on Boar's Head closed, and so closed the admirable youth or maturity of many a Sussex and Hampshire worthy.

Even now, we apprehended that a fresh forlorn hope might be demanded of the Brigade. What the Brigade felt was summed up by some sentry who, asked by the General next morning what he thought of the attack, answered in the roundest fashion, 'Like a butcher's shop.' Our own trenches had been knocked silly, and all the area of attack had been turned into an Aceldama. Every prominent point behind, Factory Trench, Chocolate Menier Corner and so on, was now unkindly ploughed up with heavy shells. Roads and tracks, hitherto securely pastoral, were blocked and exposed. The communiqué that morning, when in the far and as yet strange-seeming South a holocaust was roaring, like our own experience extended for mile upon mile, referred to the Boar's Head massacre somehow thus: 'East of Richebourg a strong raiding party penetrated the enemy's third line.' Perhaps, too, it claimed prisoners; for we were told that three Germans had found their way 'to the Divisional Cage.'

vi

Specimen of the War of Attrition

Explanations followed. Our affair had been a cat's-paw, a 'holding attack' to keep German guns and troops away from the great gamble of the Somme. This purpose, previously concealed from us with success, was unachieved, for just as our main artillery pulled out and marched southward after the battle, so did the German; and only a battalion or two of reserve infantry was needed opposite us to secure a harmless little salient. The explanations were almost as infuriating to the troops as the attack itself (I remember conversations fiercer than Bolshevik councils against the staff concerned), and deep down in the survivors there grew a bitterness of waste; one of the battalions indeed seemed never to recover from its immense laceration, though reinforcements, and good ones, made up its numbers.

Soon after this a circular appeared, which began, 'All ranks must know that the great offensive has now definitely begun,' and went on to assert the valuable creative principle that artillery and trench mortars cut the wire; infantry capture and consolidate the trenches. This promised to simplify the new warfare considerably, but as yet we were holding our sector according to precedent. If these parts were ordinarily peaceful – so peaceful that a shaky colonel was known to ask his adjutant upon hearing a single shell-burst, 'Is that on our front?' – we made up for the fact, in some degree, by our length of reign in them. We were genuine trench inhabitants as long as we were in the defences of Béthune. As yet, in spite of the fierce stories which had floated northwards from Vimy Ridge with its sixteen mine craters and its 'ploughed fields,' in spite even of the Boar's Head disaster (which had indeed been restricted in its destruction of the look of things to a few square miles), few of us had any divination of the realities of the Somme offensive. I used to rely on a sergeant who had been out before with a cyclist battalion, lately disbanded, for a sensible point of view; for days after the opening of the Somme battle he refused to admit any signs of success whatever, but when presently a telegram was passed round among us containing the news 'Cavalry ordered forward to High Wood,' he softened somewhat, and remained open to persuasion for two or three days.

We discussed these mysteries at the head of a mine-shaft in the Cambrin sector, which lies towards Loos. Why we were suddenly sent in there I do not know, and I must have wished many times that we had not been there; the fact remains that one night our entire division and its guns were on the road southwards from the Richebourg country, leaving the district of orchards for that of collieries, crossing the Canal towards a town on a small hill, called Beuvry. There was pine-apple gas, the tear-compelling kind, all along our way. An odd coincidence. For my part I was fortunate; having reported at battalion headquarters on some point, I showed signs of asthma. Wallace, the adjutant, noticing this, unconcealed his feelings; he had me remove my pack, and weighing it in his hand and saying it would be far too heavy for him, instructed that it and I should be carried on pony-back to Beuvry. The town was asleep when we arrived. The men took over billets in a large school, fitted with bunks, which I think pleased them well. I myself went into a strange cottage without a light, and, creeping after my batman through the living-room, was blessed with a clean and comfortable bed. Beuvry, we liked you well, your church, your shops, your serenity; but it was upon short acquaintance, for next day under cloudy heavens we departed, in parties of six at a time, two hundred yards apart, on what I suppose was the real, war correspondent's 'Shell-swept La Bassée Road.' I should have liked a job as storekeeper in one of the many deserted inns and dwellings, yet friendly, alongside this famous pavé; but the storekeeping genius of the nation was too abundant already. Such frowsty paradise as can be created in a cellar where the north wind of discipline never comes needs no recommendation; every man wants to be a storekeeper in some spot at once fairly safe in itself but not offering much attraction to such as give orders and handle offensives.

At Cambrin crossroads our parties of six at two hundred yards interval (or distance: I stumble at a familiar military crux) turned into a side-road by the church (which was a dressing station), and sat down by companies. While tea was dished out, a shell in the church wall, curiously embedded there, unexploded, was one topic; and another was the chocolate which a thrifty old woman – where had she sprung up from? – was peddling among us. Presently Major Harrison, now commanding us, turning from other matters, noticed this old stranger, and, recollecting that we were a relieving battalion at the foot of the communication trench – a most secret and confidential body of men! – he ordered her to be sent away. But by that time, I shrewdly fancy, the stranger had disappeared.

The communication trench was one of the longest that we ever used, and in many places it was bricked, sides and floor. It ended in a singular front line, approached by too many boyaux, known by their numbers; a front line not unhappily sited, but dominated by the enemy's higher ground, on which rose Auchy's crowding red roofs. Our company's notch of this front line was a deep trench, passing every twenty or thirty yards under roofs of iron rails or duckboards built over with sandbags. And this trench had been kept elegantly clean. On the wrong side of it, their mouths facing the German line, were several deep dugouts; forward from it reached several saps, hot chalky grooves which were by no means so tidy. And, not without their awe to the unaccustomed, there were mine-shafts in the line, mostly with wooden barriers and notices excluding infantry. 'Keep Out. This Means You,' was seen here.

The reason for the overhead coverings did not long keep me in suspense. It was my turn for trench watch, one grey morning; I walked to our left-hand post, and talked to our sentry there, when *whizz-crunch, whizz-crunch,* two small trench mortar shells of the kind called 'pine-apples' fell on the covering above us, broke it half down and strewed the place with fragments. The immediateness of these arrivals annulled fear. Taking my meditative way along to the other extremity of our trench, I was genially desired by Corporal Worley to take cocoa with him; he was just bringing it to the boil over some shreds of sandbag and tallow candle. Scarcely had I grasped the friendly mug when a rifle-grenade burst with red-hot fizzing on the parapet behind me and another on the parados behind him; and we were unhit. Worley's courtesy and warm feeling went on, undiverted as though a butterfly or two had settled on a flower. A kinder heart there never was; a gentler spirit never. With his blue eyes a little doubtfully fixed on me, his red cheeks a little redder than usual, he would speak in terms of regret for what he thought his roughness, saying dolefully that he had been in the butchering trade all his time. Where now, Frank Worley? I should like an answer. He was for ever comforting those youngsters who were so numerous among us; even as the shrapnel burst low over the fire-bay he would be saying without altered tone, 'don't fret, lay still,' and such things.

The tunnellers who were so busy under the German line were men of stubborn determination, yet, by force of the unaccustomed, they hurried nervously along the trenches above ground to spend their long hours listening or mining. At one shaft they pumped air down with Brobdingnagian bellows. The squeaking noise may have given them away, or it may have been mere bad luck, when one morning a minenwerfer smashed this entrance and the men working there. One was carried out past me, collapsing like a sack of potatoes, spouting blood at twenty places. Cambrin was beginning to terrify. Not far away from that shafthead, a young and cheerful lance-corporal of ours was making some tea as I passed one warm afternoon. Wishing him a good tea, I went along three firebays; one shell dropped without warning behind me; I saw its smoke faint out, and I thought all was as lucky as it should be. Soon a cry from that place recalled me; the shell had burst all wrong. Its butting impression was black and stinking in the parados where three minutes ago the lance-corporal's mess-tin was bubbling over a little flame. For him, how could the gobbets of blackening flesh, the earth-wall sotted with blood, with flesh, the eye under the duckboard, the pulpy bone be the only answer? At this moment, while we looked with dreadful fixity at so isolated a horror, the lance-corporal's brother came round the traverse.

He was sent to company headquarters in a kind of catalepsy. The bay had to be put right, and red-faced Sergeant Simmons, having helped himself and me to a share of rum, biting hard on his pipe, shovelled into the sandbag I held, not without self-protecting profanity, and an air of 'it's a lie; we're a lie.'

Cambrin was beginning to terrify. My excellent sentry in the longest sap, looking too faithfully through his loophole, was shot clean through the head; but the stretcher-bearers resting in a too exposed cubby-hole at the top of a boyau were mutilated in their death by the rifle-grenade which chance lobbed into their quiet dreams of home-folk. And, while these tragedies happened here in the ordinary course of trench dwelling, policy began to be more irritable and irritating. Our fire operations (every man of every employment firing his rifle, or his Lewis gun, dispatching his rifle-grenades or throwing his Mills into No Man's Land for so many minutes of the evening) called down one general answer, a sharp bombardment. The little support trench in which company headquarters was (a muddy but beloved dungeon) glowed with white-hot fragments of shells for a long while. Then, the hairy Jocks south of us made a raid, and, whether it was that, as was said, they really did bring back the enemy's mail that had just come up, or whether they did too much damage, the enemy gave proof of his anger. Forms shrouded with blankets lay still on our fire-step next morning.

Yet it was not a place in which all hours were poisonous. The summer afternoon sometimes stole past unmolested, and, sleep being now almost an abandoned archaism in the trenches, Limbery-Buse and myself would tour old diggings and admire well-carpentered loopholes or recesses, to sit with Sergeant Terry and his telescope, or shoot at fat but too clever rats with our revolvers. I fancied myself as a map-maker, but the sign which I used for trees annoyed my critics: 'Damn these Q's of yours!' – not all the offensive spirit of this quarter belonged to the Germans. Our own bombers with their rifle-grenade batteries were busy, sourly witty, sending over by one pull of a cord volleys of half a dozen, which cooed somehow like pigeons as they soared over to do mischief with a final whining. One attended these conjuring-tricks when they came off. There was some talk of using a 'West Spring Gun' which lay inert in our dump, a legacy of the ingenuity of 1915, but antiquity was respected, and our lives may have been saved from the probable miscarriage. By way of substitute I called for the company barber and sat meekly under his respectful hand, noting the distance of any disturbances.

But let us be getting out of this sector. It is too near the heats of fiercer Hulloch and the Hohenzollern. The listening-posts are not anxious to go out far into No Man's Land at nights, and I am sure I unofficially agree with them; they have had too many *pine-apples*, and not enough sleep. When we got away, it was a full moon, eternal and, so it happened, but little insulted by war's hoarse croaking. We passed the neat portcullises which were to pen the enemy in blind alleys, should he come: the loopholes, neatly set for his destruction if he would stick to the conditions; we got out of the imprisoning trench, and stretched our limbs towards Cambrin village. Daylight came to us assembled on the paved road there, and, as I said to Northcote, now commanding C Company, it seemed that we were out of range of rifle-grenades. What was this? Here were some of the old London 'buses coming, disguised with drab paint: for us! Foot soldiers to be carried to billets? I cannot believe it even now; however, according to all the available evidence, I sat on top of a 'bus that fresh morning while we rolled along into Béthune past the miners mechanically turning out with their rattling clogs to their day in the pits.

vii

Steel Helmets for All

The now familiar 'surprise' soon followed. We were needed almost at once to hold the trenches again, at Richebourg as before. A short, cool tantalization in some orchards near Lacouture, and we marched up among the ruins. In the interval three divisions had attacked near Laventie, a few miles north, without the least success; the rumours of their ordeal were not at all disbelieved in the Brigade, and when a telegram was received giving the order of battle and the approximate positions, there was bitter jesting about. My memory of the trench tour following is disordered, but there is still something to say about Richebourg L'Avoué.

It was still (even after June 30th) a sort of '1915 sector,' with a conventional performance of rifle fire swelling up and dying out at dawn and dusk. One or two mornings, this old-fashioned musketry became so voluminous that I thought something was going to happen. Sometimes Humour even adopted machine-guns. You would hear from the German line or our own the rhythm

> 'Ri-tiddley-i-ti . . .
>   Pom POM,'

done in bullets. The maps so far issued for this part were very simple, and showed our communication trenches as innocuous arrows with their names, as Fry, Cadbury, Factory, Pipe and the rest; the German lines admitted thereupon looked very humanely thin, with economical crosses for barbed wire here and there. Our own line was one breast-work, with a presumably powerful arrangement of keeps behind, and also a patchwork of derelict trenches, which had acquired superstitious fame. For instance, there was somewhere, according to somebody, a large dugout, containing six or seven old German corpses, yellow with gas; and another dugout was reputed to entomb a German officer in bed with a woman – likewise skeletonized. These bony stories might have been easily disproved, but by daylight those derelict dens were watched by the enemy's gunners, and would-be investigators soon had reasons for letting sleeping dugouts (or aluminium nose-caps) lie; at night the romance of the matter escaped attention in our other business. Old trenches towards Neuve Chapelle were safer to study; I haunted one 1915 assembly-position, beaten into humps and holes and red with shrapnel cases and duds. A huge old shell adorned the little-frequented Guards' Trench, like some brutal image in a place of sacrifice.

Port Arthur again, to which I was sent with my platoon, seemed remembering the war of a year ago. It was a brewery ruin, if our diagnosis was right – a long-shafted dray lay in its shadow; its iron boilers looked abroad in some resemblance of the pictures of the original Port Arthur. And of course the gunners had their ladder and spyglass inside the ruin; there was an excellent view from the top, but it quickly ceased to charm. The queer, disabled building was encircled with sandbag ramparts, a map of the whole looking like a diagram of the intestines. In the large cellars there was room for forty men or so; the officer had a side cellar to himself, with a sound bed, and a private stock of new sandbags for bedclothes. Opposite this unsafe but habitually trusted burrow was a little outhouse turned into a machine-gun position, with a store-room; and thence some mole of an engineer, but hopeful beyond good sense, had hollowed out a low tunnel, a secret passage, which led into the communication trench, Hun Street, some way off. We did not realize that this was the work of our enemy in days gone by, nor even that Port Arthur was a part of the Neuve Chapelle fortress. Near by was a pit, the result of much sandbag filling; among its broken spades and empty tins I found a pair of boots, still containing someone's feet.

Detached duty is pleasant. A young officer at Port Arthur was left alone in an unusual and enviable way; his main trouble was to see that, having received when he arrived a list of 146 screw pickets large, 193 screw pickets small, 53 picks, 5 mallets, and so on, he obtained on departure his successor's signature for 146, 193, 53, 5 and the others. Every night the enemy would shell and make a wide gap in the parapet; so that good exercise could be taken regularly. One had time also to study food. I worked through the several brands of bully beef while I was there, on purpose to decide whether my epicure batman's list of them in order of merit could stand. There was at Port Arthur a litter of tins of bully, as in many a dugout at that time; we did not give one thought to the question whence rations would come as time went on. Such heaps would not be found in 1917, but ours not to reason why, unless to-morrow's rations went astray. Fresh meat was often sent up to the line. The Brigade was well catered for in such things; but a trench breakfast with its fat bacon was always without charms, not to mention that a man innocently eating might at any time find a shower of dirt and shrapnel arrived in his mess-tin, or himself half buried.

We were sharply bombarded at all hours. Battalion headquarters, a group of huts Rembrandtesque enough in their rustic structure, with shell-cases of all sizes arranged in a kind of museum at the entrance, was disturbed with obvious intention. Since the tenants were at the time enforcing disliked shows of discipline upon us in the companies forward – there were three rifle inspections daily, and a programme including two hours' 'compulsory sleep' was in operation – the interlude was not distasteful to some rebels; but their turns quickly followed. One afternoon, as Worley was discussing with me the love affairs of his brother, the bay where we stood was suddenly aimed at with round after round of shrapnel and high explosive; we dropped on the duckboards, and looked up as the shells burst a yard or two too far. I watched the flame of explosion with a sort of brainless observancy; but poor Nice, a sixteen-year-old boy who had brought off some trick to get to France, lay moaning and sobbing, do what Worley could. The performance stopped; an hour later it was suddenly reopened a bay or two away, and there the adjutant, Wallace, coming up to make his inspection, was, with his runner, badly wounded. I ran to the place, and he gave me instructions for the last time. His grave gallantry and quiet conversation as he lay there, while the stretcher-bearers came, and fresh arrivals burst, were such that I wondered if, after all, the world in which these incidents happened was not normal. The Germans about this time also fired minenwerfers into our poor draggled front line; this inhumanity could not be allowed, and the rifle-grenades that went over No Man's Land in reply for once almost carried out the staff's vicarious motto, Give him three for every one. One glared hideously at the broken wood and clay flung up from our grenades and trench mortar shells in the German trenches, finding that for once a little hate was possible. To throw minnies into that ghost of a front line!

Once again we had a night or two out of trenches, and I saw anew the farmhouse where I had joined the battalion, still steadfast, still unchangeable, children and chickens and kitchen stove. It was now my luck to have a room in a farm cottage, a bed of mahogany, sheets, the usual straw mattress, with an interesting camber. Peaceful little one, standest thou yet? cool nook, earthly paradisal cupboard with leaf-green light to see poetry by, I fear much that 1918 was the ruin of thee. For my refreshment, one night's sound sleep, I'll call thee friend, 'not inanimate.' After the pause, we went without excitement into the old position east of Festubert, which was not greatly revised; the main difference was that Pioneer Trench now reached Cover Trench, allowing free communication by daylight, and the grass was thicker and taller, the ground easy and dry. The 'Islands' were there yet, on which the war was so often deplorable or agreeable according as rations worked out at seven or four 'in a loaf.' For want of something better to do, I resolved to see whether these Islands could be reached from Cover Trench in daylight, and, in spite of the accepted impossibility, got across, carrying with me little wants such as chloride of lime and the latest news. Nervous haste at the last moment drew on me the fire of a sniper or two, but I was too early. Beyond the Islands, No Man's Land was cut up with abandoned diggings, and these I looked into, scaring the rats, and lugging back old rifles, helmets, and, in the bliss of ignorance, unexploded German bombs with 'fins.' Our colonel, Harrison, who followed me in the daylight route to the Islands, met me after such an occasion, frightening me greatly. He looked at my collection, and asked, 'Been big-game hunting?' but I was tongue-tied, as I had been once in Richebourg village, where he, notebook in hand, in the heat both of the sun and my apprehension, stopped me as I led my platoon out, and asked which post I had been holding. 'Port Arthur' would not come: I stood striving for speech; he smiled, and I ruefully asked my nearest man.

Daytime was play in the Islands that summer; night was a perpetual tangle. Straight lines did not exist. If one went forward patrolling, it was almost inevitable that one would soon creep round some hole or suspect heap or stretch of wired stumps, and then, suddenly one no longer knew which was the German line, which our own. I almost joined a German working party 'in all good faith' after such a careless circuit. Puzzling dazzling lights flew up, fell in the grass beside and flared like bonfires; one heard movements, saw figures, conjectured distances, and all in that state of dilemma. Willow-trees seemed moving men. Compasses responded to old iron and failed us. At last by luck or some stroke of recognition one found oneself, but there was danger of not doing so; and the battalion which relieved us sent a patrol out, only to lose it that way. The patrol came against wire, and bombed with all its skill; the men behind the wire fired their Lewis gun with no less determination; and, when the killed and wounded amounted to a dozen or more, it was found that the patrol and the defenders were of the same battalion. I knew the officer who led that patrol; he was by temperament suited for a quiet country parsonage, and would usually have mislaid his spectacles.

The parapets were thin and treacherous in this place. One afternoon a sentry of ours was hit in the head and killed while he stood quite out of observation. I was in my tiny dugout reading Mr Masefield's *Good Friday* when I heard that shot, which at once told me that a man had gone west.

Past deaths were not so piercing. At night, men digging out Pioneer Trench found numerous bodies; but nothing extraordinary was talked of until someone disentangled a watch and some money. Lucky devil!

By now I felt myself to be an honest part of C Company, and although Northcote (he was called 'The Satire') had not been long commanding us, we were all working together in good ease. If there had to be trenches for the rest of our lives, which appeared the best possible future, the alternative being massacre in No Man's Land, well, then we should like to be left together as the happy family. Northcote was certainly paterfamilias. A little worried on every pre-text, he would pull at his light and reluctant moustache; but he was earnestly pleased with his young men. When I evolved a large and well-filled map of the sector, he more than made up for his recent reproof of me (and Limbery-Buse) on a mistake about guides. He seldom rested, plodding alone with his head thrust forward, his sad eyes seeking thoroughness, his whole face deep-lined with sense of duty. Nor did Limbery-Buse and myself, who were as thick as thieves, find much rest: the shortage of officers meant that our trench watches came oftener, and no doubt we became more confident and serviceable. Still, in daytime, we sometimes got out of the trench into the tall sorrelled grass behind, which the sun had dried, and enjoyed a warm indolence with a book (not *Infantry Training*, I think). The war seemed to have forgotten us in that placid sector. It is true that steel helmets now became the rule, their ugly useful discomfort supplanting our old friendly soft caps; and the parachute flares winding down from the cloud of night glistened here and there on those curious green mushrooms, or domes, where listening-posts perhaps listened, probably dozed among the weeds and rustlings of No Man's Land. The dethronement of the soft cap clearly symbolized the change that was coming over the war, the induration from a personal crusade into a vast machine of violence, that had come in the South, where vague victory seemed to be happening. The South! what use thinking about it? If we were doomed to go, we thought, we were, and we pressed no further. No one seemed to have any mental sight or smell of that vast battle; and it was undoubtedly better so.

viii

The Calm

With only a short interlude, in the camp among orchards towards Lacouture, by the farmhouse whose pigeon-loft caused sudden suspicious alarm and inquiry, and in the inconvenient roar and shock of a busy heavy howitzer, we moved again to relieve trenches. That afternoon we halted in the open by the La Bassée Canal, and many of us swam there in unexpected luxury, to the admiration of the small boys of the surviving houses near. One of them told me with some emphasis that he envied us; and he looked miserable as I started off my platoon in small groups towards Givenchy. He was not the only miserable one at that moment. Givenchy was not expected to give satisfaction. The long weedy canal in drowsy summer's yellow haze, with here a diver in his rubber suit exploring a sunken barge, there a solidly built battery position adjoining the bank, kept one's attention until, beyond some broad pools wherein old clumsy hulks of barges lay awaiting what we were all awaiting, the Givenchy 'village line' appeared. We hid ourselves duly in and about the village.

From the old crumpled bridge which would take us southward into Cuinchy, the street northward was not displeasing in appearance. That is to say, it had not yet lost its rows of brick dwellings, which stood up externally presentable if inwardly dismantled; and it was perhaps wholly protected against enemy observation posts by the slight ridge which gathered gently to the east of it. The ridge was still adorned with a shrine, from which a Lewis gun nightly instructed the enemy in obeisance. Between the village line and the front trenches lay another road, roughly parallel with them, and originating at Givenchy Church. Some houses here, in the thick of it, yet retained their outline, and when one had walked up the communication trench – Wolfe Road, if I am right – it was curious and touching to see them, after the thought that one was past all houses. I took a walk among their white shutters and painted garden railings in the thick mists of morning, with that compelled spirit of reverence which those village ruins awoke in me, more vividly perhaps than a Wren masterpiece can to-day. To visit such relics of a yesterday whose genial light seemed at once scarcely gone and gone for ages, relics whose luckless situation almost denied them the imagined piety of contemplation and pity, was a part of my war. There were other ruins, which we made less emotional; 'Haunted House,' an observation post, lacked the true phantom-air.

I had written and left with a publisher in London a trifling collection of verses: I had forgotten about them, but they entered my story again at Givenchy. The scene is bright in my mind's eye. Northcote and his subalterns, in their sandbagged ground floor in the village line, have had tea, and are arguing over some frivolous subject, as Mr Asquith's benignity, or the effectiveness of our Archies, when with a great clatter and abruptness a shell from our own batteries behind hits the ground before our window and sends a nosecap into our wallpaper. We are still talking about this mishit and others similar when Colonel Harrison appears and surprises us almost as much with a demand for me. I am wanted at battalion headquarters. A review of my poems has been printed in the *Times Literary Supplement* (a kind review it was, if ever there was one!), and my Colonel has seen it and is overjoyed at having an actual author in his battalion. How rosy he looks!

Paternal Northcote pleaded hard, 'Surely you won't take our young Blunden, sir – Oh no! he's quite happy here.' I, too, when Colonel Harrison had left, appealed to my admirable company commander, saying how sincerely I knew myself unequal to the lordly style of battalion headquarters. But all to no purpose; that book of verse had done its work; and the same evening I was at dinner in Harrison's presence, afraid of him and everyone else in that high command, and marvelling at the fine glass which was in use there – soon to be deposited by thoughtful Quartermaster Swain with regrets in some safe village, while we went to worse ruins and cruder warfare.

My new style was 'Field Works Officer,' and business, odd jobs about the trenches. The first Herculean labour innocently attempted by me concerned the abysmal Red Dragon Crater which had been blown here a little while before under the unfortunate Welshmen. Our posts held the 'near lip' of this devilish hole, and in order to reach them from the nearest sound trench, along a soapy brook under some hurt pollards, a longish sap had to be maintained. As the crater's rim stood at a surprising height above the surrounding ground, and the battle-line curved to the south, this sap was under observation from the flank. And further, it ran through such pulverized burnt soil that it almost filled itself without the aid of bombardment. My plan was to scrape it out and to revet it with wood and galvanized iron, and I asked for a working party. To my amazement and consternation the Brigade sent up a hundred men, or more, from a reserve battalion; it was the practice of the time to send into the line at least twice the number of men who could possibly be employed, concealed and supervised. These worthies carried up plenty of material, dug quite brilliantly, and set in position the wooden frames and the sheets of corrugated iron or expanded metal; while my good Sergeant Worley, who to my delight had joined battalion headquarters as wiring sergeant, and was with me on this piece of work through sheer love, went round with me laying on muffled mallets and risking his life. Especially so; the miracle was that the whole of my spademen were not battered into the dust. I was less like a man in fever when they were gone at last, and Worley and myself remained behind adding some practical and (as the world was then constituted) some artistical touches; sandbags and duckboards sort out your artists. These degenerate days know nothing of a stylish revetment. With a duckboard under my arm, I was suddenly pulled up by the high and dry voice of the General, who appeared to be rather more displeased by the irregularity of an officer's publicly transferring a duckboard from trench to trench than pleased by the reformation of the sap. He went off, leaving a dash of bitterness in my mild draught of content; but still it was a good afternoon's work. Worley and myself had scarcely emerged when huge crashes and dirty rolling smoke behind us needed no commentary. The memory of Lot's wife! We dropped into a tunnel-shaft and meditated audibly. It was some time before we could reasonably emerge.

But I had still a feeling that the sap might be converted, like drunkards, in confidence and secrecy, and on after days with a few skilful supporters I tidied it up. Lintott, who had sympathized, went up to inspect, whereon a minny descended and partly buried him. Others followed, and 'work done' was crossed out – on the ground, not on the report sent to higher regions. Who, I wonder, at last conquered this recreant, fulminatory alley? I should like to see that man; Madame Tussaud's has scarcely exhibited his superior.

Not only the air but the earth beneath also menaced the tenant of Givenchy. Our own miners were busy, and an engine driving pumps could be interpreted by the most youthful earth-dweller. A large sunprint on view at headquarters 'suspected' many enemy mine-shafts – one stopped counting them, they were so many – and authentic opinion promised us that the support trench near the canal would rise, Kraken-like, any day or night. This affected me, particularly as I was sent up to take a turn or two of trench watch at night in that quarter, and we were to hold the line for eight or sixteen days. However, we got nothing worse than rifle-grenades, whipping angrily down while dawn came with sinister calm, white and weary as the sentries' faces, through the sallow fog.

Givenchy with its famous keep and huge crater was no sinecure, but some memories of our incarceration there have an Arcadian quality about them. There, it was possible to send one's batman back with some francs and a sandbag, and to welcome him in a couple of hours returning with beer and chocolate. There, the doctor's monkey used to gambol like a rogue along a garden wall, in the village line, while a machine-gun at long range traversed over him. There, if you failed to see the official warning to trespassers, you might creep along the sunny canal bank in its untrodden part, and see among the weeds the most self-satisfied pike in numbers, who had almost forgotten the fact of anglers.

'Were there hooks once?'

Moreover, a heavy concrete lock, barring the canal at our support line, afforded protection on our side to bathing-parties of our men, who were marched down in the afternoon, and chaffed and splashed and plunged, with the Germans probably aware but unobjecting a few hundred yards along. Outside the stopped electrical machinery in this place was an old notice, 'Danger de Mort' – exactly. The usual nuisance was the wires which generations of field telephonists had run through the bathing pool. But, on my last occasion there, sudden shelling on the high south bank scattered unwelcome jags of iron in the still lapping water. O ho, Fritz! I never dressed quicker.

By good luck, I escaped a piece of trouble in this sector. Had I come on trench watch two hours later, not young C. but myself would have been puzzled by the appearance of a German officer and perhaps twenty of his men, who, with friendly cries of 'Good morning, Tommy, have you any biscuits?' and the like, got out of their trench and invited our men to do the same. What their object was, beyond simple fraternizing, I cannot guess; it was afterwards argued that they wished to obtain an identification of the unit opposite them. And yet I heard they had already addressed us as the 'bastard Sussek.' In any case, our men were told not to fire upon them, both by C. and the other company's officer on watch; there was some exchange of shouted remarks, and after a time both sides returned to the secrecy of their parapets. When this affair was reported to more senior members of the battalion, it took on rather a gloomy aspect; it appeared that the bounden duty of C. and R. had been to open fire on the enemy, and one hoped that the business might be kept from the ears of the Brigade Commander. Such hopes were, of course, nothing to the purpose; the story was out and growing, the unfortunate subalterns were reproved, and, what is more, placed under arrest.

Under arrest they marched towards the Somme battle of 1916. When we left Givenchy, it was known that we were at length 'going South,' and, curious as it may seem, the change produced a kind of holiday feeling among us. For some time to come, it was clear, we should be out of the trenches, and on our travels among unbroken houses, streets of life, and peaceful people; hitherto there had been very little but relieving here, and being relieved, and almost at once relieving there, a sandbag rotation. While the battalion was romantically lodged in ancient Béthune, it fell to me to haunt the sandbags a little longer. I was sent to receive instruction in trench-building from our Engineers, who inhabited a beautiful little farmhouse near Festubert. The daily plan was, after that indescribably sweet wash in well-water under leafy roofs, and a farmhouse breakfast, to cycle up to the hamlet of Le Plantin, among waterlogged grounds with willow groves of bamboo green, under which ran queer old defences and dugouts floored with ancient straw. In front of this place a support line was being made, and very nice and proper it looked to the simple mind, with its clean U-frames and footboards and symmetrical wire anchorages. Our instructor left us here with vague allusion to 'carrying on,' and several sappers also went about gravely with hammers and nails. At first we dug with medium force, but the weather was beautiful and even a little too sleepily warm, and presently we withdrew for lunch to one of the ruins behind, where thatch and brick and lath hung together still in no mean likeness of houses, and water of the most crystal dripped musically down from the tank of a well in what had been the garrets of the nearest cottage. The second morning, we took not only lunch but a walk after it; returning, we were offended by the foul smell of recent lyddite, by branches and rafters mutilated and strewn about the crossroad, by damp brown earth flung across the white summer dust. A visit to the new trench soon proved that it had been the main target; that German kite balloon which had been hanging in the blue like a boat swinging idly at mooring had not been there for nothing. We therefore elected to give time for the German observer to forget our trench, and sat simply chatting in a rustic row under a flowery bank (still smelling a little nitrous), when the instructor broke in on us. His Boer War experience, annotated in the ribbons which he wore, had given him a touch of overlordliness, which now tuned his irritable remarks. Then arose a slight argument, which seemed to promise us less of comfort in what was left of our engineering course; and I was pleased at the order a day or so later to lay down the hammer and nails and join the battalion in Béthune.

They had just come from a ceremonial parade in the yard of the Girls' School when I reached them – another escape! This was the parade on which the Colonel made the cryptic remark to the sergeant who, on the command 'Fix,' dropped his bayonet. Such things were never forgotten, while bombardments passed into oblivion. They were all as cheerful as a choir excursion, and found that Béthune agreed with them. Indeed, it was a marvellous little town to be found so near the trenches. It was old, it was young; its streets were not of 1916, but its pretty faces were immediate, and the heartiness of ordinary life prevailed. There was keen preference in hotels and restaurants. One could even go to the Banque de France and draw money in a handsome setting, instead of parading at the Field Cashier's deal table. *C'est triste, la guerre; ah, malheur, malheur.* That note was there, but above it for the time played the spirits of delight in whatever baffled war's grey tentacles. In the church the twilight bloomed with art's ancient beauty; the music adored its own centuries of grandeur. In the shops the white fingers that turned over pictures or books for one's choice were pure poetry. It is a bitter reflection that, perhaps on account of the aforesaid ceremonial parade, with the gleaming bayonets and accoutrements not unnoted by German flying Scouts, this town was shelled by heavy guns on the day that we departed, and many citizens were killed. The chemist's shop just vacated by battalion headquarters was unlucky.

And now, as I lie in bed in my billet, after a conversation on infant schools with the lady teacher whose house it is, with trees softly swaying almost to the window, and only the odd night voices of an ancient town about me, I conjecture briefly, yet with a heaving breast, of that march southward which begins to-morrow morning. It will be a new world again. The past few months have been a new world, of which the succession of sensations erratically occupies my mind; the bowed heads of working parties and reliefs moving up by 'trenches' framed of sacking and brushwood; the bullets leaping angrily from charred rafters shining in greenish flare-light; an old pump and a tiled floor in the moon; bedsteads and broken mattresses hanging over cracked and scarred walls; Germans seen as momentary shadows among wire hedges; tallowy, blood-dashed, bewildered faces – but put back the blanket; a garden gate, opening into a battlefield; boys, treating the terror and torment with the philosophy of men; cheeky newspaper-sellers passing the gunpits; stretcher-bearers on the same road an hour after; the old labourer at his cottage door, pointing out with awe and circumstance (the guns meanwhile thundering away on the next parish) his eaves chipped by anti-aircraft shrapnel; the cook's mate digging for nose-caps where a dozen shells have just exploded; the 'Mad Major' flying low over the Germans' parapet and scattering out his bombs, leaving us to settle the bill; our own parapet seen in the magnesium's glare as the Germans were seeing it; stretchers or sooty dixies being dumped round trench corners; the post-cards stuck on the corner of Coldstream Lane; the diction of the incoming and outgoing soldiers squeezing past one another in the pitch-black communication-trench; the age that has gone by since I read Young's *Night Thoughts* in the dugout at Cuinchy. And, now I think of it, I forgot to rescue that edition (1815) when it slipped down behind the bunks! We may go back again, of course: but—

> Time glides away, Lorenzo, like a brook,
> In the same brook none ever bathed him twice.

ix

The Storm

Marching west from Béthune, we had nothing to trouble us except our packs and the General, who never exhibited his talent for being in all places at once more terrifically. My own place was alongside my friends C. and R., who, with the prospect of a court-martial, were at first rather quiet, but presently began to be themselves. They rejoiced at least that their equipment was carried on the transport. Mine was not, and every halt was welcome. Our road showed us noble woods, and purling streams turning water-wheels, and cleanly green and white villages. The battalion was billeted at Auchel, a considerable mining town, for one night; I remember that well because, when we got in at eleven or so, the advance party had not completed arrangements, and I set out to find shelter for my servant and myself. Seeing a young woman at an upper window, looking out in some wonder at the sudden incursion in the streets, I addressed her with the most persuasive French I could find, and she (note it, recording Angel, or spirit of Sterne, if you did not then) hastened down to give us food and lodging, and next day piano practice and *L'Illustration*. On my asking for her address, she prudently gave me her father's. Emerging from the slag-heaps of Auchel, the battalion moved deviously, but now definitely southward, and came without unusual event and with usual misreading of the map to the flimsy outlandish village of Monchy-Breton (known, of course, as Monkey Britain), near St Pol. The weather had turned heavy and musty, the pre-ordained weather of British operations.

Near this place was an extent of open country (chiefly under wheat) which in its ups and downs and occasional dense woodlands resembled the Somme battlefield; here, therefore, we were trained for several days. The Colonel told us that the ground was held to be an excellent facsimile of the scene of our 'show.' Hardly a man knew so much as the name of the southern village from which we were to attack; but from our practice we saw with mixed feelings that the jumping-off position was one side of a valley, the position to be captured the other side, and all began to be proficient in moving to the particular 'strong point' or other objective plotted out for them. Gas was loosed over us; we ran out wire at the edge of the swiftly captured woods; we crouched down in trenches while the roaring heat of the flammenwerfer curled up in black smoke above; a Scottish expert, accompanied by well-fed, wool-clad gymnastic demonstrators, preached to us the beauty of the bayonet, though I fear his comic tales of Australians muttering 'In, out, – on guard,' and similar invocations of 'cold steel' seemed to most of us more disgusting than inspiring in that peacefully ripening farmland. In the intervals we bought chocolate from the village women who had brought their baskets far enough to reach us; and so we passed the time. Our manœuvres and marches were quite hard work, and in the evenings the calm of Monchy-Breton and its mud huts under their heavy verdure, or its crucifixes beside the downland roads, was not much insulted.

At battalion headquarters, where a French soldier, a considerable joker, was on leave, frequent conferences were called over the arrangements for our attack. 'Jake' Lintott, the clever assistant-adjutant who had been with the Canadians at Ypres, had drawn a fine bold map of the destined ground and trenches on the reverse of our waterproof table-cloth. When conferences began, the table-cloth was turned over, and the map brought into action. One sunny evening after we had been talking out the problems and proceedings of the coming battle, and making all clear with the map, it was felt that something was wrong, and someone turning noted a face at a window. We hurried out to catch a spy, but missed him, if he was one; certainly he was a stranger.

Nothing else distinguished our Monchy-Breton period; after a fine night or two sleeping under the stars, we left its chicken-runs and muddy little cart-tracks about the middle of August, and were entrained at Ligny St Flochel, between Arras and St Pol. A German aeroplane hovered above the act, and we sat waiting for the train to start, in a familiar attitude, with trying apprehensions. We travelled with the gravity due to hot summer weather, and found the process better than marching. But the Somme was growing nearer! Leaving the railway, we were billeted one night in a village called Le Souich. The occasion was marked at battalion headquarters by a roast goose, which the old farmer whose house we had invaded had shot at shortest range with the air of a mighty hunter ('*Je le tire à l'œil!*') and I joyfully recollect how Millward, that famed cricketer, gave a few of us an hour's catching practice in the orchard with apples instead of cricket-balls or bombs.

Thence the battalion took the road, in great glare and heat and dust, kilometre after kilometre. The changeful scenery of hills and woods was indeed dramatic and captivating after our long session in the flat country, but as the march wore on most of us were too used up to comment on it. Many men fell out, and officers and non-commissioned officers for the most part were carrying two or three rifles to keep others in their place. At Thièvres there was a long halt, and a demand for water; some thrifty inhabitants produced it at so much a bucket, thus giving occasion for a critical pun on the name of the place. The villagers' device for dismantling wells and pumps, and their inquisitive probing for information, disturbed our men's philosophy a little. Eventually the battalion encamped in a solemnly glorious evening at the edge of a great wood called Bois du Warnimont, with the whole divisional artillery alongside – and such was our enthusiasm that we stirred ourselves to take a look at it; the stragglers came in, and were sternly told their fault at 'orderly room' next day – we blush to think how many there were, but our experience of marching had recently been meagre.

Warnimont Wood, an unmolested green cloister, was six or seven miles west of the terrible Beaumont Hamel, one of the German masterpieces of concealed strength; but we hardly realized that yet. A reconnoitring party was soon sent up to the line, and I remember thinking (according to previous experience) that I should be able to buy a pencil in the village of Englebelmer, on the way; but when we got there its civilians had all been withdrawn. Therein lay the most conspicuous difference between this district and our old one with the cottagers and débitants continuing their affairs almost in view of the front trench. This country was truly in military hands. The majority of the reconnoitring party went on horseback, I on a bicycle; and the weather had turned rainy, and the quality of Somme mud began to assert itself. My heavy machine went slower and slower, and stopped dead; I was thrown off. The brake was clogged with most tenacious mud, typifying future miseries. Presently we passed a cemetery and reached through wide puddles an empty village called Mesnil, which, although it stood yet in the plausible mask of farmhouses and out-buildings not shattered into heaps, instantly aroused unpleasant sus-picions. These suspicions were quickly embodied in the savage rush of heavy shrapnel shells, uncoiling their dingy green masses of smoke downwards while their white-hot darts scoured the acre below. On the west side, a muddy sunken lane with thickets of nettles on one bank and some precarious dugouts in the other led us past the small brick railway station, and we turned out of it by two steps up into a communication trench chopped in discoloured chalk. It smelt omin-ous, and there was a grey powder here and there thrown by shellbursts, with some of those horrible conical holes in the trench sides, blackened and fused, which meant 'direct hits,' and by big stuff. If ever there was a vile, unnerving and desperate place in the battle zone, it was the Mesnil end of Jacob's Ladder, among the heavy battery positions, and under perfect enemy observation.

Jacob's Ladder was a long trench, good in parts, stretching from Mesnil with many angles down to Hamel on the River Ancre, requiring flights of stairs at one or two steep places. Leafy bushes and great green and yellow weeds looked into it as it dipped sharply into the green valley by Hamel, and hereabouts the aspect of peace and innocence was as yet prevailing. A cow with a crumpled horn, a harvest cart should have been visible here and there. The trenches ahead were curious, and not so pastoral. Ruined houses with rafters sticking out, with half-sloughed plaster and dangling window-frames, perched on a hillside, bleak and piteous that cloudy morning; half-filled trenches crept along below them by upheaved gardens, telling the story of wild bombardment. Further on was a small chalk cliff, facing the river, with a rambling but remarkable dugout in it called Kentish Caves. The front line was sculptured over this brow, and descended to the wooded marshes of the Ancre in winding and gluey irregularity. Running across it towards the German line went the narrow Beaucourt road, and the railway to Miramount and Bapaume; in the railway bank was a look-out post called the Crow's Nest, with a large periscope, but no one seemed very pleased to see the periscope. South of the Ancre was broad-backed high ground, and on that a black vapour of smoke and naked tree trunks or charcoal, an apparition which I found was called Thiepval Wood. The Somme indeed!

The foolish persistence of ruins that ought to have fallen but stood grimacing, and the dark day, chilled my spirit. Let us stop this war, and walk along to Beaucourt before the leaves fall. I smell autumn again. The Colonel who was showing Harrison the lie of the land betrayed no such apprehension. He walked about, with indicatory stick, speaking calmly of the night's shelling, the hard work necessary to keep the trenches open, and the enemy's advantage of observation, much as if he was showing off his rockery at home; and this confidence fortunately began to grow in me, so that I afterwards regarded the sector as nothing too bad. What my Colonel felt, who knew the battle history of this place, I perceive better to-day, and why he fixed his mind so closely on details. As we went along the slippery chalk cuttings and past large but thin-roofed and mouldy dugouts, it was my duty to detect positions for forward dumps of bombs, ammunition, water and many other needs, against the approaching battle. I was pleasantly helped by Captain Kirk, the most reticent of men; some time later we heard that he crossed No Man's Land, and fought several Germans in a dugout, the light of which had attracted his notice. However, he now seemed afraid of even me. When we had made our round, we went back across the village to the Cheshire Colonel's exemplary underground headquarters in Pottage Trench, a clean and quiet little alley near some pretty villas which might have been at Golder's Green, under the whispering shadow of aspen trees in a row, with a model firing-rack of SOS rockets; and thence, not unwillingly, back farther, up Jacob's Ladder to Mesnil, which now smelt stronger still of high explosive, and away.

The battalion moved forward to a straggling wood called from its map reference P. 18, near the little town of Mailly-Maillet. Here, three miles from the enemy's guns, it was thought sufficient to billet us in tents (and those, to round off my posthumous discontent, used specimens). Mailly-Maillet was reported to have been until recently a delightful and flourishing little place, but it was in the sere and yellow; its long château wall had been broken down by the fall of shell-struck trees; its church, piously protected against shrapnel by straw mats, had been hit. On the road to the town, we had spelt out on almost every cornfield gate the advertisement of 'Druon-Lagniez, Quincaillier à Mailly-Maillet'; but, seeking out his celebrated shop, one found it already strangely ventilated, and its dingy remnants of cheap watches or brass fittings on the floor disappointing after all the proclamation. In a garden solitude of this little town there rose a small domed building, as yet but a trifle disfigured, with plaster and glass shaken down to the mosaic floor, in the middle of which stood the marble tomb of a great lady, a princess, if I do not forget, of a better century. There the pigeons fluttered and alighted; and the light through the high pale-tinted panes seemed to rest with inviolable grace on holy ground.

Work at Hamel immediately called for me, with a party of good trench hands, duly paraded and commanded by my invincible friend Sergeant Worley. The first night that we reached the village, wild with warfare, rain was splashing down, and we willingly waited for dawn in a sepulchral cellar, wet through, yet not anxious on that account. I had already chosen the nooks and corners in the front line where I would make up in readiness for our battle small reserves of rations, rifle ammunition, grenades, reels of barbed wire, planks, screw pickets, wire netting, sandbags; my party therefore took up their burdens from the central stores in Hamel, and followed me to the different points. The chief dump in Hamel lay between a new but not weather-proof residence (its back door opened on Thiepval), and a tall hedge with brambles straying over our stacks of planks and boxes, making a scene passably like the country builder's yard. A soldiers' cemetery was open at all hours just behind this kind illusion. I may say that we worked hard, up and down, and even felt a little proud as the forward stores grew to useful size. When the Brigade bombing officer, suddenly pouncing upon me in a lonely trench, told me that my boxes of bombs, painfully stacked at that place, would all be ruined by exposure to the weather, and that he should report me to the General, I damned him and wept. My critic (an old adversary) had just arrived from England. But I was afraid of the General. Apart from that, there was no great trouble; once, carelessly pushing some bomb-boxes above the parados in sight of some enemy post, we returned with the next consignment to find nothing but new shell-holes there. All day long that valley was echoing with bombardment, but for the most part it was on Thiepval Wood that the fury thundered; and we, at meal-times, sat freely like navvies in some ruin and put away considerable quantities of bread, bully and cheese. And how well we knew our Hamel! The 'Café du Centre' was as real to us as the Ritz or the 'Marquis of Granby,' though now it was only some leaning walls obviously of cheap plaster and a silly signboard. The insurance agent's house, with its gold bee sign still inviting custom (not in our line!); the stuffed pheasant by his glass dome, drooping a melancholy beak and dishonoured plumage, opposite our duckboard and wire repository; the superior hip bath lying on the roadside towards the line; the spring of beautiful clear drink there; the level-crossing keeper's red house, with its cellars full of petrol-tins of water, in the direction of Thiepval – these and every other lineament of poor Hamel photographed themselves in us. The ridiculously fat tom-cat which had refused to run wild knew us well. We humped our boxes of deadly metal past the agricultural exhibition of innocent metal on the wayside; what were ploughs and drags and harrows to Hamel now? What rural economist had collected them there?

The date of the attack was suddenly postponed. A runner discovered me, with this news. We went back to the wood in which the battalion, not too well pleased with its surroundings, had dug short protective lengths of trench. These, however, could not protect us from a plague of wasps, and the engineers had to add to their varied service that of cleaning some monstrous nests with gun-cotton. After an agreeable evening passed in exploring the rambling streets of Mailly, and watching a huge howitzer in action in the orchards, fed with shells by means of a pulley, and those shells large enough to be seen plainly mounting up to the sky before they disappeared in an annihilating dive upon 'Thiepval Crucifix,' we turned in. I was as bold as Harrison and others, and put on my pyjamas; but at midnight the shriek of shells began, meant for our camp, and we slipped shivering into the nearest slit of trench. There were gas shells, and high explosive, and samples of both missed our trench by yards; the doctor, who was huddling next to me with his monkey in his arms, was suddenly affected by the gas, and his pet also swallowed some. They were both 'sent down the line'; but I was unharmed. When the hate was over, it seemed perhaps difficult to sleep again, warm as the blankets might be, and it was one more case of waiting for daylight.

Corporal Candler, without whom our administration would have been so much poorer from 1916 to 1918, will perhaps forgive me for telling a story of Mailly Wood for him. Perhaps it was on the occasion just mentioned that he happened to be sitting alone in the orderly-room tent, running his hands through his hair over the latest heap of orders and messages. When shelling began, he hesitated to go out to the trench; and as he sat there, he saw a man wearing a black cloak appear in the doorway. This figure stood watching him. 'Don't be funny,' said Candler, adjusting his glasses – we see and hear him exactly. The figure still paused, then went; and Candler went after, among the trees, but no explanation could be got.

Expecting that I should not again see that wood, I went up next night with some heavy materials for the dump in Hamel, carried on the limbers. The transport officer, Maycock, was with us, which is saying we talked all the way. At Mesnil church, a cracked and toppling obelisk, there were great craters in the road, and when one of the limbers fell in, it was necessary to unload it before it could be got out. While this delay lasted, in such a deadly place, my flesh crept, but luck was ours, and no fresh shells came over to that church before we were away. One still sees in rapid gunlights the surviving blue finger-post at the fork in the unknown road. It helped us. As we plodded down the dark hill, the blackness over by Thiepval Wood leapt alive with tossing flares, which made it seem a monstrous height, and with echo after echo in stammering mad pursuit the guns threshed that area; uncounted shells passed over with savage whipcracks, and travelled meteor-like with lines of flame through the brooding sultry air. One scarcely seemed to be alive and touching earth, but at the bottom of the hill, which was steep enough, the voices of other beings sounded, at Hamel Dump, like business – 'Back in 'ere, lad,' 'Any more?' The following day I had an opportunity to improve the contents of my small forward dumps, and to choose with Sergeant Rhodes, the master-cook, a 'retired spot' where he might prepare the rum and coffee, to be served to the attacking troops. This quest introduced an incident. All day, on and off, our guns were battering the German trenches, and one saw almost without a thought our salvoes bursting every few minutes on such tender points as trench junctions, whitely embossed in that sector of chalk parapets and downlands. The German guns answered this brilliant provocation at their own moment. Thus, as the thin and long cook-sergeant and I were walking comfortably in Roberts' Trench, the air about us suddenly became ferocious with whizzbangs, the parapets before and behind sprang up or collapsed in clods and roarings; there seemed no way out. They were hitting the trench. Rhodes stared at me, I at him for a suggestion; his lean face presented the wildest despair, and no doubt mine was the same; we ran, we slipped and crouched one way and the other but it was like a cataract both ways. And then, sudden quiet; more to come? Nothing; a reprieve.

Another postponement took me dustily back to the battalion in the wood watched by so many German observation-balloons in the morning sun. The wood, shelled deliberately because of its camps and accidentally because of some conspicuous horse-lines, and silhouetted movements on the hill to the west, had frayed the men's keenness; there had been casualties; and then the anti-climax twice repeated had spoiled their first energetic eagerness for a battle. Yet, still, they were a sound and capable battalion, deserving far better treatment than they were now getting, and a battle, not a massacre. On the evening of September 2, the battalion moved cautiously from Mailly-Maillet by cross-battalion tracks, through pretty Englebelmer, with ghostly Angelus on the green and dewy light, over the downs to Mesnil, and assembled in the Hamel trenches to attack the Beaucourt ridge next morning. The night all round was drugged and quiet. I stood at the junction of four advanced trenches, directing the several companies into them as had been planned. Not one man in thirty had seen the line by daylight – and it was a maze even when seen so, map in hand. Even climbing out of the narrow steep trenches with weighty equipment, and crossing others by bridges placed 'near enough' in this dark last moment, threatened to disorder the assault. Every man remembered the practice attacks at Monchy-Breton, and was ready, if conditions were equal, to act his part; among other things, the 'waves' had to form up and carry out a 'right incline' in No Man's Land – a change of direction almost impossible in the dusk, in broken and entangled ground, and under concentrated gunfire. When the rum and coffee was duly on the way to these men, I went off to my other duty. A carrying-party from another battalion was to meet me in Hamel, and for a time the officer and I, having nothing to do but wait, sat in a trench beside the village high street considering the stars in their courses. An unusual yet known voice jubilantly interrupted this unnaturally calm conversation; it was a sergeant-major, a fine soldier who had lost his rank for drunkenness, won it again, and was now going over in charge of a party carrying trench mortar ammunition. A merry man, a strong man; when we had met before, he had gained my friendliest feelings by his freedom from any feeling against a schoolboy officer. Some NCO's took care to let their superior training and general wisdom weigh on my shyness: not so C. He referred to the attack as one might speak of catching a train, and in it a few hours later he showed such wonderful Saint Christopher spirit that he was expected to be awarded a posthumous Victoria Cross. Meanwhile all waited.

The cold disturbing air and the scent of the river mist marked the approach of the morning. I got my fellow-officer to move his men nearer to my main supply of bombs, which were ready in canvas buckets; and time slipped by, until scarcely five preliminary minutes remained. My friend then took his men into cellars not far away, there to shelter while the cannonade opened; for their orders were to carry bombs to our bombing officer, young French, whose orders were to clear the suspected German dugouts under the railway bank, a short time after the attacking waves had crossed. As for me, I took off my equipment and began to set out the bomb buckets in a side trench so that the carriers could at the right moment pick them up two at a time; and while I was doing this, and the east began to unveil, a stranger in a soft cap and a trench coat approached, and asked me the way to the German lines. This visitor facing the east was white-faced as a ghost, and I liked neither his soft cap nor the mackintosh nor the right hand concealed under his coat. I, too, felt myself grow pale, and I thought it as well to direct him down the communication trench, Devial Alley, at that juncture deserted; he scanned me, deliberately, and quickly went on. Who he was, I have never explained to myself; but in two minutes the barrage was due, and his chances of doing us harm (I thought he must be a spy) were all gone.

The British barrage struck. The air gushed in hot surges along that river valley, and uproar never imagined by me swung from ridge to ridge. The east was scarlet with dawn and the flickering gunflashes; I thanked God I was not in the assault, and joined the subdued carriers nervously lighting cigarettes in one of the cellars, sitting there on the steps, studying my watch. The ruins of Hamel were soon crashing chaotically with German shells, and jags of iron and broken wood and brick whizzed past the cellar mouth. When I gave the word to move, it was obeyed with no pretence of enthusiasm. I was forced to shout and swear, and the carrying party, some with shoulders hunched, as if in a snowstorm, dully picked up their bomb buckets and went ahead. The wreckage around seemed leaping with flame. Never had we smelt high explosive so thick and foul, and there was no distinguishing one shell-burst from another, save by the black or tawny smoke that suddenly shaped in the general miasma. We walked along the river road, passed the sandbag dressing-station that had been rigged up only a night or two earlier where the front line ('Shankill Terrace') crossed the road, and had already been battered in; we entered No Man's Land, past the trifling British wire on its knife-rests, but we could make very little sense of ourselves or the battle. There were wounded Black Watch trailing down the road. They had been wading the marshes of the Ancre, trying to take a machine-gun post called Summer House. A few yards ahead, on the rising ground, the German front line could not be clearly seen, the water-mist and the smoke veiling it; and this was lucky for the carrying party. Half-way between the trenches, I wished them good-luck, and pointing out the place where they should, according to plan, hand over the bombs, I left them in charge of their own officer, returning myself, as my orders were, to my Colonel. I passed good men of ours, in our front line, staring like persons in a trance across No Man's Land, their powers of action apparently suspended.

'What's happening over there?' asked Harrison, with a face all doubt and stress, when I crawled into the candled, overcrowded frowsiness of Kentish Caves. I could not say, and sat down ineffectively on some baskets, in which were the signallers' sacred pigeons. 'What's happening the other side of the river?' All was in ominous discommunication. A runner called Gosden presently came in, with bleeding breast, bearing a message written an hour or more earlier. Unsted, my former companion and instructor in Festubert's cool wars, appeared, his exemplary bearing for once disturbed; he spoke breathlessly and as in an agony. This did not promise well, and, as the hours passed, all that could be made out was that our attacking companies were 'hanging on,' some of them in the German third trench, where they could not at all be reached by the others, dug in between the first and the second. Lintott wrote message after message, trying to share information north, east and west. South was impossible; the marsh separated us from that flank's attack. Harrison, the sweat standing on his forehead, thought out what to do in this deadlock, and repeatedly telephoned to the guns and the General. Wounded men and messengers began to crowd the scanty passages of the Caves, and curt roars of explosion just outside announced that these dugouts, shared by ourselves and the Black Watch, were now to be dealt with. Death soon arrived there, among the group at the clumsy entrance. Harrison meanwhile called for his runner, fastened the chin-strap of his steel helmet, and pushed his way out into the top trenches to see what he could; returned presently mopping his forehead, with that kind of severe laugh which tells the tale of a man who has incredibly escaped from the barrage. The day was hot outside, glaring mercilessly upon the stropped, burned, choked chalk trenches. I came in again to the squeaking field telephones and obscure candlelight. Presently Harrison, a message in his hand, said: 'Rabbit, they're short of ammunition. Get round and collect all the fellows you can and take them over – and stay over there and do what you can.' I felt my heart thud at this; went out, naming my men among headquarters' 'odds and ends' whenever I could find them squatted under the chalk-banks, noting with pleasure that my nearest dump had not been blown up and would answer our requirements; we served out bombs and ammunition, then I thrust my head in again to report that I was starting, when he delayed, and at length cancelled, the enterprise. The shells on our breathless neighbourhood seemed to fall more thickly, and the dreadful spirit of waste and impotence sank into us, when a sudden telephone call from an artillery observer warned us that there were Germans in our front trench. In that case Kentish Caves was a death-trap, a hole in which bombs would be bursting within a moment; yet here at last was something definite, and we all seemed to come to life, and prepared with our revolvers to try our luck.

The artillery observer must have made some mistake. Time passed without bombs among us or other surprise, and the collapse of the attack was wearily obvious. The bronze noon was more quiet but not less deadly than the morning. I went round the scarcely passable hillside trenches, but they were amazingly lonely: suddenly a sergeant-major and half a dozen men bounded superhumanly, gasping and excited, over the parapets. They had been lying in No Man's Land, and at last had decided to 'chance their arm' and dodge the machine-guns which had been perseveringly trying to get them. They drank pints of water, of which I had luckily a little store in a dugout there, now wrecked and gaping. I left them sitting wordless in that store. The singular part of the battle was that no one, not even these, could say what had happened, or what was happening. One vaguely understood that the waves had found their manœuvre in No Man's Land too complicated; that the Germans' supposed derelict forward trench near the railway was joined by tunnels to their main defence, and enabled them to come up behind our men's backs; that they had used the bayonet where challenged, with the boldest readiness; 'used the whole dam' lot, minnies, snipers, rifle-grenades, artillery'; that machine-guns from the Thiepval ridge south of the river were flaying all the crossings of No Man's Land. 'Don't seem as if the 49th Div. got any farther.' But the general effect was the disappearance of the attack into mystery.

Orders for withdrawal were sent out to our little groups in the

German lines towards the end of the afternoon. How the runners got there, they alone could explain, if any survived. The remaining few of the battalion in our own positions were collected in the trench along Hamel village street, and a sad gathering it was. Some who had been in the waves contrived to rejoin us now. How much more fortunate we seemed than those who were still in the German labyrinth awaiting the cover of darkness for their small chance of life! And yet, as we filed out, up Jacob's Ladder, we were warned by low-bursting shrapnel not to anticipate. Mesnil was its vile self, but we passed at length. Not much was said, then or afterwards, about those who would never again pass that hated target; among the killed were my old company commanders Penruddock and Northcote (after a great display of coolness and endurance in the German third line) – laughing French, quiet Hood and a hundred more. The Cheshires took over the front line, which the enemy might at one moment have occupied without difficulty; but neither they nor our own patrols succeeded in bringing in more than two or three of the wounded; and, the weather turning damp, the Germans increased their difficulty in the darkness and distorted battlefield with a rain of gas shells.

#

A Home from Home

For the moment, our much impaired battalion was billeted in Englebelmer, a sweet village scarcely yet spoiled. James Cassells (who had spent the day in the shell-holes between the German trenches) and myself were ordered to look after one of the two makeshift companies, who paraded for roll-call outside the clay barns, and were then given a few hours to themselves. Cassells had spoken a couple of days ago of the prospect of 'sitting in the barrage with the wind whistling through his hair,' but now he said nothing of that full experience. He was wondering how he was alive. Our billet was a chemist's house, well furnished, with ledgers and letters strewn about from bureaux, chiefly the scrawl of poor people in Thiepval and other places of the past who bemoaned the bad crops, and their consequent inability to pay up. Again autumn had come! Crops were still bad.

We were an affectionate pair, and poetically minded. With a little rum and much rhyme, taking a quiet side bedroom as our own, we gave each other a sturdy good night. Hoarse and ponderous roars of high explosive in the orchard outside interrupted that night, which we unwillingly finished in the cellar. Englebelmer, indeed, was now entering upon a dark period. Its green turf under trees loaded with apples was daily gouged out by heavy shells; its comfortable houses were struck and shattered, and the paths and entrances gagged with rubble, plaster and woodwork. Still, we explored the church, into which opened a mysterious tunnel; as if on holiday, we examined the brightly painted saints and the other sacred objects from gallery to vault; and hard by, found a large collection of the Englebelmer parish magazine, which was and was not interesting.

Religious readings were interrupted by a move to Beaussart, a village containing some sulky civilians. It was not shelled. We stood in its street, watching Colincamps smoke and flame with heavy shells. 'By way of retaliation,' our guns sent incendiary shells into a village unseen called Bihucourt – and we feared the worst. From Beaussart I was sent to railhead at Belle Église, and marched home triumphantly in twilight with large drafts of soldiers; but knew what they were for. Meanwhile, the Colonel had us all out for battalion drill in the morning dew.

Reorganized, the battalion was quickly sent back to the more obvious kind of war. My batman and a large number of his cronies used to spell the name of our new locality 'Ocean Villas,' but it appears on the map as Auchonvillers. In retrospect, I confess that we were lucky to take over trenches there, even though they faced some bases of red walls and decapitated trees, the outward signs of Beaumont Hamel. Auchonvillers at that time was a good example of the miscellaneous, picturesque, pitiable, pleasing, appalling, woundingly intimate village ruin close to the line. As we go up to the new sector, we must pass through, and we will look about us.

The direct road from Englebelmer over the downs is too generally exposed for a battalion relief. The battalion moves round through

Mailly-Maillet, in whose purlieus, where the apples are falling into disused gun-pits and the leaves beginning to change their tint, the huge throat of the howitzer is still being elevated to hurl horror at Thiepval Crucifix. For Thiepval is not yet captured; and we have heard that on September the Third the 49th Division could not get twenty yards forward from Thiepval Wood – Oh, forget September the Third. We are still in the Somme battle, and probably only just beginning. Meanwhile, between the curious concrete obelisks which here are used for telegraph posts, we enter Mailly, and turn at the church, still neatly jacketed with straw, but with a new hole or two in it, along a leafy side-road; another turn, and we are between excellent meadow-grounds, which lack only a few fat sheep, an old molecatcher and some crows. Groups of shell-holes, however, restrain the fancy from useless excursions, and, sitting under some tall slender elms on a convenient bank for a few moments' rest, we keep our ears eastwardly attentive. Crossing a light railway, we are in Auchonvillers. Here comes Hill, the new Brigade bombing officer. He arrived among us just in time for September 3. He was in the bombstore when an 8-inch shell buried itself in the floor; visited another bombstore, and it happened again; and here he is, grinning and dispensing epigrams. We walk on. The large logs by the roadside speak of former French activity here; our own engineers do not make their dugout with such timber. The mildew-ridden bombstore also has a French style, and is full of antiquated cricket-ball grenades and others with tennis-bat handles, which we had best leave alone. Outside, on a kind of gallows, hangs a church bell, beautifully dark green, the gift of some fantastic ancient 'seigneur de Mailly,' as its fair engraved inscription boasts. Perhaps the giver would not be wholly indignant if he knew that his bell was being used (as another inscription in chalk on it advises) as a gas alarm; for doubtless he intended it for the good of humanity.

The heart of the village is masked with its hedges and orchards from almost all ground observation. That heart, nevertheless, bleeds. The old homes are razed to the ground, all but one or two, which play involuntary tricks upon probability, balancing themselves like mad acrobats. One has been knocked out in such a way that its thatched roof, almost uninjured, has dropped over its broken body like a tea-cosy. The church maintains a kind of conceptional shape, and has a cliff-like beauty in the sunlight; but as at this ecclesiastical corner visitors are sometimes killed we may, in general, allow distance to lend enchantment. Up that naked road is the stern eye of Beaumont Hamel – turn, Amaryllis, turn – this way the tourist's privacy is preserved by ruins and fruitful branches.

Some prehistoric man was telling us lately he had often taken coffee in the Auchonvillers estaminets. Doubtless he could explain that roomy building with the red cross painted on it; it seems irrelevant now. Here is a walnut tree, under it a rubble-heap, and on the other side of the road another rubble-heap. Reserve company headquarters: but who's to know that? The enemy apparently knows it. Here is a sandbag sentry-box, with the inscription, 'Sam's Abode.' The roadway close to it has a distressed look. Poor Sam. But now we come to some very respectable and sizeable farm buildings, with conspicuous holes in the bottom of the walls, admitting to desired cellars, and nettles flocking rankly about the gaping windows, and even green doors hanging a little recklessly on their hinges. Odd sensation, we feel that it is good for us to be here. We look back at the church's white and grey hulk, not three hundred yards away, and do not like that look. A mound of those trench mortar bombs called footballs, shot out on the roadside like wurzels – more where these come from! – obstructs the garden of the last house-block in Auchonvillers; then we walk under cover of a damp-smelling bank of chalk along a chalky track, pick a blackberry from the bramble which takes a fancy to our khaki, and enter that long and noted trench, Second Avenue.

The French had modelled Auchonvillers comprehensively as a large redoubt, complete with a searchlight, but now it all seemed out of use and in need of an antiquary. There were many dugouts under houses and in the gardens, but of a flimsy, rotted and stagnant kind; the Somme battle had evidently swamped all old defence schemes, and destroyed the continuity of 'taking over.' Forward, the trenches were numerous and reliable, although they, too, had got out of hand, thanks to the confusion consequent upon the disaster of July 1. It was remarkable that they remained as serviceable as they were. But there was much to do for them, and Colonel Harrison soon re-elected me Field Works Officer. Meanwhile, I had spent a day or two in Auchonvillers with the reserve company, exploring everywhere for trustworthy dugouts, and finding many uncharted but uninviting ones. The post which had to be maintained near the church had scarcely been manned, and I had just visited the section there, when a shell tore its road into their cellar and killed and wounded almost all. At night, too, that company headquarters under the walnut tree was again and again treated to salvoes of shells. The servants, bringing over our dinner in the dark, judging the time – a plate of soup in each hand, for instance – felt a comical but also real terror, and when we found that our dugout roof of brickbats and earth, instead of being yards thick, was scarcely more than a decent veil against publicity, we also acknowledged the disturbance. Nor, though great energy with spades and 'air spaces' and steel girders succeeded, did I object to leaving this den for battalion headquarters alongside Second Avenue.

It was the weather when leaves begin to turn and sing a little drily in the wind; when spiders apparently spend the night in making webs on fences; and when the distances dare assume the purple as the sunset dislimns. As far as battalion headquarters, one might notice these nocturnal effects. Beyond that point the facts and probabilities of war obscured them. One's fine fancy was smothered with the succession of typewritten decrees, SECRET OR CONFIDENTIAL one and all, the collection of maps and diagrams with their gaudy green and violet and matter-of-fact symbols; my artistic appetite accepted

as its chief nourishment the eternal design – $\boxed{\text{TO DUMP} \twoheadrightarrow}$

I enjoyed my work,which took me up and down from the dreary and mutilated front line opposite Beaumont Hamel to where the lithe young poplars stood lightly sighing at the extremity of Auchonviller's orchards. The long communication trenches were daily repaired and even beautified by 'maintenance parties,' seven or eight men in each, of which I had charge; and in addition I had to keep a critical eye on all the system of trenches, and to urge the company commanders to 'do something about' this diminishing fire-step and that overwhelmed bombstore. The sector began to look extremely neat – except the front line, which remained impressionist, and bulged and silted at its own sweet will. Our nailing of duckboards and transoms, and digging of drainage pits, called 'sumps,' earned us applause; nay envy; even Harrison joined one afternoon in digging out a sump *par excellence*, six feet below the trench bottom – and it would have been deeper, but in the obsession of rapture we flung up a shovelful or two of earth over the parapet, and the observant Germans gave us notice with several large and well-placed shells.

Recollection paints these autumn weeks in the Beaumont Hamel sector as a tranquil time. Naturally, there on the edge of the Thiepval inferno, there were ungentle interludes. One night in particular the front line was stubbornly pounded with minenwerfers (it was a 'minnywafer' sector, and one often turned cold in the firetrench as one heard the approaching swish of these monsters). As we had little or no wire in front, and as the line now lay exposed and helpless, Harrison anticipated a German raid, and Cassells and I lay most of the night waiting for it in the new shell-holes, with a set of the trustiest soldiers, fingering bombs in a contemplative fashion. There was no raid; but a shock awaited me. When next morning's sun gilded even the barbed wire, I looked in early at my store dugout to decide how many duckboards were needed to make up the proper reserve. I looked in. The sun gleamed through the crannies there on the unutterably mangled heads and half-naked bloody bodies of the poor fellows, victims of the minenwerfer bombardment, who had been carried there to await burial.

Other lacerations fell on the battalion in connection with the attacks on Thiepval south of the river. This name Thiepval began to have as familiar and ugly a ring as any place ever mentioned by man; and as yet we knew it by report only. Our present business was to divert some of the enemy's heavy artillery from it when another forlorn hope was clutching the air before it: we made ostentatious 'smoke attacks,' which gave me a chance of employment. These attacks deluded some German machine-gunners, and drew some shell-fire, perhaps intended rather as a snub to impudence than as a genuine display of anxiety. The regimental sergeant-major, talented and gentlemanly Daniels, was ordered, about four one afternoon, to provide several hundred men of straw, which were to be raised above the parapet amid a heavy smoke cloud next morning. There was no straw. But with sandbags and grass and whatever trench theatricalities he could gather by the aid of the regimental police, the ingenious man produced some 190 dummies before midnight. And, I think, scarcely a dummy was lifted up next morning without becoming a casualty to the machine-guns. A good joke; but with this sub-audible meaning, that the operators might have been playing the part of these marionettes, and no doubt would be yet.

Poor Daniels, my good old friend! your Auchonvillers dugout was better than nothing, but— He shared a dark and wandering hole in 88 Trench, an underground workshop, with the Aid Post, and the stores taken over by the Aid Post included a number of ancient blankets. These blankets were probably the lousiest in all Christendom. Nevertheless, we others over the way in 86 Trench had skill to sympathize. The doctor and myself slept in a long, deep, French dugout, with a heavy timbered roof, quite warm, and scarcely less insectiferous. At night, when the red burst of shrapnel clanged over the support trench there, one was glad to go down the eight broad steps; but a scratchiness was always mingled with one's satisfaction in such a menagerie.

Days passed, weeks passed and it began to appear that we were growing like hermit crabs into the sector. Artillery liaison officers came, went, returned and renovated the wit and musical education of battalion headquarters at dinner. How charmingly Pratt (killed soon afterwards) used to parry the Colonel's propositions! The General came, insistent on the free use of chloride of lime in the trenches; he complimented us on our whitened sepulchre – but actually it was powdered chalk that had enabled us to satisfy his sanitary imagination. The apartments of those headquarters were improved within and without. Beside the old Beaumont Hamel road, in a dangerous and unvisited place, lay a large forgotten wealth of carpentering stores, ranging from thick timber to beautiful axes; on my drawing attention to these, Jake Lintott led a number of hands, glad to be busy, to the place in the evenings. (I even answered its attraction one foggy morning – and suddenly found that the fog had lifted, offering a view of 2nd Lieut. Blunden between the British front and support lines to any interested Teuton.) Plans and elevations of dugouts for the winter were pouring in from experts behind the line, and for once we produced something more or less corresponding to the scientific schedule. Honest labour. I began the private enterprise of building a new wash-house, but my excavations disturbed something, and I retired. My own job allowed me a free-lance variety which others wanted. Now I could be whiling away a foolhardy hour with a trench catapult ('Gamage's'), which, Cassells and I discovered, would readily toss a Mills bomb far enough to burst as shrapnel over the huge crater in front of the German line; now I was surveying the whole line with reference to its being prepared for winter tenancy, or listening at the foot of the mine-shaft in hateful Hunter Street for the subterraneous ticking there, spelling danger. Once I caught a stray mongrel, cleaned him and dried him in gentlemanly sort with a sandbag, kept him with me on my round, dug him a small recess, put in a couch of new bags, attached him to an old bayonet driven into the chalk. But what are human hopes? He went. I think I gave him W. H. Davies' Corned Beef by mistake, an unpopular brand; he may have thought me an agent. Once I walked back to Mailly, to gather from the Engineers' yard a consignment of duckboards and frames, and next to the dump I picked my way into the outraged house of a notary – a man after my own heart! There were books everywhere, on the floor, in cases, on chairs and even on the window-sills. On them the plaster and window-glass had been powdered, the rain had dripped and spouted; yet still they stood, a luxuriant legion of general literature in bright blue or red morocco, and ivory-smooth vellum, awaiting death. When I saw scattered about the porch and the doorsteps, unreverenced by the sappers in charge, a number of volumes less splendidly arrayed, and reflected that at battalion headquarters the charms of our library – O. Henry, the *Field Service Pocket Book* and *Spoon River* – were now rather withered, I could not but snatch up four or five, and bear them trenchwards in a sandbag. The heavyweight was a seventeenth-century treatise on Country Houses, which gave us no practicable ideas for the embellishment of our dugout, but would be a suitable kind of heirloom if we stayed much longer before Beaumont. Another passing contribution of mine to the gaieties of our home was made during a visitation of German gas shells, when it was alleged that I went to sleep in my flannel mask. (At present only the Colonel had a box respirator.) I did not recollect the details, yet this was urged as a confirmation of the feat.

But I recall the singular, phantasmal appearance of another wealthy house in Mailly. The Engineers used it as a headquarters. Its large drawing-room was furnished in delicate Arcadian style, the suite and the curtains being of a silver-grey silk, the piano of a light volatile design and clear tinge answering it; the tall windows were blocked with sandbags thoughtfully painted white, as though they, too, would harmonize! Perhaps the hues of dust and dimness helped them some-what in this impossibility. The room was unreal and supernatural, nor did I feel easy about the spirits' attitude towards my drinking my whisky by that incredible piano. Surely strange music would begin in tones of protest and prophecy. How long, I wonder, was it before the spell was snapped and the day gaped impudently through irreparable shell-holes on these exorcized haunters?

Looking back towards safety from the Auchonvillers trenches, one daily saw a high crucifix at the end of the town, silvered and silhouetted in the sunset. Before we came away, this sad sculpture had fallen, and it was penitential weather. News had indeed been solemnly circulated that the battles in the south (bigger and better battles every time!) were expected to be decisive; even the phrase occurred, 'no winter campaign might be necessary.' The first tall stories concerning the almightiness of the tank (which though so near us was as yet an unknown thing to us) had come. Something as big as a house was adumbrated, and the Germans were described as feeling completely overwhelmed. As usual, they were not overwhelmed where we hap-pened to be facing them. However, perhaps the overcast sky denied us a continual freshness, and was not much of an event after all when under that colourless cloud-veil one afternoon we were taken out of the trenches held so long – over three weeks. The General had communi-cated the move at short notice to Harrison by telephone, using some cryptographic transparency of his own invention – 'You will have your tea this evening, Harrison (are you there, Harrison?) you will have your tea, where I told you (can you hear me, Harrison?),' or something like that. The relief was accordingly confirmed with striking readiness by the German gunners, and the dirty brown smoke of their parting presents could be seen sprouting on the parapets and communications at a score of points at once while our companies handed over.

xi

Very Secret

We marched to Martinsart Wood, with its volcanic howitzers, its mud, its confusion of hutments and tents and bivouacs, and yet its sylvan genius lingering in one or two steep thorny thickets. There, the exceedingly scanty list of honours won on September 3, and consolatory remembrances from the Divisional General, were published to us. Harrison was not exalted by this diluted elixir. My batman continued to sing, 'You must sprinkle me with kisses if you want my love to grow'; he had been, as I said, a gardener. Meanwhile the men spent hours in contemplating those big guns and their shells chalked with monotonous jokes about the Kaiser and Crown Prince. Some, unluckier, were named to join some unlucky officers in a reconnaissance party to Thiepval Wood.

Thiepval, key of that region where the Ancre curves southward, had at length fallen to the British; and yet the Germans might recapture it, if they could make its north wing, Thiepval Wood, still more of an inferno than ever. This they were efficiently doing. But I anticipate – I would have you see that little reconnaissance in its natural or unnatural evolution. Date yourself 1916, and come, little as you wanted to stir this afternoon; the autumn day is moody, the ground churned and greasy; leave Martinsart Wood, and the poor dear platoon scrubbing equipment, coaxing stray dogs, hunting for canteens and scrawling letters. We cross the Nab, that sandy sunk road, and, if we are not mad, the ancient sequestered beauty of an autumn forest haunts there, just over the far ridge. Aveluy Wood, in thy orisons be all our sins remembered. Within, it is strangely uninhabited; the moss is rimy, its red leaves make a carpet not a thread less fine than those in kings' houses. But enough of this minor poetry; here the wood-path comes out on a lonely and solemn highway. There are signposts pointing between the trees beyond, 'Ride to Black Horse Bridge,' and others, French and English; but we turn along the road, unmolested, unimagining. It leads to a chasm of light between the trees, and then we have on our left hand a downland cliff or quarry, on our right hand a valley rich in trees. One tall red house stands up among them. Why? Why not? there is at the minute no roaring in the air. But here we leave the road, and file along the railway track, which, despite all the incurable entanglements of its telegraph wires, might yet be doing its duty; surely the 2.30 for Albert will come round the bend puffing and clanking in a moment?

Below, among mighty trees of golden leaf, and some that lie prone in black channels as primeval saurians, there is a track across the lagooned Ancre. A trolley-line crosses, too, but disjointedly: disjointedness now dominates the picture. When we have passed the last muddy pool and derailed truck, we come into a maze of trenches, disjointed indeed; once, plainly, of nice architecture and decoration, now a muddle of torn expanded metal and twisted rails, of discarded signboards, of foul soaked holes and huge humps – the old British system looking up towards lofty Thiepval. And Thiepval Wood is two hundred yards on, scowling, but at the moment dumb; disjointed, burnt, unchartable. Let us find, for we must, Gordon House, a company headquarters; and we scuttle in the poisoned presence of what was once fresh and green around unknown windings of trenches. 'Over the top' would be simpler and less exhausting; it is the east edge of the wood now; we must have come too far forward. Gordon House, someone finds out from his map, is behind us. We crawl or scamper along the wood edge as the plainest route, and are at once made the target for a devil's present of shells; they *must* get us; they do not. Shell after shell hurtles past our heads into the inundations of the Ancre, below this shoulder of brown earth, lifting as high as the hill wild streaming sputtering founts of foam and mud. God! Golly! Throwing gun and all at us. The next salvo – and here's that dugout. A stained face stares out among the chalk and tree-fibres. 'I shouldn't stand there, if I were you: come in.' 'No, I'm all right: don't want to be in the way.' 'Come in, blast you; just had two men killed where you are.'

Time-values have changed for a moment from furious haste to geological calm when one enters that earthy cave with its bunk beds, squatting figures under their round helmets, candles stuck longways on the woodwork, and officers at their table shared by the black-boxed field telephone, soda-bottles and mugs, revolvers and strewn papers. One of these officers, a boy who is addressed as 'Cupid,' is provoked by our naïve surprise at the highly dangerous condition of Thiepval Wood Left. 'Barrage? We *relieved* through a barrage.' (How mildly sweet might it now have appeared to be able to take over trenches at Cuinchy!) 'You can rely on a barrage here pretty well the whole time.' At last we have learned something of the defence scheme of this sector, and by way of friendly general information the present inmates of Gordon House admit that its roof, though in appearance quite generously thick, is not thick enough: not nearly! But appearance has its virtues. Even the absurd map they spread before us makes us feel safer.

Escaping as hastily and inconspicuously as our slight local know-ledge allows, we wind through the wood again, and over the causeway through the morass, while the scattered roaring lessens in our ears, and the voices of waterfowl just reach our numbed attention. Harri-son, whom we have met at an appointed corner, bustles along on the tramline sleepers, full of combat with the immediate future: 'That spot will just suit you, Rabbit. Colonel Rayley tells me that the Germans send up bombing parties of fifty every day about noon, along the CT from St Pierre Divion. There's a bombing-block for you and Cassells to keep going.' The daylight is fading now, and the red of autumn grows dusky all about us; mist, thick in the throat, comes out of the wild valley. A 'hate' begins. Flames and flashes kindle the vague wood. What a night we leave behind us!

It turned out when we reached our camp that we were after all to be spared the threatened ordeal in Thiepval Wood. New orders had come, and we were to go in again at Hamel, holding a two-battalion front. Immediately Harrison though trembling with overstrain rode off to consult authorities (Colonel Scales and, failing him, the Black

Watch headquarters at large) about that place, of which he had already had a life's experience in one inexpressible day. Gratefully now we took over the Hamel positions, the stairs and cuts in the hillside so sublimely exposed, the maze of disprivileged trenches principally useless. All eyes were drawn to the storm-centre, the savage scenery of the ridge south of the river, whence our comings and goings were so unpleasantly eyed and menaced.

Fine days succeeded, and moonlit nights, temperate nights with their irresistible poetry creating a silver lake in the borders of Thiepval's lunatical wood, a yellow harvest on the downs towards Mesnil the mortuary. It was possible for me with my odd jobs 'to go for walks' in these hours of illusion, and seldom were they spoiled by direct opposition. We had our troubles. Amongst these was the enormous British trench mortar, then called the Flying Pig, which from a cellar in the edge of Hamel hurled its shells as much into our area as the opposite trenches. We kept our sentry groups under cover during these ambiguities. There were several capricious enemy bombardments by the heaviest guns, and machine-guns were ever snarling at us: moreover, in the curiously unchartable complication of our long-stretched sub-sector, it seemed that we had in the phrase of the time 'a pet sniper,' for occasionally in daylight and in places of unquestioned security a bullet would crack past or thump into the parapet. In these days indiscriminate rifle fire, once so familiar, the ritual of the sunrise, was practically extinct. Our Lewis-gunners found themselves one or two coigns of vantage, from which the enemy's rash movements in St Pierre Division on the other side of the Ancre were seen and challenged. A horse and cart even came to a dugout entrance there one day; our artillery were also looking; the horse and cart never went back.

My trench maintenance parties with hammers and choppers, saws and nails were lodged in Hamel village; they made themselves comfortable in cellars, and went to and fro in the exact and ordinary manner of the British working man. One, by turns, stayed at home to cook; the others kept the line tidy, and left no staircase, recess nor buttress unbeautified. They enjoyed this form of active service with pathetic delight – and what men were they? willing, shy, mostly rather like invalids, thinking of their families. Barbusse would have 'got them wrong,' save in this: they were all doomed. Almost all finished their peaceful lives a few days afterwards in the fury of Stuff Trench. Leaving them at their suburban carpentering in the sunlight, I could go for an hour's exploring. Old curiosities, here a lousy mattress on ancient boxes of bombs, there a bureau or a bookcase, kept one's mind in a strange emotion. A farmer's pea-jacket hung in a shed beside the cook's wet socks; a great fuse (Dopp. KZ) and blood-stained equipment lay in the roadway beside a crimson-velvet chair lacking the hind legs. I heard an evening robin in a hawthorn, and in trampled gardens among the luggage of war, as Milton calls it, there was the fairy, affectionate immortality of the yellow rose and blue-grey crocus. Hamel Church attracted me, and though stripped and tottering still had that spirit clinging to it which would have been the richest poetry to George Herbert. Stooping along there, always instinctively listening for the field-guns opposite, and feeling the tingling physical heat due to being under observation, I found my way into a white arched cellar, half collapsed, and with some astonishment discerned that it was resting upon stacked cases of rations. This discovery quickly became the news of the day. The same night, the battalion policemen went up with me to collect the first fruits, and were able to distribute among the companies a lavish allowance of marmalade, soup squares, and other things. This home charity safely accomplished, 'the Brigade was informed'; next day the Staff Captain arrived in person, and, little relishing the hilly openness of the locality, crept along with me among the ruins to the fabulous dump. He saw, went (nimbly) – he forgives me for my accuracy – and soon afterwards our men had sent down thousands of tins of salvaged stores to the Brigade headquarters. I think I deserved any medal that may have been awarded.

One day there came to Hamel the shyest young officer imaginable. I was ordered to guide him to Captain Cooling's headquarters at Knightsbridge, the northern half of our two-battalion front. The scene still lingers. The apologetic art student, begging pardon for being so long at GHQ in charge of the guard, found a friend in the connoisseur whose name is one of the landmarks of Bond Street. Such was the arrival of Lindsey Clarke, who later became known to everyone as the most resolute of our officers.

Our tour lasted ten days, and occasionally the reminder would come that the powerful-looking German trenches opposite us were still those which we were to have 'captured and consolidated' on September 3, 1916. One would catch sight, far beyond the enemy parapets, of several coils of British barbed wire lying where the Beaumont road ran over a rise; and those coils had been there when one glanced over from Picturedome before September 3. They were the simple trophy of a still greater and more melancholy date, July 1. And now it was nearly winter. The situation southward in the wide battlefield 'remained obscure.' One afternoon, when some tremendous attempt was being made to clear it up, smiling Geoffrey Salter and myself sat on the chalk-heaps in the most easterly sap of our incomprehensible line – was it Pêche Street, or Louvercy? – with orders to record what could be seen of the battle. A moorland overwhelmed in a volume of tawny and blue smoke, thunderously murmuring, in which innumerable little lights in ones, twos, threes, white, green, red, purple, were thrown up like coloured waterdrops, was not easy to tabulate. Salter's pencil travelled at speed, but in vain. The battle died away into ordinary bad temper. The situation remained obscure. Our southmost post shared in it as much as its tenants wanted, and more. It was the burnt mill midway between our front line and Thiepval Wood positions, standing desperately alone among the waterlogged woods. One went to it and from it by grace of night, halting a moment behind the low wall of a stone bridge over the by-stream, on which a machine-gun played. My voluntary night in it, though just the expected example, was uncomfortable; the enemy exercised his field-guns regularly on the group of ruins, and with lucky monotony hit a plantation of red willows just behind it. The mill-house contained a small cupboard-dugout, stinking with old sandbags and dampness – no other protection, except a fence of barbed wire round the bare yard. *Whish – whang! sh-wang! sh-wang!* That a mill, with some steady old miller, some aproned blue-eyed daughter, with pigs in the sty and perch in the pool, should come to be so ugly even in the moon! It had been in my mind (to the amusement of Colonel Harrison) that the stream might be used for a water-expedition against the German post in the swamp; I studied the locality carefully; but the mill killed all

such mock-heroic fancies, and I never thought again of its possibilities.
A sordid cripple, it hated us all. Meanwhile the adjutant and doctor,
in better surroundings, beguiled what leisure the busy telephone left,
and the labour of supplying reports to an anxious Brigade staff, with
mouth-organs and whistle-pipes. We ate well and could keep ourselves
in trim. We had probably made an Army record in the length of time
that we had been holding the trenches without going out. At length
the Royal Naval Division relieved us in Hamel, and we accepted with
joy a story that one battalion had marched in solid column of fours
to Mesnil Church, and was not barraged: this incident, which we
refused to consider a fiction, was to us the sublimation of the impossible which happens. We smiled at this, we smiled at the blessing of
stepping westward once more, and someone whom we knew well
enough but could never catch at the essential moment was smiling at
us.

The next thing that befell us was sudden, and our smile would not
obey orders. It came in an envelope, 'Very Secret,' and stated that we
(after our extraordinary period of front-line duty) should in two
days, with the collaboration of other arms and troops, capture and
consolidate a place called Stuff Trench. The failing ancient sun shone
on the wide and shallow Ancre by Aveluy, and the green fancy-
woodwork of the mill belonged to another century, indeed another
existence, as we crossed the long causeway leading from the pleasures
of rest, and turned along the opposite hillside with its chalky excavations, old trenches and spaces of surviving meadow-like green,
towards the new arena. Then we found ourselves filing up a valley
under the noses of howitzers standing black and burnished in the
open, and loosing off with deadly clamour while the bare-chested
gunners bawled and blasphemed – Happy Valley or Blighty Valley,
which was it? Farther along stood Authuille Wood, and we went in
along a tram-line and a board walk, whereon with sweating foreheads
and sharp voices some Highland officers were numbering off some of
the most exhausted men (just relieved) I had seen. Near here was the
captured German work called Leipsic Redoubt, with its underworld
comforts, from bakehouse to boudoir; our companies were accommo-
dated there, while the battalion headquarters entered the greasy,

rotting shanties of typical British sandbags and tinware in the Wood, at a spot called Tithe Barn, and the night came on.

James Cassells and myself, when it began to rain, made ourselves a mackintosh bivouac within our dugout, and yet we rested ill, for the water ran in through many openings, and rats had here an independence and frivolity beyond any previously observed; it was with great pleasure that we got into the serene yet cannonaded morning. It fell to me then to take a party of men to the battalion's assembly position and make up a dump of tools, ammunition and other require- ments for the attack. The walk to the front line lay over the most bewil- dering battlefield, so gouged and hummocked, so denatured and dun, so crowded with brown shrapnel-cases and German long-handled grenades, shell-holes, rifles, water-bottles; a billowing desert; and yet there was not much opportunity or reason for contemplating this satire in iron brown and field grey, for the staff-supplied motive of 'offensive operations' was not yet weakening, and a rough road was being made here, and limbers were tipping and clattering ahead there, and guns being hauled forward, and signallers running out their lines and burying their cables, and little strings of burdened soldiers like mine trickling onward until they passed tragi-comically among those black accidents and emanations on the skyline.

The front trench, shallow and narrow, clean-cut by good craftsmen, soft and heavy with the night's downpour, was on the hither side of a ridge, nor could the enemy's present position be seen from it. The brown plain all round lay without landmark or distinction, though on the way up I had noticed scraps of a hawthorn hedge. Thiepval was vaguely gestured at on our left. Pozières had once been a village on our right. We got out on top, and dug a large square recess to receive the picks and shovels, the small-arms ammunition, the bombs, the water-cans, flares and what else we had carried up; and then the loud whirring of an aeroplane sounded over our heads. British! – not so: flying thirty yards above the trench was a 'plane with the formidable Prussian cross as bold as the observer looking down; the machine-gun bullets thumped the soft soil, missed us. The sarcastic visitors flew on at their ease along the trench, but our hearts sank at the knowledge that they knew about to-morrow.

That night, our attacking companies went forward and lay in a ditch with a few 'baby elephant' shelters in it, and much water, a little way behind their assembly positions. There was a white frost. Behind them, a few field-guns, covered only with netting dressed up as withered foliage, were waiting too. I went to see them on the morning of the attack, and I remember chiefly the voice of G. Salter, as he emerged from a rough shelter, stretching his stiff arms and trying to move his eyebrows like a man awake, cursing the frost; I remember the familiar song of my old companion Doogan, now for the last time, 'Everybody's doing the Charlie Chaplin walk.' He broke off, and without self-pity and almost casually he said, 'It's the third time, they've sent me over. This is the third time. They'll get me this time.' Nor would it have availed to use in reply one's familiar trench tags, or to speak out the admiring friendship which never fully found words; Doogan seemed to know; and he was tired.

The clear autumn day was a mixed blessing for Harrison, who, in his determination to send over the companies to take Stuff Trench after as much 'rest' as could be found in that Golgotha, had arranged that they should advance from the reserve trench direct to the assault. And by way of novelty the assault was ordered to be made six or seven minutes after noon; the men would therefore have to move forward in broad day and over a sufficiently long approach – liable to the air's jealous eyes. Watches were synchronized and reconsigned to the officers, the watch hands slipped round as they do at a dance or a prize distribution; then all the anxiety came to a height and piercing extreme, and the companies moving in 'artillery formation' – groups presenting a kind of diamond diagram – passed by Harrison's head-quarters in foul Zollern Trench. I watched him as he stood on the mound roof of his dugout, that simple and martial figure, calling out to those as they went in terms of faith and love. Lapworth, who had just joined us, went by at the head of his platoon, a youth with curling golden hair and drawing-room manners, swinging his most subalternish cane from its leather thong; and he was the last officer to go by.

Orders had been admirably obeyed; the waves extended, the artillery gave tongue at the exact moment. The barrage was heavy, but its uproar was diffused in this open region. Harrison had nothing to do but wait, and I with him, for I was acting as his right-hand man in this operation. News of the attack always seems to take years in reaching headquarters, and it almost always gets worse as it is supplemented. At last some messages, wildly scribbled, as may be imagined, but with a clearness of expression that may not be so readily imagined, came to Zollern Trench. One was from Doogan: Stuff Trench was taken, there were few men left, and he had 'established bombing blocks.' G. Salter had sent back some forty prisoners. A message was brought with some profanity by my old friend C. S. M. Lee, whose ripped shirt was bloody, and who could not frankly recommend Stuff Trench. The concrete emplacement half-way thither, looking so dangerous on the maps, had not been found dangerous, and the gunners' preparation there had been adequate; but, he said, we were being steadily blown out of Stuff Trench. Should we be able to hold it? We—ll, we was 'olding it when I got THIS; and so departed Lee, tall, blasphemous and brave.

Looking about in the now hazier October light, I saw some German prisoners drifting along, and I stopped them. One elderly gentleman had a jaw which seemed insecurely suspended; which I bound up with more will than skill, and obtained the deep reward of a look so fatherly and hopeful as seldom comes again; others, not wounded, sourly observed my directions down the communication trench. As they went, heavy German shells were searching thoroughly there, and I do not think they ever got through. Their countrymen lay thick in these parts. Even the great shell-hole which we hazardously used as a latrine was overlooked by the sprawling corpses of two of them, and others lay about it.

Our regimental sergeant-major was by this time in disgrace. This fine man, so swift in spirit and in intelligence, had lifted his water-bottle too often in the back-breaking business of getting the battalion into action; and he had not unreasonably filled the bottle with rum. In the horrid candlelight of the deep dugout he had endeavoured to keep going and with piteous resolution answered what he thought the substance of his Colonel's questions; but it would not do, and Sergeant Ashford, the bright and clever signaller, took his place. Again the night came on; and in the captured trench the remnant who had primed themselves with the spiritous hope of being relieved had to hear that no relief was yet forthcoming. The sharpness of their experience was to be gauged from the fact that even the company held in support in our original front line, employed on incidental tasks, was reported to be exhausted, and its commander had to appeal to Harrison for relief or reinforcement in ultimatory terms. During this battle, our contact with the gunners depended on a gentle youth named Delamain and his telephonist. Our Colonel was delighted with his tireless brightness. The next time that I met him was in Tokyo, after ten years.

Another day arrived, and the men in Stuff Trench had to eat their 'iron rations,' for we could not supply them. We had also lost touch with our battalion doctor, who was somewhere towards Thiepval, that slight protuberance on rising ground westward; the bearers of the wounded had to find another way out; yet we were in possession of Stuff Trench, and the Australians southward held its continuation, Regina. That evening, gloomy and vast, lit up with savage glares all round, a relieving battalion arrived, one disposed to quarrel with us as readily as with the Germans. 'Take the companies over to Stuff Trench,' said Harrison to me, 'and see them settled in there.' Cassells came with me. I say 'came,' for he was only coming for a kind of constitutional. We were lucky, the night being black, to muddle our way through that unholy Schwaben Redoubt, with its many charnel throats and crushed sides, but by this stage our polarity-sense was awakened and we knew how little to expect of local identifications. At last, after many doubts, we had passed (in the darkness) a fragment of road metalling in the trench side which assured me that all was right; along Lach Weg the grumbling relief followed our slow steps, which we could not hasten, even though one of many shells crashing into our neighbourhood caught the incomers and the moaning cries might have distracted more seasoned tacticians.

It was Geoffrey Salter speaking out firmly in the darkness. Stuff Trench – this was Stuff Trench; three feet deep, corpses under foot, corpses on the parapet. He told us, while still shell after shell slipped in crescendo wailing into the vibrating ground, that his brother had been killed, and he had buried him; Ivens – poor 'I won't bloody well have it sergeant-major' Ivens – was killed; Doogan had been wounded, gone downstairs into one of the dugout shafts after hours of sweat, and a shell had come downstairs to finish him; 'and,' says he, 'you can get a marvellous view of Grandcourt from this trench. We've been looking at it all day. Where's these men? Let me put 'em into the posts. No, you wait a bit, I'll see to it. That the sergeant-major?'

Moving along as he spoke with quick emotion and a new power (for hitherto his force of character had not been expressed in the less exacting sort of war), Salter began to order the new-comers into sentry-groups; and stooping down to find what it was snuffing at my boots I found it was a dog. He was seemingly trying to keep me from treading on a body. I caught sight of him by someone's torch or flare; he was black and white; and I spoke to him, and at the end of a few moments he allowed me to carry him off. Cassells and myself had finished, and returned by ourselves by the shortest way; now the strain told, our feet weighed like lead, and our hope was out of action. I put down the dog, who came limpingly round the shadowy shell-holes, stopped, whined, came on again; what was the use? he perhaps thought; that way, too, there is this maniacal sport of high explosive, and the mud is evidently the same all over the world; I shall stay here. Warmly I wished to adopt this dog, but now I could scarcely stoop, and I reflected that the mud and shell zone extended a long way on; so there he stayed; feebly I passed along.

If I was weary, what of Salter and his men? Still I hear their slouching feet at last on the footbridge over the Ancre by Aveluy, where a sad guard of trees dripping with the dankness of autumn had nothing to say but sempiternal syllables, of which we had our own interpretation. The shadows on the water were so profound and unnavigable that one felt them as the environment of a grief of gods, silent and bowed, unvisitable by breeze or star; and then we were past, and soon asleep in the tents near Aveluy Wood.

The action at Stuff Trench on October 21 and 22 had been the first in which our battalion had seized and held any of the German area, and the cost had been enormous; a not intemperate pride glowed among the survivors, but that natural vanity was held in check by the fact that we were not yet off the battlefield. The evenings were shutting in early, the roads were greasy and clogging, and along the wooded river valley the leaves had turned red and now had a frost-bitten chillier tinge; the ridges looked lonelier under the sallow clouds; but in mud and gloom the guns went on, and by our camp of tents at evening we saw the tanks – still novelties – crawl round and round in preparation for something new, and not even rumours of our being sent to Lens or Egypt were heard. Winter clothing was served out, shirts, vests, white leather gloves with fleece lining and a tape to keep them together.

xii

Cæsar Went into Winter Quarters

Then we went into the trenches round about Thiepval Wood, which not long before had been so horrible and mad; but now they had assumed a tenderer aspect, were voted 'a rest-cure sector,' and we were envied for them. The land in front was full of the dead of July 1 and other days of destruction, but our own casualties were happily few, and there was cover for all. Occasionally heavy shells blocked up parts of Inniskilling Avenue, or the waterside path to Mill Post (opposite our old mill at Hamel) which Lapworth, the mild-looking boy who had so stalwartly endured the pandemonium of Stuff Trench, now commanded. At battalion headquarters it was like old times, everyone having time and means to appear with shining face and even shining buttons, and arguments about ghosts, Lloyd George's ammunition, the German Emperor and the French artillery rising into sonorous eloquence until some near explosion put out the acety-lene lamp, or 'paper warfare' warmed up with the receipt of large envelopes from Brigade. Those not in the front trench were sheltered in mediæval-looking archways hewn through the chalk and the roots of the trees; the forward posts were chiefly manned from tunnels called Koyli West and East; and in truth everyone seemed disposed to be satisfied. In Paisley Valley, alongside the wood, some tanks were lying veiled with brown nets, and one might have translated the fact;

but a week or so passed, and nothing had happened except rain and fog. Had it not? With the aid of the sergeant cook I had built four ovens in the wood, which Wren himself would have eaten his dinner out of – or gone without.

In spite of the sylvan intricacies (a trifle damaged) of Thiepval Wood, and a bedroom in the corridored chalk bank, and the tunes of the 'Bing Boys' endlessly revolved, one was not yet quite clear of Stuff Trench; my own unwelcome but persistent retrospect was the shell-hole there used by us as a latrine, with those two flattened German bodies in it, tallow-faced and dirty-stubbled, one spectacled, with fingers hooking the handle of a bomb; and others had much worse to remember. We were merry when at length the relief was sent in and we emerged from the Ancre mists to form up and march in pale daylight to Senlis, a village six or seven miles behind the line. The road wound and twisted, but we liked it well, and as at one point the still lofty stump of Mesnil Church tower showed above the dingy trampled fields it was hard not to shout aloud. 'Not gone yet,' signalled the tower. We heard the church bell ring in Senlis, we bought beet and chocolate, and we admired with determination the girls who sold them; so vital was the hour of relaxation, so kindly was the stone of the road and the straw of the barn. We envied the troops employed as road-sweepers and ditchers in their drains and puddles. Fatuous groups of dugouts, tin and match-board, seemed unfair luxury. We heard the high-velocity gun shooting at the Bouzincourt Road with no anxiety. But, prime gift of eccentric heaven, there was the evening when Harrison took all the old originals and some others to the divisional concert-party performing in the town. The barn roof ought indeed to have floated away in the pæans and warblings that rose from us, as the pierrots chirruped and gambolled there. In sweet music is such art – and never was music sweeter than the ragtime then obtaining, if appreciation indexes merit. 'Take me back to dear old Blighty' was too much for us – we roared inanely, and when a creditable cardboard train was jerked across the stage and the performers looking out of the windows sang their chorus, 'Birmingham, Leeds or Manchester,' the force of illusion could no further go. 'Mr Bottomley – Good old Horatio' was a song scarcely less successful, though Mr Bottomley was blamed for several things scarcely under his control – as,

'When you're deep in a decline
Who provides the Number Nine?
   Mr Bottomley – John Bull.'

'On the day on which Peace is declared,' a neat little skit, and 'When you're a long, long way from home' will never cease to ring pathetically through the years between. All the performers had been over the top. Glum and droll clown, where can I now find your equal? Will time yield you such a 'house' again? and you, graceful tenor, with what glorious air can you now awaken such a sigh as when in the farmstead you sang the 'cheap sentiment' of those newly from the outer darkness? 'When you're a long, long way from home' – we seemed to be so.

Soon enough, from the huts in the orchard, from the mud-walled barns by the church, from the blankets in the straw or the mahogany beds with the mountainous straw mattresses, we were marching eastward again, with little to recommend our future to us. It was now approaching the beginning of November, and the days were melancholy and the colour of clay. We took over that deathtrap known as the Schwaben Redoubt, the way to which lay through the fallen fortress of Thiepval. One had heard the worst accounts of the place, and they were true. Crossing the Ancre again at Black Horse Bridge, one went up through the scanty skeleton houses of Authuille, and climbing the dirty little road over the steep bank, one immediately entered the land of despair. Bodies, bodies and their useless gear heaped the gross waste ground; the slimy road was soon only a mud track which passed a whitish tumulus of ruin with lurking entrances, some spikes that had been pine-trees, a bricked cellar or two, and died out. The village pond, so blue on the map, had completely disappeared. The Ligne de Pommiers had been grubbed up. The shell-holes were mostly small lakes of what was no doubt merely rusty water, but had a red and foul semblance of blood. Paths glistened weakly from tenable point to point. Of the dead, one was conspicuous. He was a Scottish soldier, and was kneeling, facing east, so that one could scarcely credit death in him; he was seen at some little distance from the usual tracks, and no one had much time in Thiepval just then for sight-seeing, or burying. Death could not kneel so, I thought, and approaching I ascertained with a sudden shrivelling of spirit that Death could and did.

Beyond the area called Thiepval on the map a trench called St Martin's Lane led forward; unhappy he who got into it! It was blasted out by intense bombardment into a broad shapeless gorge, and pools of mortar-like mud filled most of it. A few duckboards lay half submerged along the parapet, and these were perforce used by our companies, and calculatingly and fiercely shelled at moments by the enemy. The wooden track ended, and then the men fought their way on through the gluey morass, until not one nor two were reduced to tears and impotent wild cries to God. They were not yet at the worst of their duty, for the Schwaben Redoubt ahead was an almost obliterated cocoon of trenches in which mud, and death, and life were much the same thing – and there the deep dugouts, which faced the German guns, were cancerous with torn bodies, and to pass an entrance was to gulp poison; in one place a corpse had apparently been thrust in to stop up a doorway's dangerous displacement, and an arm swung stupidly. Men of the next battalion were found in mud up to the armpits, and their fate was not spoken of; those who found them could not get them out. The whole zone was a corpse, and the mud itself mortified. Here we were to 'hold the line,' for an uncertain sentence of days.

Harrison had his headquarters at the Thiepval end of St Martin's Lane, and, while the place was deep down and even decorated with German drawings, its use was suspected by its former occupants, whose shells fell nightly with sudden mangling smash on the roof and in the trench at the exits. Nevertheless, he had a lantern put out in the night, to guide those who made the awful journey from the line; it took an experienced messenger, such as our still smiling runner Norman, four or five hours to come and return. The nights were long, but the Colonel could not sleep; ordering me to watch, he might lie down for a time, but, if a visitor or a signaller with his pink forms came and spoke with me, he at once called out the instruction wanted. At Hamel he had once remarked to me, 'We're going to lose this war, Rabbit – we don't *work* hard enough;' and he seemed to be trying to make up for the general defect by his own labours. His face was red and pallid with the strain; he buckled his coat, and forced his body round the eastward mud-holes in the early morning, and on returning would find the General paying a call, with 'Well, Harrison, the air of Thiepval is most bracing.'

In saying this, the General was perfectly serious, and he was not less so in many other remarks of a more military and not less tangential kind, which caused Harrison to carry with him habitually a letter of resignation. One day some unforewarned and desperate order led to the display of this letter. 'No, Harrison,' piped the now amazed General, 'no, I shall not look at it. I shall put it in my breeches pocket;' and the event ended in Harrison's gaining his point and a personal anecdote of the General which never failed to charm. But the background of such humours was a filthy, limb-strewn, and most lonely world's-end, where a Picard village had been, and where still a foundation of bricks, or the stump of an apple-tree, or even a leaf or two of ivy might be found – at your own risk.

Of all the strange artifices of war, Thiepval was then a huge and bewildering repository. The old German front line on its west slope still retained its outline, after the lightnings of explosive which it had swallowed month after month. Steel rails and concrete had there been used with that remorseless logic which might be called real imagination, had been combined and fixed, reduplicated and thickened until the trench was as solid as a pyramid. In front of it here and there were concealed concrete emplacements, formerly lurking in the weeds and flowers of No Man's Land, the fountains of whole rivers of sudden death; beneath it, where now our reserve company lived, were prodigious dugouts, arranged even in two storeys, and in the lower storey of one of these was a little door in the wall. Opening, one went steadily descending along dark galleries, soon discovering that the stacks of boxes which seemed to go on for ever were boxes of explosive; then one arrived at two deep well-shafts, with windlasses and buckets ready for further descent, but at that point it seemed as if one's duty lay rather upstairs. This mine in due course would have hurled the former British line over the Ancre. In another great dugout were elaborate surgical appliances and medical supplies; another, again, was a kind of quartermaster's store, in which, although in one of the crushed staircases were some corpses not to be meddled with, one stooped and turned over heaps of new, smart, but now inapplicable German greatcoats, or tins of preserved meat with Russian labels (I tried it, but made no converts), or heavy packages of ration tobacco which extremest want would not force us to approve – and egg bombs japanned black, and 'windy bombs' with their bat-handles and porcelain buttons, and maps in violet and green and scarlet, and letters in slant hand with many an exclamation mark, and black and gold helmets, and steel ones with cubist camouflaging, and horse-hide packs, and leather-faced respirators, all in one plethora and miscellany, bloodstained here and there. The smell of the German dugouts was peculiar to them, heavy and clothy.

There was, moreover, one vault here which was arrayed with mirrors, no doubt collected from the château whose white ruin still exposed the interior of a cellar, and on which a tall image of the Virgin was dreaming in the sullen sunlight. One could find books in Thiepval; I am guilty of taking my copy of Ferdinand von Freiligrath's bombastic poems from that uncatalogued library. (Von Freiligrath had been a regular contributor to the London *Athenæum*. I did not know it in 1916, but I was to become a writer for that journal too.) But it is time to return from these abysmal peregrinations to the world up aloft, where still here and there in outlying pits a minenwerfer (without its team) thrusts up its steel mouth towards the Old British Line; where the ration party uses the 'dry places' in the mud – those bemired carcasses which have not yet ceased to serve 'the great adventure' – and the passer-by hates the plosh of the whizzing fuse-top into the muck worse than the fierce darts of the shrapnel itself; where men howl out angry imprecation at officers whom they love; where our poor half-wit and battalion joke, whom red tape will not let us send away, is running out above the Schwaben half-naked, slobbering and yet at times aware that he is not in his perfect mind,

> 'Waking in the wet trench,
> Loaded with more cold iron than a gaol
> Would give a murderer.'

We came away for a couple of nights, and were billeted in dugouts by Authuille, built against the high sheltering bank called 'The Bluff,' and there we passed pleasant hours. They were not shelling us here. The blue Ancre swirled along as though it could not be beaten from its brookish gayness and motion, right against our feet; songs sounded sweetly there, and the simple tune 'We were sailing along on a moonlight bay' held me enchanted; I can never escape from that voice in that place. The cold and clear stream was a blessing, and many a soldier dipped his hands in it spontaneously and in happiness, or crossed to the islands midstream to wash out a haversack or a shirt. Poetry with her euphrasy had her triumph, no matter how brief, with many of those pale weary men; nor could she find it strange when they were hurrying up to the canteen kept open there by the South African heavy artillery, or when their song changed to 'When the beer is on the table, I'll be there.'

Now November's advancing date seemed to warrant us in believing that actual battle was finished for the present, and when we took over the Schwaben again we did not think of anything worse than a trench tour – ordeal enough in that den of misery. Sluggish, soaking mists, or cold stinging wind, loaded the air and the spirit of man; the ruins of the world looked black and unalterable; Thiepval Wood's ghostly gallows-trees made no sound nor movement. Thus, then, beyond doubt, the gigantic clangour of the Somme offensive had ceased, and once or twice one heard it alleged that Cæsar went into winter quarters, and if so—. The fog, dewing one's khaki, scarcely let the sun rise, and the grey chalky mud, as though to claim the only victory, crawled down the dugout entrances, whether those still had stairs, or were mere gullets, their woodwork burnt out by phosphorus bombs or shells. Where it had the chance, the mud filled these to the top. We fell into a routine, relieving companies at short intervals, clearing our wounded and concealing our dead; to indicate how steady the look of things was, let me mention that one day someone had to report at advanced Army headquarters and view a new patent oven (constructed of five oil drums) in operation. The victim, myself, left Thiepval and arrived duly by a course of lorry-jumping at Toutencourt, at least a dozen miles back; the miraculous oven was displayed to a selection of ordinary officers by a selection of staff officers, and an aroma of roasting sirloin (or it may not have been sirloin) was detected; it should have been served to the audience. Thence 'home' from aristocratic Toutencourt through the best villages imagination could paint to democratic Thiepval, and a night of the usual blended notes – chiefly the double bass of high explosives on the dugout exit.

'And this,' said Lupton, the adjutant, one gaunt morning (Lintott had become temporary transport officer) – 'this,' remarked Lupton casually, pulling his moustache, 'is Z day minus two.' My eye must have looked like a pickled onion. 'Really,' he continued. 'The biggest attack of the lot.' That had been the case before. But – anyway, the news was right, and whatever Z day might do, there was a little affair for the battalion to administer at once. A German strong-point thirty or forty yards ahead of the Schwaben was awkwardly situated in regard to the proposed 'doings,' and would be cleaned up by us. I received this information with distaste, and Harrison seemed at first to think it applied specially to me, as odd-job man; then he changed his mind, and sent James Cassells and Sergeant Stickland out with a fighting patrol that night; if this failed, it was intended that I should try my hand the night after. As soon as Cassells and his men moved, they were bombed and fusilladed, whereupon they lay down in confusion round the inconvenient saphead, and, by the grace of God, suddenly two of the enemy from another direction wandered among them and surrendered. These prisoners duly arrived at battalion headquarters, seemingly half expecting to be eaten alive – a milkman and an elementary schoolmaster – most welcome guests. They blinked, gestured, accepted cigarettes, became natural. The back areas were so well pleased with these samples that they accepted the perfectly sound report of Cassells, finding the enemy's post too thickly wired and resolutely held for any but a carefully studied assault.

By a foolish error in taste, I, who was then 'mess president,' had brought up to Thiepval an ample bottle of Benedictine, but little whisky; and on the eve of attack that little had disappeared. Poor Harrison gazed as one in a trance at the deplorable bottle of Benedictine, and more in sorrow than in anger at me. I felt that I had to recover my position, but whisky does not appear at a wish. In double gloom the short day decayed, and the noise of shelling swelled until my Colonel sent me up above to listen occasionally if there was any sound of rifle fire. For during this battle of the Somme, there must have been a hundred shells for one rifle-shot; and the cracking of bullets from the front trench in the general stormsong would have been a danger signal. But the night dragged its muddy length without German interference, and the attacking troops assembled in the ravenous holes more or less as was planned on paper. Our own part was subsidiary, and the main blow was to be struck northward towards Grandcourt and Beaumont Hamel. Struck it was in the shabby clammy morning of November 13.

That was a feat of arms vieing with any recorded. The enemy was surprised and beaten. From Thiepval Wood battalions of our own division sprang out, passed our old dead, mud-craters and wire and took the tiny village of St Pierre Divion with its enormous labyrinth, and almost 2,000 Germans in the galleries there. Beyond the curving Ancre, the Highlanders and the Royal Naval Division overran Beaucourt and Beaumont, strongholds of the finest; and as this news came in fragments and rumours to us in Thiepval, we felt as if we were being left behind. But the day was short. Towards four o'clock orders came that we were to supply 300 men that night, to carry up wiring materials to positions in advance of those newly captured, those positions to be reconnoitred immediately. This meant me.

A runner called Johnson, a red-cheeked silent youth, was the only man available, and we set off at once, seeing that there was a heavy barrage eastward, but knowing that it was best not to think about it. What light the grudging day had permitted was now almost extinct, and the mist had changed into a drizzle; we passed the site of Thiepval Crucifix, and the junction of Fiennes Trench and St Martin's Lane (a wide pond of grey cement), then the scrawled Schwaben – few people about, white lights whirling up north of the Ancre, and the shouldering hills north and east gathering inimical mass in their wan illusion. Crossing scarcely discernible remains of redoubts and communications, I saw an officer peering from a little furrow of trench ahead, and went to him. 'Is this our front line?' 'Dunno: you get down off there, you'll be hit.' He shivered in his mackintosh sheet. His chin quivered; this night's echoing blackness was coming down cruelly fast. 'Get down.' He spoke with a sort of anger. Through some curious inward concentration on the matter of finding the way, I had not noticed the furious dance of high explosive now almost enclosing us. At this minute, a man, or a ghost, went by, and I tried to follow his course down the next slope and along a desperate valley; then I said to Johnson, 'The front line must be ahead here still; come on.' We were now in the dark and, before we realized it, inside a barrage; never had shells seemed so torrentially swift, so murderous; each seemed to swoop over one's shoulder. We ran, we tore ourselves out of the clay to run, and lived. The shells at last skidded and spattered behind us, and now where were we? We went on.

Monstrously black a hill rose up before us; we crossed; then I thought I knew where we were. These heavy timber shelters with the great openings were evidently German howitzer positions, and they had not been long evacuated, I thought, stooping hurriedly over those dead men in field grey overcoats at the entrances, and others flung down by their last 'fox-holes' near by. It is strange how carefully, though rapidly, I looked at these bodies. The lights flying up northward, where the most deafening noise was roaring along the river valley, showed things in an unnatural glimmer; and the men's coats were yet comparatively clean, and their attitudes most like life. Again we went on, and climbed the false immensity of another ridge, when several rifles and a maxim opened upon us, and very close they were. We retreated zig-zagging down the slope, and as we did so I saw far off the wide lagoons of the Ancre silvering in the Beaucourt lights, knew where we were, and decided our course. Now running, crouching, we worked along the valley, then sharply turning, through crumbled pits and over mounds and heaps, came along high ground above what had been St Pierre Divion, expecting to be caught at every second; then we plunged through that waterfall of shells, the British and German barrages mingling, now slackening; and were challenged at last, in English. We had come back from an accidental tour into enemy country, and blessed with silent gladness the shell-hole in which, blowing their own trumpets in the spirit of their morning's success, were members of four or five different units of our division.

We lay down in the mud a moment or two, and recovered our senses.

The way to Thiepval was simpler. At the edge of the wood a couple of great shells burst almost on top of us; thence we had no opposition, and, hitting a duckboard track, returned to the battalion headquarters. Johnson slipped down the greasy stairway, and turned very white down below. We were received as Lazarus was. The shelling of the Schwaben had been 'a blaze of light,' and our death had been taken for granted. Cooling, second in command, shone with pleasure at our good luck. Harrison was speaking over the telephone to Hornby, and I just had vitality enough to hear him say, 'They have come back, and report an extraordinary barrage; say it would be disaster to attempt to send up that party. Certain disaster. Yes, they say so, and from their appearance one can see that these are men who have been through terrific shelling . . . Yes, I'll bring him along. *That's* all right,' he turned to his second in command. 'No wiring party. Carry up to Point 86 instead. I said it would all come out in the wash. Seven o'clock – take it easy, Rabbit, we'll go and see the General when you feel a bit better.'

xiii

The Impossible Happens

It seemed far away from war's unruly ravings, that lamplit but damp dugout at Passerelle de Magenta (the better side of the Ancre) in which the General was resting on his bed, his arms folded on his breast; but the occasion made me bold. Closely following the map, with my narrative, then I hope much plainer than now, Harrison decided that we had nearly been into Grandcourt (still a name of distance and wild desire) and that we had come up against the real line which the Germans were holding. But, however these things might be, one immense fact came out like the sun at midnight: our division had almost done with the Somme. The misty trees might have been Hyde Park, and my feet moved with a rhythm, as I kept pace with the Colonel's always vigorous but now champion pace.

A Highland unit was filing into the line. At the ration-party's rendezvous below Thiepval, our hearty Quartermaster Swain had arrived with his transport, and in particular he was guarding, with all the skill of years of suspicion and incident, our issue of rum. When he called at headquarters presently, he was distressed, and his 'eyes were wild.' Two jars of the rum had been 'lifted' under his very nose by the infallible Jocks. It was a feat of arms indeed, but poor Swain felt his occupation was gone. A few hours later we took our belongings from Thiepval, and went down the track and surviving country road, still being shelled in a casual way, and busy with men and transport, to the Bluff dugouts. These were gradually deteriorating, and Harrison sent in an ironical report on their condition, in case they were being relied upon for 'the coming winter.' A pleasing incident of the course of inspections which occupied that day of rest was the quenching of a pushful officer, who was ever to the fore with accounts of his unrewarded perspicuity and daring, by the Doctor, who, seizing as his pretext a more insolent phrase than the other usually snapped out, put down a scintillating barrage of army satire and even sanctimonious benedictions, to the joy of all who were present. Warmed by his success, Doc. Ford proceeded the same evening to serve the general good again, entering the dugout of the Lewis-gun officer, who was not thought the most energetic altruist among us, and disturbing his rest in an ingenious and sociable manner. I loved this Doctor, athletic, bright and young – I particularly remember his beautiful opposition to our conventional explanations of Patriotism, his 'No, that's Jingoism' – but already he was sickening for trench fever, and after a short time he had to give way to its heavy siege.

The first kit inspection proved that we were short of all sorts of things, rifles, leather equipment, gas masks and all the rest, and next morning early I took a party of men and a couple of limbers up towards Thiepval and set about salvaging what was wanted. The inward upheaval of our promised exodus made this seem one adventure too many, and we observed the grouping of the customary big shells snouting up the grey mud and derelict timber with great care; but we needed not range far, for the greying haversacked British dead were all round – not many of the German thereabouts, but what should one want with their red-hide hairy knapsacks, their leather respirators, curious but somehow inhuman? There was no time for deep feeling in the mysterious presence of all these masked men. My explorers did their work with vigour, the limbers were soon more than brimful, and we hustled down through Authuille and over Black Horse Bridge, 'for ever and for ever.' The battalion was on the roadside ready to step off, and amid humorous and artful smiles and glances we fell in. Lancashire Dump in the verge of Aveluy Wood, and the old French finger-posts and notices, and the mossy clear places between the trees, and the straight, damp, firm highway, good-bye to you all; there in the sedge the wild duck and moorcock noise, and farther behind one hears the stinging lash of shells in the swamp, but we are marching. Not the same 'we' who in the golden dusty summer tramped down into the verdant valley, even then a haunt of every leafy spirit and the blue-eyed ephydriads, now Nature's slimy wound with spikes of blackened bone; not that 'we,' but yet here and there was the same face that had belonged to them, and above all Harrison with his merry eye and life-giving soldierly gesture was riding up and down the column.

After a night's respite in huts in the Nab Valley, not far from our old cover, Martinsart Wood, we were able to add a few more kilometres to our distance from the line, and, passing Albert with songs and in some amazement, left the pools of the Ancre behind, and came to the substantial village of Warloy. There, too, we stayed one luxurious night. The house in which some of us were lodged was the quietest conceivable, the most puritan, with little square plots of grass and tiled paths between it and the road; our beds were in the attics, and during the night we had scarcely thrown down the French novels which we picked up there and put out our candles, when, it seemed, an aeroplane was buzzing overhead and something hit the tiles. This dream was confirmed next morning, for the raider had killed some transport-men in the village with machine-gun fire.

We now marched in earnest. Of all the treasured romances of the world, is there anything to make the blood sing itself along, to brighten the eye, to fill the ear with unheard melodies, like a marching battalion in which one's own body is going? From the pit, arise and shine, let the drum and trumpet mark the pride of your measure; you have now learned that the light is sweet, that a day in peace is a jewel whose radiances vary and frolic innumerably as memory turns it in her hand, infinitude of mercy. Here is this jewel; kind Nature will shield it from the corrosions of yesterday; yield yourself to this magical hour; a starling curving among tens of thousands above the blue mere, a star spinning in the bright magnetic pilgrimage of old God; follow that God, and look you mock him not.

So inexpressible was the exaltation of that day, and the solid ground was ethereal, not much being uttered from man to man for many miles. An old friend of ours, however, did not feel this. In his grimmer mood and best red tabs he rode up, shrilly calling me out of my planetary dream to him, and ordered me to arrest the transport sergeant for the offence of allowing what he called 'super-structures' on his vehicles. Poor Sergeant Luck on his black horse came up in confusion, accepted his fate and observations on his gross unmilitary character, and the General reluctantly went devouring elsewhere. The super-structures ('surely you can see them, Blunden? Why did you not immediately place this non-commissioned officer under arrest?') consisted chiefly of the illegal extra blankets which the batmen had contrived to collect for their winter campaign; and once again one innocent suffered while many guilty went free. I condoled with Luck, and he with tears in his eyes thought of his hitherto spotless name in the world of limbers and Maltese carts and horse-lines.

Hardly believing what was happening, we came through places which had been so remote from possibility that their names were unmeaning to us. Greenness, even if it was only November greenness, was our dream scenery. There was to have been green country on the victorious far side of the Somme battlefield. Ridges and valleys disappeared behind. We passed Beauquesne, where somebody said, was Advanced General Headquarters. Well, you say so. We ended our resurrection road in Doullens, a placid town, with cobbled complicated streets, withdrawing courtyards under archways, and curtains, and clocks, and mantelpiece ornaments, and roast fowl, and white and red wine. One longed to take one's ease in that miniature triumph of domesticity, but it was no more than a stage, only long enough for some claims for damages to be registered against A Company. I was soon reporting at the station yard, trying to obtain all the information about the battalion's train journey northward, and the sunset flared the brazen news that it would be a cold one, while the shifting wind whistled through the black chains and waggon-wheels of the waiting cattle-trucks. But it was a beautiful world even then.

xiv

An Ypres Christmas

So we have come North. We did not expect this, ten days ago. It is midnight, with intense stars and darkness, and one has rarely felt the frost strike sharper (the ponderous journey scarcely having aided those bodies so long in the mud and gunning to repel the climate); but we have come North, and the ground is solid and clean. The battalion detrains at an unknown siding and its forerunners guide it in to unknown M Camp. I am warmed by the sight of my old confederate Sergeant Worley, in the exit of the siding; he gives his usual candid views on the situation, but is on the whole favourable to it; and we go along the cobbled road between level fields. Suddenly turning aside we find the Quartermaster and the Transport Officer, Swain and Maycock, who, stamping their feet, rejoice with me, and Maycock seizes my shoulders with gloved hand and pretends to dance. These invincible officers have a pleasant surprise for us, and, although it is midnight, there is soon a sound of revelry. In a large wooden tavern a cheerful Belgian girl, under the argus-eyed direction of a masculine mother, is soon running hither and thither among the veterans, from colonel to subaltern, with some of the best victuals ever known. Rave on, you savage east, and gloom, you small hours: we will take our ease in our inn, by the red-hot stoves. We have come through.

Life in M Camp was sweet, and lasted quite a long time. Our quarters were a set of huts and tents surrounding a small ugly farmhouse, a mile or less from the road to Poperinghe, with field paths leading past the biscuit-tin and sugar-box dwellings of refugees around it. The frost broke up, the air grew sleepy and the ground sloppy, forewarning us of what we hardly yet troubled to discuss or fancy, the real object of our journey – the Ypres Salient. We had been in the mud of the Somme, and could not be forewarned. Epicurus would have liked the mood of M Camp. Inspections soon multiplied upon us, and the new Corps Commander, of whom already dry anecdotes were current among us, enraged us by a short speech in which he said, jovially enough, that we were very dirty. Training schemes were enjoined, modified, supplanted. Harrison took us out for running and walking in the morning's ashen gloom under the avenue of dripping poplars, and caused a riding school for officers to be instituted by Maycock. I may claim to have popularized this by my extreme inefficiency in the new crisis. Maycock, brilliantly and sublimely horsey, his opportunity even adding an unusual rosiness to his cheek and jockeyism to his shoulders and legs, stood in the middle of the circus, cracking his whip and giving the most terrible orders about the stirrups, and the elbows, and trotting, and what not. A body of spectators was soon on the scene. Sergeant Ashford would say to me afterwards, with the smile of Ah Sin, 'Yes, the first time they went round you were there. The second time you weren't. It was very puzzling.' Not content with this atrocity, Harrison obliged me to ride out with him over the ploughlands westward, broken as they were with low brushwood boundaries, ditches and coppices. How I rebelled, with Absalom's fate ever impending! In the evenings, I would confer with my co-juvenile confidant James Cassells, upon the matter of the Colonel's hardness of heart, his morning 'physical jerks,' his afternoon prancings. We resolved to lampoon him if these went on. His likeness cannot come again in this life, nor can man be more beloved.

During our enthralment in the Somme offensive, we had seen little of the country but what was raving mad, and no civilians were permitted within many miles of our usual haunts. That bad spell was broken. Here we saw life in her rural petty beauties. The windmills with their swinging sails beat off a white world of deathly oblivion, and the ploughman driving his share straight and glistening through the brown loam was a glory to see as we marched in the pale winter sun. We imitated his cacophonous but delightful orders to his massive horses with joy and thanksgiving. We had eyes alike to see the curiosities of weathercocks, such as represented a running fox or a coach and horses, and to lift up our souls to the hills whereon a monastery towered. The spires were gilded with our unhoped-for emancipation, and the streets rang with our surprising steps.

Poperinghe was a great town then – one of the seven wonders of the world. The other six, indeed, were temporarily disregarded. Poperinghe streets are narrow, and there were thousands of soldiers there, coming and going; yet the town disappointed none, except when the enemy spoiled an afternoon with gas or long-range guns. One of our first impressions here was caused by the prominent notices against the Post Office (open!) concerning gas and the state of the wind; the skeleton of Ypres thus began to give us a nudge and a whisper. Meanwhile, we marketed and strolled about in contentment, allured from one shop window to another – all were bright (though splashed with mud from the columns of lorries), all were alive. If one could not buy a new razor, or a new cap, or O. Henry's works here, then Bohemia was nothing. The ladies spoke English with adroitness and amiable looks. Some observers preferred 'La Poupée,' the daughters of which tea-house were certainly fair and gentle; the youngest, 'Ginger,' was daily attending school in Hazebrouck, a courageous feat. 'Ypriana' also boasted some beautiful young persons who condescendingly sold gramophones, postcards of Ypres, and fountain pens. Up in the higher windows, the milder air once or twice allowing, one saw old women making lace or some such thing. There was one church into which we could go, white-walled and airy and cold, the delight of any who admired the Netherlands of the painters; another church in a tranquil side-street defied doubt with its strong and scarcely impaired tower. By the station, in a brick storehouse among many spacious buildings belonging to the hop factors, the 'Red Roses' in song and dance never ceased to gild the clouds of fate. The simple legend Box Office had its epic majesty, and one still sees the muddy track leading thither across the railway as the high road to Parnassus, and hurries to the feast.

In M Camp I acquired an extraordinary facility in issuing the mighty rum ration. There were so many (I forget the exact tally) to be served from each jar; each man brought his own favourite vessel at the welcome call 'Roll up for your Rum,' and the dispenser was confronted with need for all sorts of mental mensurations. The indefatigable dear Worley held up his candle, or turned on his pocket torch, as I stood at the door of each billet, and it was rare that anyone went short. The precious drops were fairly distributed, and when all was done Worley would prolong my visitation, in defiance of military principles, by luring me into his tent to join a party of old stagers whose bread and cheese was the emblem of an unforgettable kindness. And there was an occasion or two in which Cassells and myself were the guests of those good souls at a veritable banquet. An estaminet by St Jans ter Biezen was then the scene of much music, much champagne and a dinner of the best: there's no higher honour to come. Daniels, Davey, Ashford, Roberts, Worley, Clifford, Seall, Unsted, do you remember me yet? I should know you among ten thousand. Your voices are heard, and each man longed for, beyond the maze of mutability.

There naturally began some mention of Ypres, and I was intending an unofficial visit (much to the cynical amusement of Lintott, who knew the place), when, instead of going forward, we went still farther away. This excess of good fortune was less real than it ought to have been, for we could not place it at all – it was out of our line. We went back to a nook of quietude and antiquity discoverable on the map some few miles behind St Omer. At Poperinghe station, as we entrained, we saw two officers standing beside the line, evidently pleased to see us; and one was waving his hand and singing out messages to the old hands. This was Vidler, who had been one of the battalion's first casualties, and with him was his old schoolfellow Amon, a survivor from battles long ago in the Loos district. These joined us, and the life of the battalion was enriched beyond words. Not so can I mention the advent of another officer who had turned up at M Camp with a sinister, dry and staffy accent, recommending himself to Harrison on technical grounds and the claims of training, and being accepted by that good old soldier, whose sole weakness seemed to be a prejudice for the professional. (Or was the Colonel only allowing us to think, in the interests of discipline, that he accepted him?) The intruder was immediately given the duties of second in command; and, strutting with redoubled vanity and heel-clicking, on Harrison's going on leave, actually reigned over the battalion for a short time. In vain did we mutter and hint that this man was a liar, for Harrison was glad to receive someone with what he thought 'discipline' in him, and easily allowed old tenets to deceive him into misplaced enthusiasm. It was felt by most of us that this was no good omen. Our second in command that should have been, Cooling, who had served continuously in and out of our trench sectors, went off as a Staff Learner. The family atmosphere was altered. The Silver Age was upon us.

In our village we trained ourselves in many subjects, which did not burden the spirits overmuch; or if they did, had alleviations, as the following memorandum shows:

Sergt.	SEALL	Frs.	40
Sergt.	CRADDOCK		40
	AUGUR		15
	BARNARD		15
	LOVELAND		15
	RACKLEY		15
	HUNT		15
	MITCHELL		15

Francs were still ninepenny ones.

The speedy putting on of gas helmets – the new 'box respirators' – was made a day's business. We were employed to dig a large rifle-range in storms of rain and wind near the road from St Omer to Calais, and there were conferences and lectures. The French language became very popular and, the lectures being held in the evenings in the village school, suggestions for the children's instruction next day were written on the blackboard – 'Hommes 40 Chevaux 8' and 'Wait and See.' The remembrance comes with kind modest voices and nun-like faces of the teachers, who seemed (unusual in their perception) to think of us as men wearied with a brutal war; I wish that I could name them, for their grace; far otherwise seemed the lady of the curé's house in which

I was lodged. She, with hostile rays of repellence, scarcely let me pass the door into that dim religious atmosphere as of cassock and taper, but perhaps something had gone wrong in the days before me. My room was adorned with inexpensive angels, who also seemed distant and cold. Another billet here was the lair of a most formidable woman of bosomy immenseness, who assailed me in full fury out of the void. Her children, who all rejoiced to inherit a bass voice and a squint, were very handy in filching our meat and coal. I was tempted to avenge myself and us by leaving her a safety razor as a parting gift. But these little charities were interrupted when suddenly the furious news reached me that I was to go on leave, and the mess-cart was driving down to St Omer with me in it and a yellow warrant in my hand.

How to express that hour?
Do not try.

At St Omer the expected report hit me a punch combining the talent of Spring, Fitzsimmons and Dempsey. 'All leave stopped.'

This was a lie.

I wore a little warm-coat, a cyclist's coat, experimentally made. Harrison had given it to me, and had repeated these words: 'Rabbit, you are not to go on leave in that coat.' As I was standing on Victoria Station about to enter the return train for Folkestone and France, I caught sight of my Colonel in conversation with someone even more Olympian than himself. There was no help for it. I ran up, and saluted. 'Rabbit!' Harrison roared with laughter. 'That coat!' His friend smiled sympathy at me, but I was in torment, and as usual, in the words of one of our contemporaries, I had only myself to blame.

Going on leave, I had heard a colonel on the seat opposite indulge in a little eloquence about the evil iciness of some gunpits by Zillebeke Lake, just out of Ypres, the winter before; and returning, I guessed by my movement order that the battalion was in the line, and meditated a little. Still, however, the weather was misty and peaceful, and the worst was not yet to be feared by a healthy youth. At Poperinghe a draft of perhaps sixty soldiers was put in my charge, and I was told to make my way to the Red Hart Estaminet on the canal bank near Ypres. It did not strike me at first that an estaminet with a name like that would be a foolish ruin, not dealing in malaga, thin beer or grenadine.

Nor, even when I arrived there, did the unholy Salient at first reveal itself. The battalion was in the long terrace of dugouts along the broad Yser Canal, with its pedestalled lines of slender trees, and its neat wooden bridges. Handing over my reinforcements to Daniels, whose swift glance and fine word of command immediately shepherded them into our fighting strength, I went along to the headquarters dugout, and, looking round first, asked 'How's things?' The battalion had been in the trenches above, and a wonderful, almost woundless tranquillity had blessed it. There was only one flaw, and that was the presence of the 'fraud,' who at the moment was elsewhere. I meanly rejoiced to hear that he had slunk about the trenches with his head well down (whether he had or not), and we all hoped Harrison would shake off his trance and, like Lear, 'see better' when he returned. For two or three days we stayed here, in the remarkable line of shelters on the embankment of that drowsy canal, and working parties and wanderings were all that happened. Machine-guns did homage to Night, and that was almost the only unrest. A spy was reported to be lurking about some bricks called Wilson Farm, but nobody could catch him; and from company headquarters and cook-houses one heard such cheerful singings and improvisations as seemed to hail the Salient as the garden of Adonis. Here first I came upon Olive, a new officer younger than myself, and duly addressed him with the gravity and the superior philosophy of old age; and here Whitley, soon styled 'OC Daily-Mirror,' enlivened the day's work.

The ruined wharves of Ypres were conspicuous enough a short way along the Canal, but no occasion arose as yet to go nearer. Clambering along the greasy black duckboards beside the water was not specially pleasant. The sluggish weather, the general silence and warlessness encouraged us to take life easy; and yet it was at this time that one poor fellow was charged with a self-inflicted wound, the first instance in the battalion. Perhaps he divined the devilish truth beyond this peaceful veil. It was easier to be deluded by the newness of the communication trenches and the appearance of quite good farmhouse walls in the area of the foremost trenches. This was, I think, the end of the quietest period ever known in the Salient, and one exploited the recent standards of carelessness and freedom of movement, unthinking that the enemy was looking on and taking notes from the low ridge ahead. The lowness of High Command Redoubt was stultifying, for it did not strike the eye; yet it was all that was needed for overwhelming observation of our flat territory, right back to the Poperinghe road, the artery.

Now winter, throwing aside his sleep and drowse, came out fierce and determined: first there was a heavy snow, then the steel-blue sky of hard frost. To our pleasure, we were back in a camp in the woods by Elverdinghe to celebrate Christmas. The snow was crystal-clean, the trees filigreed and golden. It was a place that retained its boorish loneliness, though hundreds invaded it: its odd buildings had the suggestion of Teniers. Harrison's Christmas was appreciated by his followers perhaps more than by himself. He held a Church Parade and, while officiating, reading a Lesson or so, was interrupted by the Band, which somehow mistook its cue. The Colonel is thought to have said, 'Hold your b— noise' on this contretemps, which did not damp the ardour of the congregation, especially the back part of the room, as they thundered out 'While Shepherds Watched.' After prayers we were free for the rest of the day, and the Colonel visited all the men at their Christmas dinner. At each hut, he was required by tradition to perfect the joy of his stalwarts by drinking some specially and cunningly provided liquid, varying with each company, and 'in a mug.' He got round, but it was almost as much as intrepidity could accomplish.

XV

Theatre of War

And soon afterwards we began to discover the War again. In gusty rain we relieved the Welsh on the extreme left of the British Line, where it adjoined the Belgian trenches. The village of Boesinghe, which named this part, lay on the edge of the Yser Canal, and was now no ornament to it; but in the light of earlier troubles and later ones we were not so badly off.

Our way up was through Elverdinghe with its tower mill and its miraculously preserved château ('von Kluck's country seat'), past its little gasworks, and along shallow trenches pontifically screened, hitherto left alone by our German cousins. Houses in quite good shape appeased the anxious eye as one advanced, fine stone roads plotted out the country, and there was a general simplicity and complaisance in the martial arrangements which pleased one's civilian self. But there are certain possibilities and indeed occurrences in war which a soldier cannot entirely dismiss, and by the time that one had looked into Boesinghe and its system of defences, one was not amused. The burnt château was only a useless case; the battalion headquarters was an iron vault in an outbuilding, with fragile huts and coop-like sandbag annexes obviously clustered round. Boesinghe village street, though approached over a rustic bridge past an Arcadian lake, was a litter of jutting roof-timbers, roomless doorways, and plaster and brick rubbish. The tawny and white tumulus of stones that represented the church was very avoidable. No protection against anything more violent than a tennis-ball was easily discernible along that village street. Uncommon feebleness of design and performance was plain in the communication trenches, Hunter Street and Bridge Street; the wicker-work support line was scarcely strong enough to keep white mice in, but muddy enough to destroy tempers; the gabioned front line was in the massive canal bank, than which a finer parapet could not be demanded, but just behind it and parallel with it ran the awkward stream Yperlee. Our future, in short, depended on the observance of the 'Live and Let Live' principle, one of the soundest elements in trench war.

Unfortunately it was not invariably observed. The Germans possessed a magnificent minenwerfer, well masked under the wreckage of a place known as Steam Mill. With this weapon they celebrated the new year and demonstrated that enormous explosions could be induced at any moment on Boesinghe Church and the parts adjacent. The crash of their presents was not in keeping with the evergreens that led along to the pretty bridge and winding water. Once or twice the operators amused themselves by lobbing their trench mortar bombs into the area of the Belgians, accurately leaving ours (from the extremest of our posts) unassailed; and the action of our neighbours, who made the best of their way out through our lines, was no doubt watched with interest by the German observers. The situation was such that at any moment, and especially in the intense frost, we feared that the Germans might cross the canal and drive in our left flank. Alarmed, with redder cheeks and sharper tone than usual, the General urged on our wirers and insisted that they should not do their work under cover, but emerge down the canal bank and drive in their stakes and criss-cross their entanglements there. Barbed wire is noisy gear to handle, and the bobbins on which it is supplied and from which it is uncoiled have tin protections which clank and twang at most unsuitable moments. The German parapet on the other side of the canal was perhaps fifty yards away. Worley managed to set some wire out, without casualties, but he was lucky. I watched him scrambling about the steep bank in some pain, and afterwards heard his opinions with equal pleasure.

Another feature of this 'bit' was the broken railway bridge across the canal, which promised two hateful excitements – the order to raid the enemy thereabouts, the receipt of a raiding party from him. Both events happened, but to our successors. Life for us was daily less delightful, despite that; shells fell much too frequently about the silly allotment-sheds of battalion headquarters, where I lived and made my nightly tea in a bomb-store, and snipers and machine-guns performed artistically on the front and village lines. A domestic impediment still remained with us; and, being visited while I was in charge of a digging party by this lisping emperor, I was enabled to observe for myself the speed with which he denied himself the pleasure of walking about on top when flares and maxims were hunting us. This excessive caution of his at last became discernible to Harrison, and somehow the Colonel's discovery disappeared into the unbeloved mysterious country behind. 'I was never so taken in in my life,' Harrison would sometimes say, later on; but he felt too keen a remorse to discuss the case at length.

The stand-to billets in this sector were at a quiet camp called Roussel Farm, a place with hutments of Belgian make, like barns; where perhaps no one was more conspicuous than a sergeant-major, who in the temporary absence of Daniels acted as 'Regimental.' The substitute, a tall, baggy-trousered and agreeably boastful man, was one who spluttered and swung his arm up and down like a pump-handle whenever a chance of important conversation arose. At Roussel Farm he planned and with the labour of defaulters completed a slight drainage scheme, which was afterwards associated more or less mischievously with his name. Imitations of his bellowing, stammering, good-hearted style were highly popular: 'I've done it, Sir. [The arm sawing the air.] I've laid the duckboard just where you said. – 'Ere, you, catch 'old o' that angle iron and carry it to my place. – I told that damn fool of a batman to fill my case with Gold Flake and 'e's gone and crammed it with Red 'Ussars. – Speakin' of 'Amel, I wasn't 'arf glad when I see you at that water store,' and so forth. His drains and duckboards served us well at Roussel Farm; if you missed the duckboard in the dark you were at least sure to find the drain, and that led ultimately in the required direction.

One morning, dark and liquid and wild, Colonel Harrison and a number of us went off in a lorry to reconnoitre in Ypres proper, and to visit the trenches we were to hold. The sad Salient lay under a heavy silence, broken here and there by the ponderous muffled thump of trench mortar shells round the line. We passed big houses, one or two glimmering whitely, life in death; we found light come by the time that we passed the famous Asylum, a red ruin with some gildings and ornaments still surviving over its doorway, and an ambulance pulling up outside. There was in the town itself the same strange silence, and the staring pallor of the streets in that daybreak was unlike anything that I had known. The Middle Ages had here contrived to lurk, and this was their torture at last. We all felt this, as the tattered picture swung by like accidents of vision; and when we got out of the lorry by the Menin Gate (that unlovely hiatus) we scarcely seemed awake and aware. The Ramparts defended the town on the east and seemed to concentrate whatever of life and actuality dared to be in it. After the distant and alien secrecy of the Grande Place, the sound of dripping water-taps put in here by British soldiers, and the sight of dispatch-riders going in and out, had an effect of reanimation. Here we entered headquarters, or waited at the entrances among the tins of soapy water and the wet rubber boots. We went into the naked eastward area, studied the trenches and their bleak-faced sentries, shivered in the wind. Then, later in the day, we heard for the first time the bursting of shells in Ypres. Their shattering impact sent out a different noise to any before heard by me – a flat and battering, locked-in concussion. Then silence and solitude recaptured the wilderness of looped and windowed walls, unless the wind roused old voices in flues and wrenched vanes. More and more shells leapt down with the same dull and weary smashing. Our motor moved out without further delay.

I had longed to see Ypres, under the old faith that things are always described in blacker colours than they deserve; but this first view was a tribute to the soldier's philosophy. The bleakness of events had found its proper theatre. The sun could surely never shine on such a simulacrum of divine aberration.

The new year was yet very young when the battalion filed through Ypres to take over trenches at Potijze, which we came to know very well. It was not the worst place in the Salient. I had seen it already, and its arrangement was simple – a breastwork front line, running across the Zonnebeke road to a railway bank on the south; a support line; two good (or not too bad) communication trenches – Haymarket and Piccadilly. Battalion headquarters dugout was near Potijze Château, beside the road. It boasted a handsome cheval-glass and a harmonium, but not a satisfactory roof.

This headquarters also enjoyed a kind of Arcadian environment, for the late owner had constructed two or three ponds in the grounds with white airy bridges spanning them, sweeping willows at their marges, and there were even statues of Venus and other handsome deities on little eminences, although I did not examine them closely. The château itself, much injured as it was, was not destroyed, and in the upper storey my observers gazed through a telescope on a dubious landscape; lucky these, whose day could not begin before eight, and ended at four with the thickening of what little light there had been. Littered on the damp floor beside them were maps of parts of the estate, some of great age, and log-books of the number of woodcock, hares, rabbits and I forget what, formerly laid low by shooting parties of this fine house. At least we had not done that! The antiquarian instinct was not assisted by the exposed situation of that garret, though Chatterton might have refused to leave the muniment room of St Mary Redcliff whether five-nines were occasionally whooping past or not.

In the ground floor of this white château, which still had a conservatory door, and a painted metal chair and table near that, was a dressing-station; outside lay a dump of steel rails, concertina wire, planks and pit-props, now mostly frozen into the ground; opposite was a low farm building, Lancer Farm, in which was the bomb store. The stream Bellewaardebeek flowing by (under its ice) supplied the ponds. Presently its depth was daily measured, in case the enemy (who owned the upper stretches of the stream) was preparing any new deluge like that which drove Noah to sea. If one lived much in the district, one evolved a sense when to use the Haymarket communication trench, when Piccadilly. The men, unable to keep their footing on the glazed boards, bound sandbags round their boots; but the 'practice' had to be 'discontinued forthwith.' Going forward, one finds St James' Street, the support trench, none too comfortable: it is narrow, its sandbags are worn out (and the thaw will come presently), its dugouts are only dugouts by name, for they are small hutches of galvanized iron and revetting materials, blackened with wood-smoke, and inside dusky and suffocating. Sit down, and cower, for the 'air' is best near the floor. At the extreme left one may find Amon and Vidler playing cards in the worst canopy of all these flim-flam constructions, and one shudders in the evil, iced draught that darts through, and marvels at this tenacity.

The front line was crude and inhuman. Our new doctor, Moore, with lean cheek and red nose, went round with his flask in the foul cold, and was admired for his courage and charity at once. (He had won his DSO near here in 1914.) The parapet was low, and such a man had to stoop all the way along. On the right, a telegraph pole leaning over at 45 degrees or so was our landmark and boundary; there a great mine-crater interrupted our prettily alternating bays and traverses, which on the map look like a wainscot design. There were no dugouts in the front line, and even recesses for bombs and ammunition were scarce. Still farther ahead was the British wire, a thin brambly pretence, nor was the German wire at this point the usual series of iron thickets. Their front trench was much higher than our own, and behind it the ground made a gradual ascent, whereon one identified such bony remains as Oskar Copse and Wilde Wood.

Deathly blue, sable, hung the pall of the great cold over this battlefield. It was bad enough to be standing or moving there at all, but our business was more than that. From an 'absolutely reliable Belgian source, which had never hitherto failed,' it was reported that a German offensive was maturing here, and our alertness had to be impeccable. Ignorant of the secret news, I went round with Harrison, and was startled by his merciless arrest of a sentry, who, contrary to orders, was wearing a knitted comforter to keep his ears from freezing as he stood on duty in a saphead. Our patrols were frequent and even foolhardy. Vidler and Amon excelled in them. They lay in that arctic fierceness and listened to the conversation of sentries, and the common night routine of the Germans, which Vidler readily completed with his amusing imagination.

As intelligence officer, I, too, was many times out in No Man's Land here. It may be well to say more, since those times and tortures are now almost forgotten. The wirers were out already, clanking and whispering with what seemed a desperate energy, straining to screw their pickets into the granite. The men lying at each listening-post were freezing stiff, and would take half an hour's buffeting and rubbing on return to avoid becoming casualties. Moonlight, steely and steady, flooded the flat space between us and the Germans. I sent my name along, 'Patrol going out,' and, followed by my batman, blundered

over the parapet, down the borrow-pit, and through our meagre but
mazy wire. Come, once again.

The snow is hardened and crunches with a sort of music. Only me,
Worley. He lays a gloved hand on my sleeve, puts his head close, and
says, 'God bless you, sir – don't stay out too long.' Then, we stoop
along his wire to a row of willows, crop-headed, nine in a row,
pointing to the German line. We go along these. At the third we stop.
This may have been a farm track – a waggon way. But, the question
for us is, what about that German ambush, or waiting patrol? Somewhere, just about here, officers were taken prisoner, or killed, a
fortnight ago. There is no sound as we kneel. A German flare rises,
but the moonlight will not be much enkindled. I have counted our
steps from the first pollard. We come to the last. There are black,
crouching forms, if our eyes do not lie, not far ahead; but, patience at
last exhausted, we move on again. The forms are harmless shapes of
earth or timber, though we still think someone besides ourselves has
moved. I am looking for two saps, which the aeroplane photographs
disclose boldly enough, and one of which is held at times. And here
is one. Hold hard.

This one is vague and shallow. We enter, and creep along, but it
does not promise well; then we step up, and cross over to the other.
At the extremity is a small brushwood shelter, and this *may* mean –
it does, but not now: yet this mess-tin and this unfrosty overcoat are
not so derelict. We cannot avoid the feeling that we are being stalked,
and we are equally amazed that in this moonlight we are not riddled
with bullets. The enemy's parapet is scarcely out of bombing range.
Far off we hear German wheels; but the trenches are silent. Probably
we are being studied as a typical patrol. I do not like this telegraph
wire here, which is not so continuously buried in snow as it ought to
be. I have put my foot on it gently, and it *is* a wire. It leads to a stick
bomb ready to be exploded. We move again, with our trophies. I still
keep count of our paces.

Spike-like tree-trunks here stand surrounding an oval moat, which
in turn encloses a curious mound. We must carry in some idea of
this, and we coast it, but nothing happens, and so far as the difficult
moonlight shows it is desolate and harmless as its two lean elm-trees.

And now turning home, we see that our wirers have packed up, and we are amazed that we have been out over two hours. It is not so easy (once we have slipped over our parapet again) to leave the front line for battalion headquarters; it has magnetized the mind; and for a moment one leans, delaying, looking out over the scene of war, and feeling that to 'break the horrid silence' would be an act of creation.

Things did not always end so. One night, when I was far out, our artillery suddenly and for no obvious reason began to shrapnel the German front line at savage speed, and north and south a hideous noise began. The Germans flung up volleys of flares and alarm lights, and my small party sunk to the ground in terrible anticipation. The British guns raked the German line, the shells only just missing us. We presently ran and stumbled into the miserable British breastwork, and asked why all the banging; the reply was that someone along the line had given the gas alarm. With us there was no gas, and we shook in the prospect of a retaliation. Strange acquiescence! the enemy made no immediate sign; and after a time the patrollers went down by way of Haymarket. Suddenly a stupefying fury of shells lashed that black-shadowed alley, and we ran (myself asthmatical, but swifter than a hare); shells burst slap in the trench, and we half choked in the reek and fume. Then the sharp and well-calculated German answer to British offensiveness stopped, and we panted and pitied ourselves in the candle-light of company headquarters in St James'.

It was thought by the staff that we should do well to patrol the snowy ground in white suits. One day a large package of what we expected to be snow-suits came up, by the hand of Q. M. Swain. On being opened, it was found to contain a number of ladies' becoming night-gowns.

xvi

A German Performance

I do not know what opinion prevailed among other battalions, but I can say that our greatest distress at this period was due to that short and dry word 'raid.' Adducing one reason or another, the lowering of the enemy's spirits, the raising of our own, the identification of some supposedly new troops opposite, the damaging of the German trenches, the Great Unknowns behind us were growing infatuated with this same word. Rumours often sprang up, promising us that we were to carry out one of these nightly suicide operations, in which, one point being fastened on by one side, the guns and machine-guns of the offended party for miles were turned on to the danger-spot – not to mention the minor problems of cutting the German wire and assembling under the sentries' noses, of 'establishing superiority' with the bayonet and so on. The patrols of which I have revived some memory were partly intended as the preparations for a raid. There were to be these raiders – Amon, myself and thirty 'other ranks'; and we were to enter the German line, destroy dugouts and procure samples of the young men. Amon and myself, knowing the ground and the enemy's habits (he was hereabouts noisy and inattentive) decided on a 'silent raid'; but, our scheme being sent down to the General in the old bakehouse in the Ramparts, this plan was imperially rejected. I have somewhere still a copy of the official arrangements, which sent more than that winter's ugly cold down our spines, with their time-table of barrages by guns and trench mortars of all sizes. And this seemed the end of our careers. Why was that raid cancelled? I do not know, and was careful to ask no questions after a day or two of inertia; cancelled it was.

It was as bad to raid as to be raided, and the battalion was able to give an interpretation of that before long. The occasion was perhaps the coldest night in which we ever manned a trench. About midnight, I had been wandering through No Man's Land, visiting a good deal of our front – but not all. I had had a heavy day, and the patrol was dreary and laborious; so that afterwards I went down to the battalion headquarters and there, in my small sandbag house (not then to be exchanged for any other), 'got down to it.' Two or three hours afterwards the most brutal bombardment began on the right of our line, and, as I hurried out and watched, it seemed to be falling on the battalion there adjoining us – but this was wrong. Harrison, who had been in the middle of his nightly tour, came panting down the road and along the duckboards to his headquarters; the cruel and shattering concentration went on, and no news came through from the right company, though the telephones were busy. To vary the game, the German artillery scattered some hundreds of shells round the statues of Venus and Mars and our dugouts, and finally dismantled the greenhouse of the château garden. Presently, the bombardment ended, and it was the general conviction that it had fallen on the flanking battalion's line in Railway Wood.

I went back to my blanket, and at eight or so was out ready for the day; meeting Harrison, I was taken aback by his looks of reproach and disappointment. 'A nasty bit of bombardment on the 12th, sir.' 'Not on the 12th, on us. We have lost ten men killed and prisoners. Clarke took his company over the top to reinforce. You'd better go up and see what you can see.' This bad news surprised me, and I knew that I ought to have gone up at the time of the bombardment; but I had given in to the customary feeling, 'business as usual,' and the usual illusion that we were the lucky ones. It was a sparkling, frost-clad morning, and the guns were still. As I slipped along that lonely little trench by Gully Farm, I found that there were many new details of landscape, great holes and hunks and jags of timber; one had to take a chance exposed over mounds that had been excavations; the raided bombing-post soon after appeared, trampled, pulverized, blood-stained, its edges slurred into the level of the general wilderness. An unexploded shell lay in it, and many scraps of iron. Like fragments of masonry here and there, ponderous frozen clods had been hurled out by the minenwerfers, which had blown enormous pits in the stony ground. Our own dead had been carried away, but just ahead were stretched two or three of the raiders. One was an officer of forty, sullen-faced, pig-nosed, scarred, and still seemingly hostile. In his coat pocket were thirty or forty whistles which evidently he had meant to issue to his party before the raid. Another corpse was that of a youth, perhaps eighteen years old, fair-haired, rough-chinned. He was lying in the snow on his back, staring at the blue day with eyes as blue and icy; his feet were towards the German lines, and his right hand clutched the wooden handle of a bomb.

We had been raided with great ingenuity. The raiders had approached the British lines where our sentries could not see them, on the south side of the railway embankment which marked our battalion boundary; then they had turned under the railway at a little culvert, and waited for their guns and mortars to send over the barrage which had so completely shut in our unfortunate bombing post. That culvert, hitherto unnoticed, although only twenty yards ahead of our trench, now appeared painfully prominent. Some few details of the fighting came to light; one of the Lewis-gunners had carried his gun forward and fired it, it seemed, from the shoulder at the coming raiders. He was found dead among the hummocks with his hand to his gun.

One more glimpse; the German bodies are carried down to Potijze Château. We are required to send back specimens of German army underclothing. Paige and Babbage, most mild of garden-loving men, have to cut the clothing off with jack-knives. The frost has made it particularly difficult.

Whether the Germans really intended a great attack on the Salient at this time, their own archives may tell; but their aim was feared by our authorities. They pounded away at all our shelter, which was not to be concealed. Much defensive work was done, even though conditions were opposed to field engineering, and a reserve trench called Half Moon Street was neatly furnished with small iron-roofed shelters and wooden fire-steps. They would have been almost useless in any bombardment, but it was clever to construct them at all. Reconnaissances were frequent. We examined the land just behind the line for the best reinforcement routes, knowing well enough that almost all were equally unprotected, and suppressing the unpleasant premonition of what it would be like to come out of the Menin Gate, or the adjacent exits, in the height of a special bombardment. It was my own business to know in detail all the houses along the Potijze road, and I conceived a liking for many of them, a smithy here, a summer-house or a lodge there and one red-brick dwelling with a bassinette, a supply of tracts on Sunday observance, two sewing-machines, and a huge mahogany bed full of lath and plaster. Your East Anglian huckster might have made a fortune with a pony and van here. The tower of St Jean Church stood yet in broken but shining prominence, while along the Menin Road itself a suburb of tallish red houses (ambulances hiding behind them) brought to mind the causeways of the La Bassée district. The railway running past them lifted itself into the air in absurd wormy loops, the Ypres cemetery wall had been bitten through by some Wellsian and unclassified insect, and artificial lakes appeared in the centre of the roadway; yet there was an insistent echo of old life still, and the gate-pillars signalized the definite ownership of certain large, ornamented, but heavily mort-gaged buildings.

xvii

Departures

The battalion, being relieved from Potijze breastworks, occupied various cavities of less or more insecurity in Ypres. Though many cellars existed in the town, most of them were battered in and water-logged, and the Ramparts were overcrowded. Our principal shelter was the Convent, then the husk of a building, but concealing a many-chambered underground lodging for a considerable number of men, who could parade for working or carrying parties in its court-yard; that cobbled yard will ever be to me the stage on which Maycock stands glaring at the round white moon, and shaking his fist at her, and crying, 'It's that bloody old witch – until she changes we'll keep being frozen.' At one corner was the entrance to a garden, the paths of which had been adorned by some patient enthusiasts of the autumn before with their regimental badges done in coloured glass; and, passing that way, one had the choice of admiring their workmanship, or the sweet simplicity of the pigeons curving and glinting round the Cathedral's tattered tower, or the fact that the German gunners were shooting high explosives to burst in the air innocuously round that aiming-mark of theirs.

Over the sepulchral, catacombed city, aeroplanes flew and fought in the cold winter sun. Sentries blew their whistles from broken archways; the brass shell-cases used for gas-gongs gleamed with a meaning beside them; and all of a sudden flights of shells came sliding into the town. Few people were seen on the streets, and it is difficult to recall in realistic sensation one's compulsory walks in Ypres. The flimsy red post-office, a blue poster for Sunlight Zeep, a similar advertisement for Singer's Naaimaschinen, the noble fragment of a gateway to Saint Martin's Cathedral, interior walls with paintings of swans on green ponds, the rusty mass of ironware belonging to some small factory with an undestroyed chimney, ancient church music nobly inscribed on noble parchment, scattered among legless wicker chairs, in the roadway outside St Jacques, a scaffolded white building in the Place (the relic of a soon disillusioned optimist), a pinnacle, a railing, a gilded ceiling – those details one received, but without vivacity. One set out to arrive at a destination in Ypres, and even in quiet times one was not quiet. As if by some fantastic dream, the flush and abundance of antique life and memorial and achievement, such as blend into the great spirit-harmony of the cities in that part of Europe, stole suddenly and faintly over the mind; then departed. This city had been like St Omer, like Amiens. How obvious, and how impossible!

Man, ruddy-cheeked under your squat chin-strapped iron helmet, sturdy under your leather jerkin, clapping your hands together as you dropped your burden of burning-cold steel, grinning and flinging old-home repartee at your pal passing by, you endured that winter of winters, as it seems to me, in the best way of manliness. I forgot your name. I remember your superscriptions, 'OAS' and 'BEF,' your perpetual copying-ink pencil's 'in the pink,' 'as it leaves me'; you played House, read Mr Bottomley, sang 'If I wore a tulip,' and your rifle was as clean as new from an armoury. It is time to hint to a new age what your value, what your love was; your Ypres is gone, and you are gone; we were lucky to see you 'in the pink' against white-ribbed and socket-eyed despair.

We suffered much from death and wounds, but still there existed a warm fraternity, a family understanding, for a large proportion of those who saw the Somme battle together still formed the cordial opinion of the battalion. Harrison, with his gift of being friend and commander alike to all his legion, was at our head; everyone was outwardly censorious and inwardly happy when he paraded the battalion by the bleak hop-garden at Vlamertinghe for arms drill. It was cold, but he put life into us, and there is a religious or poetic element in perfecting even one's dressing by the right. We still had our Colonel when we were sent back amid hootings, and swervings, and bangings on a quaint railway (with the usual desperate palaverings over entraining, at the Cheesemarket Station, Poperinghe) to an untouched and sociable village called Bollezeele (tins of Oxblood Polish and salmon in every window!). It was near St Omer. There we ate and slept excellently, and for myself, I was in the house of the local doctor, whose talk was in the best style of wisdom and tolerance. We endlessly played the gramophone, and we had concerts at which the metre and tune of

'England was England when Germany was a pup,'

served for numerous additional verses of personalities. 'Harrison' was rhymed thus: 'The listening posts they think it hot, the noisy way he carries on,' and 'Allen': 'who issued the troops with a small tot of rum and reserved for himself One Gallon.'

Innocent activities like the famous Sergeant-Major's drainage improvements at Roussel Farm, needed but to be mentioned – a magnificent and general laugh at once burst forth, echoing through the rafters. The Medical Officer's simple remedies were sufficiently ridiculed, and he himself, battering away at the piano and roaring out in a most parching voice 'The Battle Cry of Freedom,' was declared on all sides to be 'a cure.'

A thaw came on, and dirty rainstorms swept the open fields. I felt how lucky I was to have received almost at that moment a pair of new and ponderous Wellingtons, though my size in boots was different;

and in these I worked with Worley on a new plan for putting up barbed wire in a hurry, which we had ourselves pencilled out. The Divisional General rode by one morning as we were beginning, with our squad of learners, and when he returned we had put up quite a maze of rusty inconvenience. The good old Duke – no, the General, called me all trepidant to him, smiled, asked my age and service, liked the wire, and passed into the village. At lunch Harrison also smiled upon me. 'Rabbit, I hear you were wiring this morning. . . The General said you surprised him. He asked me, "Who was that subaltern in the extraordinary boots, Harrison? Well, he got that wire up very quick. We went down the street, and there wasn't a yard of it: we came back and there was a real belt." You've found another friend.' He began to laugh very heartily as he added, 'Those boots, Rabbit!' This painful memory must be exorcized by being noted here. I presented my batman shortly afterwards with a pair of new jack-boots.

With a sudden surprise order to return to the trenches, these affectionate times came to an end. We marched that great march of the British from Poperinghe, past hop-gardens and estaminets, past shattered estaminets and withered fields and battery shelters and naked hearths dripping with rain – perhaps the most significant and sad of all domestic ruin – to the screened corner by Ypres Asylum, thence turning along Posthoornstraat into Kruisstraat, a suburb of Ypres, where, we heard, the inhabitants had longest lingered on and sold wines against the fates. A reconnaissance of the trenches which we were to hold came next. They were those on a rising ground in Sanctuary Wood, near Hill 60, and were indifferently known as Tor Tops, Mount Sorrel and Observatory Ridge. On arriving in the wood, we found it an unprepossessing one. 'What about Thiepval?' said Sergeant Ashford to me as we moved taciturnly up the duckboards, not the imagined communication trench. 'Looks exactly the same.' The scene was deathly, and if we had known then the German points of vantage we should have disliked it still more.

Meeting me outside a high red house in Kruisstraat, Harrison walked along the road to tell me some news, and his face was overcast. He was ordered to return to England, and at once. But more followed. He had arranged that I was to go to Brigade as Intelligence Officer;

the General had previously desired him to let me go, and now he thought it would do me good. These facts caused the Ypres-Comines Canal, over which our short walk led us, to look particularly desolate and grey. That night Harrison went his way, and I reported anxiously at the seat of terror in the Ramparts; the battalion relieved in wild blackness on Observatory Ridge. They had hardly taken over the trenches when a fierce brief bout of shelling fell upon Valley Cottages, the foolish wreckage used as battalion headquarters, and among the victims was our kind, witty and fearless Sergeant-Major Daniels. He was struck in the head, and being carried away to the casualty clearing station in Vlamertinghe white mill, lived a day or two and said good-bye to Harrison, who heard of the bad business in time to see him once more.

These men being lost to me, Cassells having transferred to the Flying Corps, and Lintott having collapsed and disappeared in a deathly state from among us, I felt myself in the void. I made an attempt to master the position at Brigade headquarters, and there was certainly work to do. It was my business to compile all the information that our front yielded, and to write daily reports which were signed by the General before being sent to higher quarters and circulated in the Brigade. The battalions manned various observation posts and snipers' lairs, and, while their work came under my control, we had a section of specialists attached to the Brigade headquarters. Moreover, I could now claim to be a bureaucrat, for there were two clerks to draw maps and produce manifold copies of reports and programmes. I received several ancient and some modern maps and archives as my weapons of war.

Such was the subject of my interest; and now for the surroundings. Brigade headquarters was compendiously concealed in an ancient bricked vault under the Ramparts, not far from the Lille Gate – not far enough.

This cavern was reputed to have stored barrels of beer in recent, and Marlborough's horses in remote, antiquity. It produced in the mind of the visitor a confidence in its prodigious strength, but some absurd stickler for accuracy presently proved that a very few feet of earth protected it above. At least, it was roomy, and contained a suite of cubicles (divided with best mailbags), a dining-room at the moat end, and an office at the Ypres end. There next the exit I had my table and my mysterious heap of pamphlets, codes (one never spoke nowadays of the 11th R. Sussex, but of 'Arthur' or similar pseudonym) and papers. Outside, men were killed from time to time, but there were generally a good many, cleaning up, delivering messages, awaiting inspection or instructions, acting as if it was a normal rendezvous.

From the time of my arrival here and the severance from the companionship and duty which had grown preternaturally mine, I find that my memory relaxes and chronology withers away. But much topographical and personal impression persists, and I can still pick up my tin hat and the General's periscope ('Albert') and get out to my daily round. The moat was often as placid as John Crome as one crossed it into the exposed flats beyond. There I soon left behind the often remarked gunner's grave, honoured with the small statue of a child bearing a basket of flowers, borrowed with a genuine poetical pathos 'for the duration.' Thence the way over the watery grass did not detain anyone. As time went on, the Germans practised more and more the ingenious but dangerous by-play of 'sniping' even at a single passenger here with shells, and one's more fantastic thoughts ran upon the rumour that there existed below a conduit from the Ramparts to the dam of Zillebeke Lake ahead – a very nice conduit, but closed to the public. Half-way across to the dam, a precarious battery position lined the Ypres-Roulers railway, in the middle of a morass; and it was here, at an unpleasant moment for the gunners, that I actually saw the dark body of a huge shell in the air as it swooped into the muck just ahead. Our gunners in the Salient were at the mercy of their opponents, and their gunpits hardly looked strong enough to store potatoes. Not much better were the numerous shanties and holes, all in a row, along the Zillebeke Lake dam, called The Bund. Here I would call for my observer-corporal, Kenward, who daily bumped his head over the entrance as he came out with telescope and logbook, after which we tramped under the rags of camouflage round the corner of the lake into the handsome communication trench to Zillebeke village. Daily that corner grew more of a slough. A line of slender trees, and a strip of grass, gave us a hint of pastoral as we looked out, but what one was most aware of was the interminable clump, clump of boots on trench boards.

This route was known to so many uncomplaining tourists that I may be forgiven a quantity of detail. Presently one turned from the lake at Hallebast Corner, easily redesignated Hellblast, where usually one might see not far off what enthusiasts called 'splendid bursts' of five-nines, occasionally with water-music. A short ditch led to Zillebeke Church by a little stream which murmured over pots and pans, as having no reason to change its habits because of a dull war; ruined brickwork hugged the ground, and among it some headquarters officers were answering questions and finding a little whisky left, unseen but not unsuspected. A cat or two, or their ghosts, glossily crossed the linenless backyards. Zillebeke tileyard had ceased work and a little smoke there was naturally a dangerous thing. The church tower was not yet altogether down, but one lost its architectural distinctions in one's quick movement over the road, under German observation; one's eye managed to register nevertheless a number of wooden crosses.

From that point, two trenches went on to the firing line, and it depended on incident or instinct which we took. Vince Street, the north one, was solidly made, and commanded a pretty view of a farm called Dormy House, in the court of which a cart stood with a load of musty straw, scarcely to be considered extant. So Oberon might have deceived. The trench led into the brutalized little wood known to mournful history as Maple Copse; and so did the other trench from the south, Zillebeke Street, which had shallowly twisted along past a battalion headquarters, Valley Cottages. The only way to get to Valley Cottages was to hoist oneself out of Zillebeke Street into the full gaze of competent German observers and walk 'over the top,' into the back door. There were many wooden crosses here. It was best to have no business in daylight at those cottages; but even so one went into Maple Copse, the pretended shield of some field-guns with the additional harmless fraud of brown-leafed camouflage, and one left Maple Copse with a serious mind to walk on in the open to support trench, Stafford Trench. The greensward, suited by nature for the raising of sheep, was all holes, and new ones appeared with great uproar as one crossed. A German battery at close range made beautiful groups round Kenward and myself one day, and the interested faces looking on from Stafford Trench had the pleasure of seeing us refuse to quicken our pace. As we expected to receive the next salvo on our persons, we felt that running would be a little tedious. I looked down and saw a shrapnel helmet, with blood and hair in it.

The land rose to the south and east, and formed positions of decided strength in spite of the wretched approach. East, ahead, we climbed up Observatory Ridge, scantily covered with the verges of Sanctuary Wood, and still we were under the telescopes of the enemy, who had Hill 60 and other observation posts. By a peculiarity of remembrance I see there a dugout like a cairn in the open, at first a cookhouse, but shelled out of that use; then the terrible little trees of the brown ridge posture on the sky, with the terraced 1914 shelters, useless and bulged, below them. Trenches began among these. It was a deep front line, but to the south there was an end to it – 'The Gap.' The sandy soil otherwise was carefully dug and sapped, with tremendous dugouts beneath, entered from the malodorous cutting Krab Krawl. In that trench there was a surprising little nook for two, one the observer, and the other his mate with the logbook. My old friend Sergeant Clifford would always be fondly lingering at this point for me, with marvellous exposition of German subtlety more or less based on what he had seen. This man loved his work, and wrestled with its problems as nowadays people struggle to prepare huge strikes. I am meeting him again one posthumous morning, and shall expect him to have news of Satan tunnelling under Zion Hill, with exact map references. From his post in the Low Countries, strange contrasts of happenings were to be seen. Here, a little iron pipe, puffing out vapour in moment-jets. There, a party of bluish Germans, apparently all sage elders with swarthy beards, gingerly filing through a copse – past old British crosses and new German monuments. Shrapnel sends them scampering off the track. There, a white-headed boy carrying a mess-tin. Dogs, with the usual habits. Beyond, a pushing-party bringing up trolleys bristling with the iron rods used for reinforced concrete. The same party scuttling away from sudden white cloudlets – our shrapnel again. Curious that one did not notice it going over. Farther, a street emerging from a clean village, white linen on the lines, civilians, horsemen and dogcarts spanking along; resting troops out in a field at physical exercises, even women in dark blue skirts pushing trucks. One day, the grand spectacle of a church steeple in flames, finally toppling to earth. With such varieties our observers were in clover, even if they usually recorded about four in the afternoon, with a flourish, that the 'light prevented further observations.'

Not nearly so good was the look-out at Rudkin House, the little hillock facing towards Hill 60, although the cardboard chart of landmarks there claimed a spacious survey. It was an odd place, being actually in the mouth of an old well, the bottom of which was in a tunnelled dugout; and, as a cookhouse was installed there for battalion headquarters, the observers had domestic difficulties. Wood-smoke in dugouts already short of air was one of the war's little miseries; and I never visited this dungeon without repeating from Young's *Night Thoughts*, often in my pocket, the just words,

> 'Dreadful post
> Of observation! darker every hour.'

From Rudkin House a subway provided safe but awkward communication with the front line, and one morning early, calling there with the Brigade-Major, I was thunderstruck to see troops coming up from the emergency exits between the front and support systems and smoke rising also. The German gunners, whose opportunity filled one with horrid apprehension, stood by and no doubt preferred the information they got by watching to other action. Men crowded out and doubled and ducked back into Stafford Trench, while the Brigade-Major rapidly organized a working-party to block up the fire below with sandbags. This was the result of some machine-gunner's mistaking a can of petrol for his washing water. Such fires happening in tunnelled dugouts ended a number of lives. On this occasion I believe one man was suffocated.

xviii

Domesticities

The advancing spring of 1917, with its ever brightening green even round Rudkin House and its prismatic play of sunbeams on that gurgling, persistent brook in Zillebeke, yet meant advancing war, and our sector began to warm up. Our own flying corps were brilliantly active, but there were on occasion four or five German airplanes in the early day over our forward positions. Great shells were sent into our area in the endeavour to destroy the deep dugouts, shells which from a flank could be plainly seen in the final seconds of their descent. I was fascinated by that violent spectacle. A long-range trench mortar one afternoon fired with weary iteration and accurate inaccuracy, its visible missiles plunging into the muck and tinware just over the trench in which I talked with the inimitable Vidler, who felt friendly towards this region from its connection with the Canadians, his brothers by adoption. He took me on little explorations in the wood, and we found old German uniforms, bones and shovels, and British graves. (They are still finding them, in 1930.) Vancouver Street was anti-German at this time. It was, however, not a good platform, as its mud-filled entrance to the front trench suddenly exposed one's head and shoulders to the snipers opposite. But being on this ridge at all was rather like being in a deadly pillory.

My observers' reports grew extensive and sometimes valuable; the more valuable they were, the worse for me, for an officer at Divisional headquarters could never be satisfied with what I transmitted. He came along himself to Ypres at a gentlemanly hour to press for more facts, and this usually meant my going up to the front trenches and round the positions for the second time that day. This steely youth had the bad habit of crossing the infantryman's country between trenches where that was not the convention, on the principle of 'après moi les 5.9.' One day a footsore Blunden was just back in the Ramparts, perhaps noting down a poetical hint on the swans in the moat or more probably wondering if the mess corporal had got back from

Poperinghe and forgotten the Beaune, certainly feeling he had earned an interval, when his tormentor called, requiring instant conduct to a point in the front line where the authentic eye could examine a mass of new earth reported by Sergeant Clifford in the German support line. Good, in a military sense. Shell-holes, duckboards, trenches, again drearily footed, we chose a point looking towards Stirling Castle. When the Divisional eye had rested on this phenomenon, but not with such insight that any brilliant interpretation followed, we turned, and my friend strode over the open, stepping westward, and singing some rhymes by Mr Belloc. This excursion proved a little too bold, and suddenly a shell or two fell behind; then with the familiar breath-stopping suddenness a large one rushed into the mould beside us, kicking up some lumps of it, and then another, quite as large. We removed from this disturbance in different directions, and my high-booted inspector made his own way to Ypres, thenceforward leaving me to myself for some time.

Long tramps day and night ruined my feet, but I had to walk to Poperinghe in great misery to have a tooth put to rest or die in the attempt. In daylight one might be unlucky over getting a lift on that hazardous road, which could be seen between its trees from the German and from our front line. I was. The tooth was pulled, back I went, and saw again the tipsy water-tower and the sole surviving pinnacle along the road through Ypres with illogical happiness. By the station I noticed some newly installed howitzers, and there was a suspicious quickness among those now passing out of the Lille Gate, but even so, the dentist had been settled with. In the very prime of my content, seeking the home from home across the rubble, and instinctively avoiding the pits leading swiftly into the Ypres sewers, I was chilled by the recollection that as 'mess president' I was due to receive the evening admonition from the General, as he sat down and scanned the seats to note the absentees. He was quite right; I had no faculty for turning the young mess corporal, though he looked rather like a Frenchman, into a Soyer. The satisfaction with which poor Hornby could say to his visitor, 'Do try this cream cheese, made at Mont-des-Cats, quite a local product,' or 'These cauliflowers are uncommonly good, Clark,' was sure to be knocked of a heap by some horrid hiatus or ruination; by charred sardines or marine coffee.

One evening his thoughts were distracted from these unhappy imperfections by the unprecedented characteristics of the visitor. This was a Major, attached to the tunnelling company and living, apparently for ever and from the beginning, along by the Lille Gate; a Canadian, a big, slow-paced but unescapable being; and he had 'dropped in' to inform Brigade of emergency exits from the Krab Krawl tunnels, requiring our considered defence in case of a German raid. There was to my sense indication that this evangelist had drunk our health occasionally before calling, and at dinner his gold-digger's fraternity of style appealed to all except the General, who at every vivid question and proposition and even critical shaking of head went redder, but could not impress his guest with the due gravity. At last, he seized an opportunity. 'You wish an officer to inspect the tunnel exits; very well; Mr Blunden will go with you immediately,' with a look towards me in which a rudimentary wink strove for dignified expression. I went many times round the Observatory Ridge trenches, but this was the most picturesque of my tours. The Major seemed to have an enormous physique, eyes independent of light, and a preternatural affinity with this trench area. Everywhere we passed, he murmured over past and present stages of sandbags, junctions, revetments, drains, even patting the side of Vince Street like a horse as he said, 'It's a good trench, Vince Street, and it always was, young man. What's that? The man who made it? Yes, knew Vince well. Now just here we'll turn off (see the steps?) and look at Yeomanry post,' a formless site, shelled an hour earlier. On Observatory Ridge it was blackness profound, and not only did the veteran pry about all the emergency exits with dangling barbed wire to them, but also he felt very much attracted to various derelict sapheads and cuttings, thick to the knees with cold mud. 'This was a very promising communication,' 'I myself preferred this to Living Trench,' 'Well, d'ye know, your General ought to be up here – see, there's nothing to stop 'em.' At last he went downstairs into the tunnels, and in a sort of wooden sepulchre found two mining officers and one bottle of whisky. They were in a grave mood, and as he went in dismissed a non-commissioned officer from the doorway. 'Fresh, fresh, fresh,' one commented in deep bass on the departing soldier, and the other nodded assent, though in that cave of spoiled air and fuscous lamplight the word 'fresh' was misleading; then they welcomed the Major as he seated himself on the wood bench, and (to use a contemporary elliptical expression) I had one, too. They talked of drives and parallels and countermines, spreading out a magical but terrible map of the underworld, and all with a stolid permanency resembling the Major's, who finally hauled his bulk up again into the moist darkness and we arrived in Ypres (one of us having grown a little stupid) in the moody hush of the darkest hour.

It was at that stern time when the Brigade-Major, Clark, would often take a walk round the line, and his route was likewise an individual choice, though he avoided half-choked derelicts. 'I like,' he said, 'to see something of the country we are fighting for,' and so he moved mazily in the mist from point to point inaccessible by day, often with some recollection of local history, tantalizing me in my sympathy with these overwhelmed barns and hovels and beetfields; but he was not really occupied in antiquarian studies. He was under orders to gather ideas for bloodthirsty battle, but he kept that secret. The first notion I had of it was when, on the extreme right of our territory, close to a hopeless drowned support-trench, we came on a rough trench tramway, which made me say, 'This must have been put down in 1914 by the Spanish Onions' (he belonged to the regiment so nicknamed); whereon he replied, 'I'll bet you it wasn't there three weeks ago.' It was in fact part of the preparation for the Messines attack, which was shortly afterwards rumoured, with expansive stories of our mines ready to be sent up under German Brigade headquarters, a modern miracle if it was so, and the even colder announcement that the British staff were allowing for I forget how many thousand casualties on the first day.

Do I loiter too long among little things? It may be so, but those whom I foresee as my readers will pardon the propensity. Each circumstance of the British experience that is still with me has ceased for me to be big or little, and now appeals to me more even than the highest exaltation of pain or scene in the 'Dynasts,' and thank the heaven of adoration incarnadined with Desdemona's handkerchief.

Was it nearer the soul of war to adjust armies in coloured inks on vast maps at Montreuil or Whitehall, to hear of or to project colossal shocks in a sort of mathematical symbol, than to rub knees with some poor jaw-dropping resting sentry, under the dripping rubber sheet, balanced on the greasy fire-step, a fragment of some rural newspaper or Mr Bottomley's oracle beside him? That thrusting past men achingly asleep in narrow chilly firetrenches, their mechanical shifting of their sodden legs to let you go on your way, pierces deep enough. That watching the sparks of trench mortar bombs converge on some shell-hole a few hundred yards towards the still dawnless east, with their fiendish play on Aristophanes' comic syllables 'tophlattothratt, tophlattothratt,' the lunge and whirr of such malignity against a few simple lives, pierces deep enough. Towards Hooge one brazen morning, running in a shower of shells along 'The Great Wall of China' (one dull shell struck within a rifle's length of us, and exploded something else), Kenward the corporal and I saw a sentry crouching and peering one way and another like a birdboy in an October storm. He spoke, grinned and shivered; we passed; and duly the sentry was hit by a shell. So that in this vicinity a peculiar difficulty would exist for the artist to select the sights, faces, words, incidents, which characterized the time. The art is rather to collect them, in their original form of incoherence. I have not noticed any compelling similarity between a bomb used as an inkpot and a bomb in the hand of a corpse, or even between the look of a footballer after a goal all the way and that of a sergeant inspecting whale-oiled feet. There was a difference prevailing in all things. Let the smoke of the German breakfast fires, yes, and the savour of their coffee, rise in these pages, and be kindly mused upon in our neighbouring saps of retrogression. Let my own curiosity have its little day, among the men of action and war-imagination.

The Brigade was withdrawn to Poperinghe for rest. We had our meals where we wished, and I chose a little table in the 'British Hostel,' where the gramophone was chiefly employed on a minuet by Boccherini and something 'Hawaiian' – not bad accompaniments (for the uncritical young) to Madame's chickens and wines. The Officers' Club was usually overcrowded, but none the worse for that; one could exercise oneself in the delicate operation of identifying badges and divisional symbols, thus always gaining power of conjecture about possible reliefs for our own division. Even the General took some wine one evening at the invitation of Clark, and I reflected that he might even have gone to see Charlie Chaplin if we had pressed the point. However, he was called off on momentous affairs. Chaplin was showing, but in a microscopic size; better things were given us at the great hop-warehouse by the station, by our own divisional party, 'The Tivolies.' These oscillated round that well-known entertainer Du Calion, who perched on a ladder in the middle of the stage, wearing a pseudo-naval uniform and let fall on the lordly brass-hats below his licensed satire beginning, 'I should like to inform you young fellows of the junior service.' O, then there was clowning, then there was antic; Robinson, the tall immaculate in evening dress, danced with the tubby little 'wench,' who snivelled to perfection, in lovely incongruity – what a roar went up when the 'wench' appeared again as a Lancashire lad of rather limited sense and confronted some tremendous stage colleague, with

'Get out of 'ere.'

'I'll knock yer 'ead off.'

'You won't.'

'I will.'

'You'd never do it' (advancing firmly).

'I will.'

(Recoiling, and very rationally) 'Ah, and I believe he would.'

Or that other commonplace, fortune-telling.

The 'wench' was listening earnestly. The wizard read 'her' hand, scratching it. 'Ah, there's a bit of luck for you. I can see it. There's the firing line. We don't 'ave no breastworks in this part. Ah, there's that bit of luck again. You're going to 'ave a letter. Your sweetheart's on the road to Poperinghe. He's been awarded the YMCA with Triangles. He's got off at the station. He's been told off by the RTO. He's gone in for a glass of stoot. He's come out again – they don't give credit. He's in the street outside. He's coming in to this 'all. He's —' (commotion at the back, shouting and blundering over forms; a red-nosed gruesome figure, the like of which never rewarded Shakespeare's fancy, comes hurrying up the middle passage. Applause *crescendo*, all heads turned to the new Adonis) 'he's coming on to this platform!!' (He does, and with one final tremendous gesture, glaring horribly at the gasping 'wench,' flings out his scraggy arms in awful invitation. 'Alarums. Chambers go off.')

This elementary but then glorious comedy was the last that some of the audience were ever to enjoy. But they had not expected even that much. One sees why they roared with laughter. Shakespeare died too soon.

xix

The Spring Passes

Returning to the line, the Brigade took over the rather uninteresting positions north of Ypres, spread out under the superior enemy strongholds called High Command. The weather grew quite warm, and answerable to May; there seemed no special operation in the air, although at night one might pass the time by taking compass bearings on the most usual gunflashes. That notwithstanding, a change for the worse in the treatment of the support and reserve area was now clear enough, and the German counter-battery firing had to be watched by us passers-by. The most terrific punishment fell in the golden evening upon one or two battery positions recently perfected, such violence on such points exceeding our previous experience, and attracting numerous spectators out of the dugouts along the Yser Canal. One strange fact in the area often provided discussion. A little way behind the canal, beside the high road, stood a pretty ornamented house, among trees, called Reigersburg Château. It was unmolested by the German gunners, or practically so. Similar non-combatant's privilege was allowed to another château a short distance westward, the Trois Tours, although the village of Brielen which it overtopped had become the usual three-verse fandango of brick mounds and water-holes. Of the White Mill, which artillery had been occupying, nothing but the crushed base was left, but the winged structure was easily fancied in

that spring sun and wakened zephyr, a fair and blessed ghost. Even
the Yser Canal, in whose high bank we lived, was fresh and twinkling,
crossed with bridges of light timber almost like a Chinese lake. In the
dugout of Vidler, when the 11th were relieved, there was particular
joy, for his old schoolfellow Tice had now joined the battalion, and
in conclave threatened solemn war against any German who crossed
his track. With his stiff, cropped hair he looked an unmistakable
German himself. Vidler now had a fresh audience for his school
recollections and mimicry; he almost gave his orders on parade in the
nasal tones of our famous writing-master, and filled the desert air
with imitations which a starling would have been proud of. Amon
and Collyer, his old school-fellows, bore the burden, Tice with his
sweet mournfulness listened and gave suggestions and approval, while
I made up the party of five and the colloquy of Sussex in her days of
peace with all my heart.

The Brigade took its full turn of sixteen days, and at headquarters,
in the absence of the General, the temporary command of kindly
Colonel Draffen well suited the mild season. Draffen 'never tried to
be his own lance-corporal,' and sympathetically regarded us as trying
hard to perfect ourselves in our special jobs. At table, in his office, he
was fatherly. I knew about Jeshurun, and how when he waxed fat he
kicked, yet I am sorry to recall that my confidence ran a little too high
in these easier conditions. First I began to air my convictions that
the war was useless and inhuman, even inflicting these on a highly
conservative General (an unnaturally fearless man) who dined with
us one evening, and who asked me, 'why I wasn't fighting for the
Germans?' to which I answered with all too triumphant a simplicity
that it was only due to my having been born in England, not Germany.
Probably I was growing reckless after a year of war. And then our old
commander came back, on the eve of our relief, with the result that
he quickly sent for me and ordered me to keep my observers manning
their present posts during the tour of the incoming Brigade. At this I
dared to complain that the men had already worked day and night
for sixteen days, under dangerous – 'Good God, man,' the General
broke in with just indignation, 'don't talk to me about the men being
in danger; don't we all' – and I forgot what more, for I took an early

opportunity to go. I went to the Brigade Major, and, mentioning my escapade, petitioned for my return to the 11th Royal Sussex, where indeed I still felt my companionship was. Clark gently but firmly supported this idea. The next time that the General saw me was on a country road; he told me he was returning to me a manuscript of poems on Ypres which he had done me the honour to read, and observed that he had perused them with interest. This he reinforced later in his own handwriting, 'I have read these with great pleasure.' I do not aspire to any more unexpected critical commendation.

The relief was completed, and we migrated into the world of ivied dovecotes and orchards, where a battalion sees itself as a united family, horses and all within the same hedgerow; but those who heard Olympian voices on the wind were a little depressed to think that we were due back after our week or so in the country, to attack Pilkem Ridge, of which High Command was one bastion.

Training in a new mode of offensive approach now occupied the Foot. I was once more a genuine infantryman, and with less enthusiasm than was apparent I controlled my platoon as they plodded through the ploughed ups and downs beyond St Omer to outflank a prearranged and harmless enemy. Several mild and lengthening days went by as we yawned over this exercise; it was the season of Love. Accordingly the old farmer in the yard of his, and our, headquarters protested that we had stolen his new irreplaceable bucket worth several hundred francs, and was hardly convinced that his claim was too bold even when the bucket was produced from beneath some trusses of straw in his loft. The cars of authority came and went; the mossy banks of the country roads smiled more sweetly every morning with celandine and violet, with primrose and starflower. One day when I was ordered to serve at a court-martial a few miles off, I was rewarded as I went for my trouble; after a walk across a moor with ancient quarryings all solitary and primeval, the village of Acquin to which I was sent was shown suddenly like a jewel in the valley below, through a sparkling wave of sun and dewy haze. The roofs were rosy bright, and the lusty speech of the farmyards resounded.

The only consolation that one could find in being warned that an attack was coming was the frequent unfulfilment of such warnings;

and this time the proposed capture of Pilken Ridge was postponed after all. I personally profited by the changed intention, for I was sent to the seaside for a rest. At Ambleteuse there was little to do but to idle among the tents or downs, as was prescribed, and now a somnolent, apathetic mood had come over me, so that I kept little reckoning of events. By luck or judgment in lorry-hopping (the snarls of the Portuguese drivers were amusing, seeing that the lorries they drove were British), one reached Boulogne and looked at the shops. A French poet (there are as many in France as this side), Albert Sautteau, who always added to his name the dignity 'des Gens de Lettres,' used to receive me kindly at 'Le Home' near our rest camp, and we read together his clockwork rhymes from the local papers. Like the curious Eclympastere in Chaucer's poem, nearly, 'he slept and did none other work,' still dreaming on and refusing to believe in the war save in verses 'pour les blessés' and 'à mes amis à Verdun.' Madame was his very opposite, elegant and energetic; mademoiselle was only able to speak in blushes and smiles; and the small boy Gustave, dressed up like a young Highlander, haunted the camp and seemed to hold a better command than the Major in charge there. These were my friends, and I contrived to return to 'Le Home' once or twice more during the war. But now, I think, that home would be found in some leisurely by-street of Valenciennes, agreeable to the patient Muse of my good old friend.

And now away again to the outer world, where the tide of British power is gathering imperiously and insolently already for the onrush of 1917. I was now eager once more to share the regular life of my battalion, whose friendship outweighed all sorrows, but to my disgust I was once more detached from it to suffer a course of musketry. The countryside round St Omer and the dusty highway were nothing to me without my old familiar faces, and the terms and technicalities of the rifle and its use were like grains of sand working into my skull. There were accordingly some petulant remarks over the telephone at the rifle-range when I was in charge of practice; and I was at least more skilful with the shots of epigram than with the three-o-three of the small-arms factory. The village where we lived was marvellously cloaked and embosomed in huge old trees, the grass and herbs ran high above its churchyard wall, there were oak benches and books and beer; but I was in my glory the day we ended the course and marched away through the burning glare of dusty summer. I had been longing for the fragrance of ancient peace:

> 'Now to attune my dull soul if I can
> To the contentment of this countryside,
> Where man is not for ever killing man
> But quiet days and quiet waters glide.'

That was the note which my verses struck (memory retains these things capriciously), but officialdom and military manuals struck a louder and a harsher one. The heartiness of tried companions was the only real refuge; and so I went to find it with a lightened step. At Watten station something happened which you may laugh at, but I shall not. The train was not due to leave till the evening; after a visit to an estaminet, listening to a hero who was not ashamed of it, I sauntered by the canal, and then settled myself with my book in an empty cattle-truck. There came along a girl of fourteen or so, with a small brother, and looked in. We talked, and – we fell in love. That 'I' may be still in love with her, Marie-Louise of course, so black-eyed, and serious, and early-old with the inheritance of peasant experience – I have seen her alone since in many a moment of escape and fantasy. Still she looks in on this life's sultry cattle-truck, halted awhile in some drab siding, and once again we kiss, innocent as petals in the breeze. With what sad resignation to the tyrannical moment, which she hardly credits to be true, lifting her slow hand doubtfully to wave farewell, does that child-love of only one day's courting watch me pass into the voluminous, angry, darkening distance: ah, Marie-Louise!

Canal bank: Coney Street: and almost the first face I saw in the communication trench beyond battalion headquarters was Sergeant Davey's, covered with sweat and mud. He was emerging from the explosion of a couple of shells in the trench, which had killed two of the runners before and behind him. It had required many frightful shocks to impress on Davey's noble looks this appealing misery. 'Is this the promised End, or image of that horror?' However, Davey went on, one of the essential men of all our changing battalion; and soon a healing liberty from the gridiron of new labours and new lightnings was afforded. Out we went to a merry round of work and pleasure at Houlle in the marsh of St Omer, one of the battalion's best times. In 1917 old expressions such as 'a bon time' and 'trays beans' were not much heard; another had arisen, 'The BEF will all go home – in one boat': but at least we now had a week or two of camp life, some in tents, some in brewery warehouses, some in fine bedrooms, all in high summer. The lonely ponds and canals were a delight after the day's strenuous business, which began often before dawn. Having attacked and trenched and reinforced and counter-attacked through the yellowing corn, and discussed this manœuvre, that quarry, that cross-road until the afternoon, we came into the splendid silences of evening with intense joy. It was during this rest that Vidler, Amon, Collyer, Tice and myself, all of Christ's Hospital, went together into St Omer, and roamed the streets, the cathedral, the cafés and the shops with such exhilarations of wit and irony that we felt no other feast like this could ever come again; nor was the feeling wrong.

The picture taken that day is by me now; the vine winds over the white wall, a happy emblem of our occasion; and the five of us, all young and with an expression of subdued resoluteness and direct action, are looking on the world together. What do we care for your Three Musketeers? And after all, we know their very roads better than they did.

I recollect the battalion on the march through grey and pink boulevards and faubourgs, in misty morning dripping dew; and there was a night when we slept on doorsteps by the road; I recollect the enormous sidings at Hazebrouck station, and one more languid, unconversational, clumsy journey in the open trucks to Poperinghe, Olive and myself sitting swinging our legs over the track, noting ominous new shell-holes in the fields alongside; but most of all, out of a deranged chronology and dimmed picture, I recollect the strange sight of red rose-like fires on the eastward horizon at dusk, the conflagrations of incendiary shells tumbling into that *ghat* called Ypres with which we must now renew acquaintance.

XX

Like Samson in his Wrath

The preparations for the new battle were perforce as obvious to the Germans, with their complete dominance in observation posts, as they were to us. All the available open space through the Ypres Salient, which is sparsely dotted with farmhouses, tail-ends of villages and copses, was crammed with men, animals, stores, guns and transport; from Poperinghe forward the place was like a circus ground on the eve of a benefit. New roads and railways had changed the map so completely in a few weeks that one was a stranger here. The instinct revolted against the inevitable punishment to come, already tokened by those big holes now met in walls and crossings. Not the famous footprint in the sand contained a sharper shock than the shell-hole unerringly torn out by the far-off gunner 'registering' his targets in the middle of some previously secure trackway; and whatever had been formerly by some mercy peaceful, sleep-inviting ground in the Salient was not so now. A fever was in the midsummer air, and it has left a disordered recollection of the sequence of events, so that I find myself in unexpected sympathy with Tennyson's oracle:

> 'Who can say
> Why to-day
> To-morrow will be yesterday?'

What the infantryman in France knew about the war as a whole was seldom worth knowing, and we had little time or taste for studying the probable effect upon us of events beyond the skyline of immediate orders; yet before Third Ypres we heard without delight that a store of ammunition and battle requirements, covering several square miles, had been exploded by an enemy airman, and that the Germans had driven in the English trenches at Nieuport in the most blunt and unintimidated style. Such news got about very slowly, but made a mark where it touched. Then there was the usual soul-sapping doubt about the date of our push. Before it came, there were opportunities enough for death or glory. But the experienced sense observed that people did not espouse these with the comparatively bright eye of a year before; 1917 was distasteful.

The battalion camped in readiness among the familiar woods west of Vlamertinghe, but the woods were changed and the parting genius must have gone on a stretcher. No Belgian artisans were hammering strips of tarred canvas on the hut roofs now in the homely style of our original visits here; there were ugly holes of various sizes among the huts. Wooden tracks led this way and that in puzzling number through the crowded airless shadows, and new roads threw open to the public a district only suited for the movements of a small and careful party. At the corner where one swaggering new highway left the wood eastward, an enormous model of the German systems now considered due to Britain was open for inspection, whether from the ground or from step-ladders raised beside, and this was popular, though whether from its charm as a model or value as a military aid is uncertain. Vidler and Tice inspected it, at least, as stern utilitarians, and infallible officers. No great way off, a large ammunition dump was in use, and those who had ignored it previously became aware of it one night when something from above hit it. The irritated crackling of myriads of cartridges and small explosive, interspersed with thunder-shocks, woke everyone up; but sleep when it had come was precious in those days.

German airmen adventured over in daytime to drive down the observation balloons helplessly wallowing there, and the troops, who appreciated such displays, saw one German machine race along only a few yards above the trees, with machine-gun playing, in an attempt to escape two British machines; all ran like boys to see it brought down and its occupants captured. But the wood was a sultry and offensive place, and when one was out of it (Collyer and I were somehow allowed a few hours in Poperinghe) the relief was surprising; return after dark was from the frankness of a restaurant with white cloths and glittering glasses into a gross darkness and surcharged crucible.

The road towards Vlamertinghe, newly constructed of planks, forced a publicity on farmlands into which I had only gone before on some pleasant trespass. It took one presently through a gorgeous and careless multitude of poppies and sorrels and bull-daisies to the grounds of Vlamertinghe Château, many-windowed, not much hurt, but looking very dismal in the pitiless perfect sun. Its orchards yet clung to some pale apples, but the gunners were aware of that, the twelve-inch gunners, whose business here seemed like a dizzy dream. Under several splendid untrimmed trees, among full-flooding grass, shone certain rails, and on these rails were some tremendous iron engines, with gaping mouths; standing behind, if you could keep your eye unblurred at the titanic second of their speaking, you could see their mortal monosyllables of inferno climbing dead straight into the sky. But these metaphors occurred later. Continuing eastward, one might pass that other remarkably complete country house called Reigersburg, but one would be shocked at the new broad-gauge railway thrust past it into conspicuous open ground, and the trucks waiting on it, no doubt at liberty for a speedy transit to Brussels after the 39th Division had 'gone over' and tidied up. This was one of various fantastic tricks which as we went up gave us the anticipatory chill – 'Not on us?' the Oysters cried. The Yser Canal itself had been drastically rearranged. New bridges crossed it, powerful works, carrying real roadways. On the far side, the old bank which alone afforded cover from view and splinters to all those who lived or moved along the canal had been hewn through for the roadways and other tracks. Great heaps of warlike materials stood up naked and unashamed; batteries glinted and bellowed in transparent air. These gay grimaces had not failed to upset the enemy, who was tearing up the once idle ground and venerable shelters with long-range guns. The most solid bridge, No. 4, was a ferocious target; but at the Ypres end, called the Dead End, the new causeway was swollen with dead mules, pushed out of the road on to the sloping bank. The water below, foul yellow and brown, was strewn with full-sized eels, bream and jack, seething and bulged in death. Gases of several kinds oozed from the crumbled banks and shapeless ditches, souring the air. One needed no occult gift to notice the shadow of death on the bread and cheese in one's hand, the discoloured tepid water in one's bottle.

On one of the preliminary evenings the new Colonel, with his habitual bad luck, sent forward from C Camp an officer fresh from England, and one or two men with him, to patrol the land over which our assault was intended, with a special eye to the enemy's concern with some ancient gunpits there. This officer took with him his set of the maps, panoramas, photographs and assault programmes which had been served round with such generosity for this battle. He never returned. The next night a seasoned officer, from another battalion, patrolling the same ground, disappeared. It was believed that these had been taken prisoner, but I was not much inclined to that view when, the third night, I was sent up with one or two old hands to see what I could see. We reached the very sketchy front line before it was quite dark, soon afterwards crawled over the top and were carefully making our way through our own wire – not that its puny tendrils needed much care! – when with a crash and flame on all sides at once a barrage began. Shells struck so fast that we seemed to be one shell-hole away, and no more, from the latest, and as we dodged and measured our length in wild disorder, we drifted a long way into No Man's Land. The barrage followed our direction like a net, and when it stopped, as we lay panting and muttering in the smell of explosive mixed with that of the dewy weeds and broken clods, I saw that we were a few yards from a German sap, and I heard stealthy movement in that sap. This might have been the secret of my predecessors' misfortune. After the shelling we were not much good for observation or offence, and found out no more. On our shaky way down from the line, we passed two cottages, called Pittsburg and Frascati – formerly picturesque studies for amateur water-colour. We quickly found that we should have chosen any other route, for, as we passed, shells flinging out bright terrible phosphorus howled into these thatched hovels. Running along another of the new plank roads, uncertain where it led, we beheld in the sickening brightness a column of artillery waggons, noiseless, smashed, capsized, the remains of mules and drivers sprawling among the wreckage.

We passed, and I determined that we must rest the few hours till day in the canal bank. In order to save us a weary search among blown-in dugouts, and others specially allotted already, I called upon the Canal Bank Major, who was normally in control of the accommodations. No sooner was I inside the sandbag porch of his lair than a shell knocked the porch in, and some more of my nerve system with it. The Major knew nothing up-to-date about the canal bank, which was (in Vidler's phrase) 'not quite itself' at the time; so my call was mere formality, and we soon were running over the canal to the old familiar places, in the middle of some gas shelling, which seemed to increase the foul mist sneaking along, and worried us. There is a hypocritical tunelessness about a gas shell in flight and in explosion. With that, there was the thought of being pitched bleeding into the gummy filths and mortifications below. At last we were in a 'small elephant' dugout, which if hit would be smashed like an egg, and I stretched myself on the dusty boards. I woke with a stiff neck in slightly gasiferous sunlight, mechanically receiving a mug of lurid tea with a dash of petrol from one of my invincibles.

I could dilate upon other drama that occurred towards July 31, 1917; there was, for instance, that tooth of mine, which our Irish doctor painfully extracted for me by muscular Christianity in the wood, surely the last afternoon we were there; as many of my signallers as were off duty stood round with a hideous pleasure, and one or two begged to offer their compliments on so great a fortitude! But the battle cannot be postponed longer. I had to thrust aside my *Cambridge Magazine* with Siegfried Sassoon's splendid war on the war in it; sent my valise along to the dump; and fell in, wondering how Sassoon could pass one or two technical imperfections (as I thought them) in his fine verse. The spirit of battle was not rampant among us that turgid, thirsty night; our route was complicated by design and by accident, and the travelling companionship of numbers of tanks and other troops confused us. The unfamiliar way was now narrow as a lane, now broad and undefined as a football ground, sometimes dark, then lit whitely at a distance. At last we occupied trenches on the scene of our proposed business. Two days – was it? – elapsed; nature tried her hand at a thunderstorm; then the last colourless afternoon arrived. Before that a number of our men had been killed, and all drenched and shaken. That afternoon I saw the miserable state of a little group of houses called La Brique, now the object of a dozen German guns, and, escaping death, I well understood the number of bodies lying there. Everyone was moving in the open, without any help for it, and yet we were beating away at every point of importance opposite. Presently I stood with my friend Tice looking over the front parapet at the German line. Tice, though blue-chinned and heavy-eyed, showed his usual extreme attention to detail, identifying whatever features he could, and growing quite excited and joyful at the recognition of 'Kitchener's Wood' in the background. To-morrow morning— The afternoon grew pale with cloud. Tice went along one trench and I along another, with some absurd familiarity as, 'See you in the morning, old boy.'

xxi

The Crash of Pillars

The hour of attack had been fixed by the staff much earlier than the infantry wanted or thought suitable. The night had passed as such nights often do, shelling being less than was anticipated, silent altogether at times. I suppose it was about three when I shook hands with Colonel Millward, mounted the black-oozing steps of battle headquarters in the burrows below Bilge Street, and got into the assembly ditch ('Hornby Trench') with my signallers. It was thick darkness and slippery going, but we used an old road part of the way. Where we lay, there were in the darkness several tall tree-stumps above, and it felt like a friendly ghost that watched the proceedings. A runner came round distributing our watches, which had been synchronized at Bilge Street. At 3.50, if I am right, shortly after Vidler had passed me growling epigrams at some recent shell-burst which had covered him with mud, the British guns spoke; a flooded Amazon of steel flowed roaring, immensely fast, over our heads, and the machine-gun bullets made a pattern of sharper purpose and maniac language against that diluvian rush. Flaring lights, small ones, great ones, flew up and went spinning sideways in the cloud of night; one's eyes seemed not quick enough; one heard nothing from one's shouting neighbour, and only by the quality of the noise and flame did I know that the German shells crashing among the tree-stumps were big ones and practically on top of us. We rose, scrambled ahead, found No Man's Land a comparatively good surface, were amazed at the puny tags and rags of once multiplicative German wire, and blundered over the once feared trench behind them without seeing that it was a trench. Good men as they were, my party were almost all half-stunned by the unearthliness of our own barrage, and when two were wounded it was left to me to bandage them in my ineffective way. (I have been reminded that two of our party were killed, but at the time the fact was lost in the insane unrealities all round.) The dark began to dilute itself into daylight, and as we went on we saw concrete emplacements, apparently unattended to as yet, which had to be treated with care and suspicion; walking to the slanted low entrances with my revolver, I was well satisfied to prove them empty. And indeed the whole area seemed to be deserted! German dead, so obvious at every yard of a 1916 battlefield, were hardly to be seen. We still went ahead, and the mist whitened into dawn; through it came running a number of Germans – a momentary doubt; we prepared for a fight; no – 'Prisoners!' shouted my batman. Where they went I don't know; we took no more notice. A minute more, and my advanced guard of signallers had come into touch with our companies, digging in by fours and fives along their captured objective. Meanwhile, I went ahead to see all that the mist allowed; there were troops of our Brigade advancing through the lines of men consolidating shell-holes, and with map before me I could recognize some of the places which we had certainly captured. It seemed marvellous, for the moment. All ours – all these German trenches. Caliban Support, Calf Avenue, Calf Reserve. But, stay – even now a pity looks one in the face, for these trenches are mostly mere hedges of brushwood, hurdles, work for a sheepfold, with a shallow ditch behind; and they have been taking our weeks of gunfire in these!

The reflection and the sympathy actually occurred to me, but were soon obliterated by the day's work, and an increase in the German gunfire upon us. The slow twisting passage of the tanks through our position was thought to be the reason, for as these machines wheeled aside from the pits where our men were digging, heavy shells came down in plenty with formidable accuracy. Besides, the enemy must have captured a set of operation maps with all the stages of advance displayed. I remember that I was talking with somebody about one 'Charlie' Aston, an officer's servant, who had been running here and there to collect watches from German dead. He had just returned to his chosen shell-hole with several specimens, when a huge shell burst in the very place. But not much notice was taken, or elegy uttered, for everywhere the same instant destruction threatened. And Tice and Collyer were already killed – news as yet failing to have its full painfulness in the thick of things.

The battalion headquarters soon advanced from the old British front line, still conspicuous with the tall tree-stumps, and crushed itself into a little concrete dugout with a cupola over it, formerly used for a perfect survey of the British defences. I tried to throw up enough earth to protect an annexe next door, but was driven from the work by a machine-gun, hanging on no great way off. Road-making parties behind us had lost no time and, strung out among the shell-bursts, were shovelling and pummelling tracks across old No Man's Land. And then the Brigade headquarters came, beautiful to look upon, and their red tabs glowed out of several shell-holes. This was more than the German observers could endure, and in a short time there was such a storm of high explosive on that small space that the brains of the Brigade withdrew, a trifle disillusioned, to the old British trenches. Another storm, and a more serious and incontestable one, was now creeping on miserably with grey vapour of rain over the whole field. It was one of the many which caused the legend, not altogether dismissed even by junior officers, that the Germans could make it rain when they wanted to. Now, too, we were half certain that the attack had failed farther on, and one more brilliant hope, expressed a few hours before in shouts of joy, sank into the mud.

It was wet and it was cold. The marvel was that the day wore on, so heavy it was, and yet the day wore on, and I found by my watch that it was afternoon. At battalion headquarters in the concrete look-out there were long faces, not in expression of despair but what is almost as bad – indefiniteness. In the doorway, where the wounds of several men were dressed, a man with a mortal wound in the back was propped up. This poor wretch again and again moaned, 'I'm cold, cold,' but seemed to have no other awareness of life. The doctor looked at him, and shook his head at me. A medical orderly looked at him, and answered me he could do no good. I went out to visit company headquarters, which were now (with bombs and notebooks) under waterproof sheets stretched over shell-holes, swiftly becoming swimming-baths. As the unprepossessing evening came, N. C. Olive and myself were sharing a tin of 'Sunshine' sausages in one of these pools.

The position grew no better during the night, and the succeeding day was dismal, noisy and horrid with sudden death. Tempers were not good, and I found myself suddenly threatening a sergeant-major with arrest for some unfriendly view which he was urging on the headquarters in general. Then, there were such incidents as the death of a runner called Rackley, a sensitive and willing youth, just as he set out for the companies; intercepted by a shrapnel bullet he fell on one knee, and his stretched-out hand still clutched his message. Vidler, that invincible soldier, came in a little afterwards through explosions, observing, 'That was a quick one, 'Erb. I was feeling round my backside for a few lumps of shrapnel – didn't find any though.' This second day was on the whole drab in the extreme, and at the end of it we were ordered to relieve the 14th Hampshires in their position ahead, justly termed the Black Line, along the Steenbeck. The order presented no great intellectual difficulty, for our reduced battalion merely had to rise from its water-holes, plod through the mud of an already beaten track and crouch on the watch in other holes. Darkness clammy and complete, save for the flames of shells, masked that movement, but one stunted willow tree at which the track changed direction must haunt the memories of some of us. Trees in the battlefield are already described by Dante.

Headquarters – officers, signallers, servants, runners and specialists – arrived in the blind gloom at the trench occupied by the Hampshire headquarters, and it is sufficient to indicate the insensate condition of the relief when I say that we did not notice any unusually close arrival of shells as we drew near to the trench, but as we entered it we found that there had just been one. It had blown in some concrete shelters, and killed and wounded several of our predecessors; I was aware of mummy-like half-bodies, and struggling figures, crying and cursing. Passing along towards the officers' dugout, we found the Hampshire colonel, sardonic and unshaken, who waited with us long hours while the relief, so simple in the mention, so perplexing in the midnight morass, was being completed. He told us that in daylight one only reached the front companies through a machine-gun barrage. He intended to have taken out with him a German soft cap, but eventually he forgot it; and perhaps I ought to be ashamed of saying that I have it to this day. It was the chief museum-piece in the dugout, except for a stack of German ration tobacco, which made a pretty comfortable seat. The smell of this little concrete hutch, like all other German dugouts, was peculiar and heavy; I do not know how they found the British lines, but probably their experience would be parallel. It is a matter which W. H. Hudson should have heard of, when he was writing *A Hind in Richmond Park*.

The night spent itself somehow. Already it seemed ages since I had last seen poor Tice, and looked at this very patch of ground with him ('To give five ducats, five, I would not farm it'), but the gulf between this and three days before was indeed a black and lethal abyss, which had swallowed up the hopes of the Allies for this summer. I do not remember what was said. Day brought a little promise of better weather, and the guns were for a time quiet enough; I explored here and there, and my signallers got their wires to 'all stations' into working order. A tank officer looked in, asking help to salve some equipment from his wrecked machine, lying just behind our pill-box. Presently the drizzle was thronging down mistily again, and shelling grew more regular and searching. There were a number of concrete shelters along the trench, and it was not hard to see that their dispossessed makers were determined to do them in. Our doctor, an Irishman named Gatchell, who seemed utterly to scorn such annoyances of Krupp, went out to find a much discussed bottle of whisky which he had left in his medical post. He returned, the bottle in his hand; 'Now, you toping rascals' – a thump like a thunderbolt stopped him. He fell mute, white, face down, the bottle still in his hand; 'Ginger' Lewis, the unshakable Adjutant, whose face I chanced to see particularly, went as chalky-white, and collapsed; the Colonel, shaking and staring, passed me as I stopped to pull the doctor out, and tottered, not knowing where he was going, along the trench. This was not surprising. Over my seat, at the entrance the direct hit had made a gash in the concrete, and the place was full of fragments and dust. The shell struck just over my head, and I suppose it was a 5.9. But we had escaped, and outside, scared from some shattered nook a number of field mice were peeping and turning as though as puzzled as ourselves. A German listening-set with its delicate valves stood in the rain there, too, unfractured. But these details were perceived in a flash, and meanwhile shells were coming down remorselessly all along our alley. Other direct hits occurred, the Aid Post and the signallers' dugout were shattered. Men stood in the trench under their steel hats and capes, resigned to their fate. I said to Sergeant Seall, 'This is thick'; he tried to smile. A veterinary surgeon, Gatfield, with his droll, sleepy, profoundly kind manner, filled the doctor's place, and attended as best he could to the doctor and the other wounded. The continuous and ponderous blasts of shells seemed to me to imply that an attack was to be made on us, and being now more or less the only head-quarters officer operating, after an inconclusive conference with the Colonel, I sent the SOS to the artillery; the telephone wire went almost immediately afterwards. Our wonderful artillery answered, and at length the pulverization of our place slackened, to the relief of the starting nerves; whereon, Sergeant Ashford came to tell me that our linesmen had put us in touch with the 13th Royal Sussex on our right, and that the Adjutant of that battalion wanted me at the 'phone. Bartlett, a genial and gallant man, bright-haired Bartlett called me by name – I hear his self-control still in those telephoned words – and told me what made our own 'direct hit' not worth mentioning. His headquarters had been pierced by a great shell, and over thirty killed or wounded. 'A gunpit – Van Heule Farm'; I knew it by the map. What could we do to help? It was little enough; we called the RAMC to send rescuers to that gunpit, and I heard later that a driver actually succeeded in getting an ambulance to it, up the gouged and eruptioned St Julien Road.

The tragedy of the 13th came home to me more than all the rest, and from the moment of that telephone call my power of endurance lay gasping. Two chaplains visited us, to their glory and our pleasure, but not to our final comfort, for they brought no guess nor hint of our relief. One's range of effect, and of conception, seemed to close in, and the hole overhead in the resumed ill-smelling pillbox was ever catching the eye. I managed to fill in my diary for the day, and could not keep out some thoughts of better days. That night about twelve o'clock we were relieved ('all in billets by 3.30 a.m.'), and even those who like myself had been for the last twenty-four hours in a gully or pit were scarcely able to credit it. Hobbling down the muddy mule-track, one found that the soles of one's feet had become corrugated, and the journey was desperately slow. No ordinary burst of shells could make us hurry now, but as we approached the dark earth wall of the Yser Canal, the notion of having a chance of escape quickened our dragging steps; and my own little group, passing a familiar spot called Irish Farm, went still quicker because of the most appalling missile we had ever heard. It was a high-velocity shell, and a big one; it came suddenly with a shriek beyond expression, entered the mud a few yards away, and rocked the earth and air. Perhaps the gunners were accustomed to this sort of nightmare, which in its solitary horror impressed me more even than the rolling storms of shell of the last few days.

The second-in-command, Frank Cassells, met us on the canal bank, and by his excellent household arrangements we got under cover there, and warmed ourselves with unforgettable, though very simple stew. Officers were herded together in a grimy dugout, with bunk beds; the men were in the long tunnels; and after a few hours of impervious sleep all woke to a sense of renewed misery. For one thing, we were expecting to be sent up again almost at once (the following night) into the battle. For another, a heavy battery in the field behind, next my old Red Hart Estaminet, was firing straight over our quarters, and at every discharge the roof of the dugout and our scalps seemed to be lifted and jarred with acute pain. Then, the desolate sky was still dropping rain, and the stricken landscape offered no relief. It would have been a poor day even by the Arun. Two dumps of timber and ammunition flared and snapped along the transport track. In the tunnels the men were humbly dozing or cleaning up, one degree farther from the pale happiness of knowing 'what it was all about' than we were. But that evening the Brigade-Major, Clark, who saw me going by his temporary 'office,' called me in for a word or two, in his usual tranquil tones disclosed some of the mistakes of the attack (our 15-inch artillery had fired for two hours on one of the positions already overrun by us, for example!) and told me the strange news that we were going out, the whole Division. I was sent ahead to seize enough tents for the battalion's accommodation.

Poperinghe again! even more divisional emblems, more badges and uniforms; more mud on the white house-fronts, more shutters up, fewer tiles on the roofs; the smell of petrol, veritably as sweet as life – we ask no violets yet. Through Poperinghe, among the wooden shops and taverns, to St Jans ter Biezen; a hop-garden or two, a shrine or two, peasants, dog-carts, poplars waving in the watery breeze. It is a real relief, but the battle has already become a vile and inglorious waste of our spirit; indeed to most of us it had from the first appeared a deal too ambitious, to vaunt it at Ypres. And even our pastoral retreat is now being visited at night by aircraft well accustomed to the art of murdering sleep if not life. Out of the line was out of the line in 1916, but we are older now.

xxii

Backwaters

In a day or two I was sent on leave. After an unpleasant delay at Poperinghe station, about which now hung an atmosphere of anticipated terror thick as mist, the train went its way through Haze-brouck and St Omer, formerly a secure region; but now an enemy aeroplane flew part of the way with us, and bomb after bomb burst flaming in the fields alongside, until 'wished morn' whitely appeared. During my leave, I remember principally observing the large decay of lively bright love of country, the crystallization of dull civilian hatred on the basis of 'the last drop of blood'; the fact that the German air raids had almost persuaded my London friends that London was the sole battle front; the illusion that the British Army beyond Ypres was going from success to success; the ration system. Perhaps the ration system weighed most upon us. This was not the ancient reward of the warrior! He had never had a sugar-card in Marlborough's wars, or even 1916. Meanwhile Hampton Court, and even the Palladium, seemed to be standing where they did.

The return from leave was none the better because I heard that the battalion had made a big move, but after all they had not gone far. I got off the train at Bailleul, which recalled Béthune to my mind, and, although it stood as near the line as Poperinghe, had as yet escaped the look of raggedness and weariness and punishment. The shops were coloured, artistic, and many amusing trade placards and concert announcements seemed to show prosperity and vivacity. The battalion was not in this graceful old town, but in the outskirts of Meteren, a village on the highroad westward, whose church tower serenely faced, along the straight stone road, the beautiful Moorish turrets of Bailleul church. In this village I found some of the officers (Amon, of course, among them) hobnobbing with a French gentleman whose pretty house was a cabinet of water-colours chiefly of racehorses. I fear those cannot have survived the subsequent surge of war over Meteren. Here I would have gladly stayed, but I had hardly found the farm at the end of a sandy lane, in which our billets were taken, when I was ordered to be ready for attending a Signalling School in the real 'back area.' This development, promising in itself a period of rest and safety, was bad news; for experience proved that to be with one's battalion, or part of it, alone nourished the infantryman's spirit. Now amid a thousand tables I should pine and want food.

Next morning, therefore, while the young sunlight freshened the darkened greenery of the year, I was sitting among a load of equipment, officers, NCO's and men in a lorry, hurtling along the causeway towards Cassel, through villages where one imagined one would like to come from a normal trench tour, past cottages at whose doors women sat on chairs to pick the hopbines heaped about them. A lorry is not the vehicle for enjoying the Barbizon aspect; the travellers grew comatose long before the end of the journey, which was at a dull little village called Zuytpeene. The Signalling School was a series of huts in a long meadow, with an ugly house posing as a 'château' at the far end. Here days went by without incident; above, the sky was usually clear and calm; around, the spirit of apathy and unconcern with the war was languidly puffing at its cigarette or warbling revue melody. Yet only a few miles off was that commanding hill Cassel, whence radiated constantly the challenge and dynasty of battle at Ypres. The road thither was secluded, and hardly anyone noticed the fantastic fruitage of blackberries in the low hedges; one climbed until presently at a bold curve the track joined the stone road, with its rattling railway. At the top, the cool streets of Cassel led between ancient shop-fronts and courtyards, maintaining in their dignity that war was nothing to do with Cassel. There was one memorable inn in whose shadowy dining-room officers from highest to lowest congregated. Far below its balcony the plain stretched in all the semblance of untroubled harvest, golden, tranquil and lucent as ever painter's eye rested upon. Some confused noise of guns contested one's happy acquiescence. But what one saw and what one felt at Cassel's watchtower that September is taken from time by the poet-historian, C. E. Montague.

As I dreamed over this landscape of richness and repose I was tapped on the shoulder. It was our old fellow-sufferer Kapp, who recognized the battalion colours on my shoulders; he was still wearing his on his back, having heard nothing of our modifications. He had been away from us, with the Press Bureau, since June 1916, and he could not withhold his questions about the battalion. But they were few; he had now become a temporary proprietor of motor-cars and châteaux, and our news sounded very silly and coarse as I tried to give it. He, however, was not listening much; he asked after names and passed quickly to others. It was too late! the war had changed as well as the battalion. Why change your profession in middle age? Kapp's momentary flicker of romance soon died down, and he went out, promising to call on me in his car one day soon.

The course of signalling imposed no burden, beyond that of estrangement from one's battalion, upon the officers attending. Many of them, to my joy, were Australians, at whose resourceful wit and confidence one refreshed the parched mind. I hear still the gay and easy Captain Bath, reciting the 'Nancy Brig,' or offering sermons on the Uncertainty of Life. I see his towzled hair, bright eyes, and vinous flush such as jolly Bacchus must have had. I hear also his laments for Adelaide, while we were wandering through benighted farm buildings in performance of 'a scheme.' His companions were worthy of him, and they revealed every day that it is possible for an army to be highly efficient without a sign of pedantry.

This period ended, I returned to the battalion, not without difficulty, for they had been on the move. The first news I had of them, on arriving at a field where they had been, towards the south of the Ypres Salient, was from a transport driver, who said they 'were going over the top in the morning.' The suggestion was unpleasing, for my servant and myself had already been carrying our burdens for miles, and it was still many kilometres to the battlefield. At the end of another dusty trudge we met the transport officer, Maycock, friendliest and most impulsive of our officers, who told me I should ride up to the battalion with him, and we set off at once. The battalion was drawn up in a field by the scanty ruins of Vierstraat, nearly ready to move; the sun shone with autumn light on the kind round faces, and dun uniforms, and sack-clothed helmets, and broken trees with yellowing leaves, and trodden strings of grass under foot. Dixies of tea were passing round among the companies. To my surprise Colonel Millward, though hailing me affectionately, did not want me for the coming tour in the line, and I found myself riding away with Maycock, while the battalion marched into the ruins of Hollebeke and Battle Wood. It was that evening that a shell fell among the headquarters staff on the way up, and killed Naylor, the philosophic and artistic lieutenant who had served in the battalion almost all my time, whose quiet presence was a safeguard against the insolence of fortune. I do not see many allusions to him in these memoirs, but he was one of those silent, modest, and ubiquitous men whose quality is consistent and therefore taken for granted. Another shell, bursting on a small party of non-commissioned officers as they were about to leave the trenches after relief, robbed us instantly of Sergeant Clifford, a man of similar sweetness of character and for months past invaluable in all necessities. These losses I felt, but with a sensibility blurred by the general grossness of the war. The uselessness of the offensive, the contrast in the quality of ourselves with the quality of the year before, the conviction that the civilian population realized nothing of our state, the rarity of thought, the growing intensity and sweep of destructive forces – these views brought on a mood of selfishness. We should all die, presumably, round Ypres.

The transport camp was at Rozenhil, near Reninghelst, a small hill among small farms, now five or six miles from the battlefield; and here I acted as assistant to Maycock, though I hardly knew a horse from a dromedary, and as Anglican opponent at table to two Roman Catholic chaplains who lived in the camp. Their rest, like ours, was broken by bombing raids, which night and day came near enough. It was a bad season for mules and horses, which, as they stood in regular lines, could not be protected, and made a simple target. The camps of the men were only tents and shanties, round which low walls of earth were cast up to catch flying splinters from the explosions near by. If the bomb fell on top, clearly there was no more to be said about it. Night was streaked and dissected with searchlight beams, but the raiding went on thoroughly, turning the area in which troops rest into a floor of Hades. As for the forward area, from the glimpses which I had of it, no unstable invention of dreams could be more dizzily dreadful. Taking up the rations used to be almost a laughing matter – not so now. Merely to find the way through the multiplying tracks and desperate obliteration of local identity would have been a problem; to get horses and vehicles through, in the foundering night of dazzling wildfire and sweltering darkness, with shells coming and going in enormous shocks and gnashing ferocity, to the ration or working party crouching by some old shelters, was the problem. Maycock could do it. While I was admiring him, I found my horse suddenly going his own wild way because an anti-aircraft battery opened up furiously beside our heads, or because he smelt danger. A view of the then notorious Spoil Bank under these conditions is in my mind's eye – a hump of slimy soil, with low lurching frames of dugout entrances seen in some too gaudy glare; a swilling pool of dirty water beside it, among many pools not so big (the record shell-hole?); tree-spikes, shells of waggons, bony spokes forking upwards; lightnings east and west of it, dingy splashes of searchlights in the clouds above; drivers on their seats, looking straight onwards; gunners with electric torches finding their way; infantry silhouettes and shadows bowed and laden, and the plank road, tilted, breached, blocked, upheaved, still stretching ahead. The plank road was at once the salvation and the slaughter-house of the forward area in this battle. To leave it was to plunge into a swamp, to remain on it was to pass through accurate and ruthless shell-fire.

These wooden roads began at some distance from the line, for now all this countryside was more than defaced, and drainage was unthinkable. As I entered the destroyed plain and passed along the loathed planks, one day, I saw a little knot of Chinese labourers, carrying shells from a lorry to a dump, hopping, grinning, singing. It was near Voormezeele, where the wreckage of a convent could be seen in a thinned grove of trees. Looking through a bookseller's list lately, I found a devotional book there entered with the place of publication 'Voormezeele.' The printing office was not open when the Chinese and I were there, and the convent bell was mute. Still, there were spots of greenery in the dried moats and the gardens, and the general desolation with which they must be compared was worse. The battalion, having undergone its torture at Hollebeke, was withdrawn into dreary, flimsy dugouts, an old British support position, beneath the Wytschate Ridge; no relief for the mind other than physical rest could be found there, and rain set in cold and dark to depress them, when I made my way to them. Behind, along the road to Kemmel, still stood the column of tree-stumps among which our sniping authorities had formerly smuggled in one or two steel trees, now lagging superfluous on the stage, their green paint and tubular trunks being out of season.

xxiii

The Cataract

The companionship of Maycock was so happy, and our odd jobs on horseback or by foot so pleasantly scattered about the countryside, now among the ruins, now among the farms and villages, by windmill and by busy railhead, by hop-garden and by white house, that I soon accepted the situation and wished for no other. Eight or ten days after my first arrival in the camp, suddenly a call came from the battalion, and we rode up in haste to find them once more about to move from a halting-place in a field into a new attack. This time I was wanted; my horse was sent back, and the adjutant, Lewis, told me to go up immediately to the new front with him. No one knew, except in the vaguest form, what the situation was, or where it was.

Suddenly, therefore, I was plucked forth from my comparative satisfaction into a wild adventure. Lewis, a reticent man, hurried along, for the afternoon sun already gave warning, and to attempt to find our position after nightfall would have been madness. First of all he led his little party to our old familiar place, Observatory Ridge, and Sanctuary Wood, across which we looked for those once solid trenches, Hedge Street and Canada Street; but never was a transformation more surprising. The shapeless Ridge had lost every tree; the brown hummock, flayed and clawed up, was traversed by no likeness of trenches. Only a short length of shallow half-choked ditch stood for Hedge Street or Canada Street, with the entrance to the dugouts there in danger of being buried altogether. I asked a bystander where we were, and gasped at his answer. Waiting there in the gashed hillside for Lewis, who had gone below for instructions, we looked over the befouled fragments of Ypres, the solitary sheet of water, Zillebeke Lake, the completed hopelessness. The denuded scene had acquired a strange abruptness of outline; the lake and the ashy city lay unprotected, isolated, dominated finally. But farther off against the sunset one saw the hills beyond Mount Kemmel, and the simple message of nature's health and human worthiness again beckoned in the windmills resting there. There – and here!

'God knows!' was all the answer our adjutant gave us as he emerged into the air again, fixing the strap of his shrapnel helmet, and clambering out of the holes. He went ahead, and before the glow of the splendid evening had paled he had cleverly led us to the new headquarters, a set of huge square pillboxes (forts, in fact) on a bluff, which the low-shot light caused to appear steep and big. Here he again entered for a conference, and his party had time and inclination to linger behind one of the pillboxes, and to observe that the next one had been uprooted and smashed into massy boulders. We did not misinterpret that; but, as luck would have it, there was no bombardment proceeding just then. At length our battalion was guided through the starlight into the sector, its business being to attack some buildings on the road to Gheluvelt, in conjunction with an attack on a wider front; but the orders were never clear and during the next three days confusion reached its maximum. The companies held a site called Tower Hamlets, known to me in the early spring through a telescope as a pretty little nook among hazy trees, with the best part of a mill and a serviceable barn still standing.

What the companies in the forward craters experienced now I never heard in detail. Their narrative would make mine seem petty and ridiculous. The hero was Lindsey Clarke, already mentioned; nowadays known for his imaginative sculptures, then for his hoarse voice, modesty and inexhàustible courage. He took charge of all fighting, apparently, and despite being blown off his feet by shells, and struck about the helmet with shrapnel, and otherwise physically harassed, he was ubiquitous and invincible. While Clarke was stalking round the line like a local Cromwell in his great boots, poor Burgess in a pillbox just behind was wringing his hands in excess of pity, and his headquarters was full of wounded men. With him sat one Andrews, a brilliant young officer, not of our battalion, on some duty of liaison with Brigade headquarters. But as even we hardly ever had certain contact with him, his lot was not a happy one.

At our headquarters, two pillboxes were used, one by the adjutant and his clerks and messengers, with the doctor (Gatchell, already named); one by my signallers, men of all work, and myself. The entrances of these places, of course, faced the German guns, but my doorway was shielded by a concrete portico. About forty men of various vocations used the place, and I sat in a corner near the door, directing the work of the signallers, and waiting for orders. By night it was cold, by day roasting hot. Water was desperately scarce here and everywhere. There was little to do but to see that all means of communication were open and ready. The carrier pigeons which we had brought up suffered from the bad air of the place. The men drowsed and yawned. Time went by, but no one felt the passage of it, for the shadow of death lay over the dial.

Never (to our judgment) had such shelling fallen upon us. For what reason? The Germans had clearly no idea of letting the British advance any further along the Menin Road. Their guns of all calibres poured their fury into our small area. It was one continuous din and impact. Reports of casualties were the principal messages from the front line, and we had no reason to think them exaggerated, with such a perpetual rain of shells. The trenches immediately about our pillboxes were already full of bodies. One man in my headquarters died of shock from a heavy shell striking just outside. We endeavoured to send off a pigeon, but the pigeon, scared by the gunfire, found his way into the dugout again, and presently a fluttering sound under the floor-boards led to his discovery. The men thought that many shells struck the pillbox. The only question seemed to be when one would pierce it, and make an end.

Next door, so to speak, the adjutant, doctor and their helpers had a slightly worse position, more exposed to enemy observation. The Aid-Post was hit, and the doctor continued to dress the wounded at incredible speed, though with only an appearance of protection overhead; the wounded came in great number. I went over to ask for orders and information; Lewis, as though defying this extreme fury of warfare, was in an almost smiling mood, and quizzed me about 'coming to dinner.' Old Auger, the mess corporal, winked at me over the adjutant's shoulder, and raised a tempting bottle from his stores. Even here he had managed to bring a full box of supplies. I returned, and presently the firing decreased. Lewis called on us to see how we were, and told me that he really meant some sort of dinner would be going soon, and I was to be there. Colonel Millward had just rejoined, from leave, and I had seen him in the headquarters just now; surely, I thought, the news he brings is promising. A runner visited me, and went back over the thirty yards to the other pillbox – his last journey. He had arrived in the doorway there, and joined the five or six men sheltering there, including the doctor consulting about something, when the lull in the shelling was interrupted. I was called upon the telephone (we had some inexhaustible linesmen out in the open incessantly repairing the wire) by Andrews at the forward station. 'I say, hasn't something happened at your headquarters?' 'Not that I know of – all right, I believe.' (The sound of shelling had long ceased to impinge.) 'Yes, I'm afraid something's wrong; will you find out?' My servant, Shearing, hurried across, and hurried back, wild-eyed, straining: 'Don't go over, sir; it's awful. A shell came into the door.' He added more details after a moment or two. The doctor and those with him had been killed.

The rate of shelling even seemed to increase after this, and yet outside the late September sun shone 'as on a bridal.' That 'serene, exasperating sunlight!' But already the thought was in our minds: What will happen to this front when it rains? Behind our pillboxes the low ground had formerly been ornamental lakes in château grounds. Besides, there would assuredly be no pillboxes in a couple of days. Meanwhile bullets began to strike round the entrance of my pillbox, as if the Germans had advanced their machine-guns. We were supposed to have been making advances on this front, too.

During this period my indebtedness to an eighteenth-century poet became enormous. At every spare moment I read in Young's *Night Thoughts on Life, Death and Immortality*, and I felt the benefit of this grave and intellectual voice, speaking out of a profound eighteenth-century calm, often in metaphor which came home to one even in a pillbox. The mere amusement of discovering lines applicable to our crisis kept me from despair.

We were relieved in broad daylight, under every sort of observation, but nobody refused to move. The estimate of our casualties was 400, and although the real number was 280 or so, the battalion had had enough. When all my men had gone, including Sergeant Worley, who had been my fearless, tireless 'second' all the time, I found Sergeant

Craddock, of the Orderly Room, also ready to depart. We stared over the 'ornamental lakes,' now a swamp with a dry crust of a surface, and tree-stubs here and there offering substantial foothold. Already there was a marked track across, and shells were thundering and smoking along it. Craddock seized his portfolios (the paper war always accompanied its rival) and I my belongings; we looked silently at one another, and went. We immediately passed the bodies of two men just killed, the sweat on their faces, and with shouts of uncontrol we ran for life through the shelling and the swamps. These were called Dombarton Lakes. The screech and smashing filled a square of the old pleasure-garden; you could almost feel the German gunners loading for you; we emerged short of breath. Beyond, one of my signallers whom I had not seen lately approached us, and showed the inimitable superiority of man to fate by speaking, even then and there, in appreciation of the German artillery's brilliance. 'Never did see such shelling,' he said. It was exactly as if he had been talking of a break by Willie Smith, or art for art's sake. A machine-gun at long range interrupted this moment of conversation, and moved us on.

Then I met Sergeant Worley again, just as the shelling was waking up afresh. He caught my arm, and pointed out a spire far off, but glittering clearly in the westering light, beyond the battle line. 'It's that bloody old church spire,' he said, 'that's the cause of all this big stuff: enfilades the lot: why don't the 'eavies get on to it?' That spire, so cool, so calm, so bright, looked as though it deserved to escape, but it would hardly do so: even as we gazed, volumes of smoke began to burst out in the air around it.

The battalion united in the neighbourhood of a small and wiry wood called Bodmin Copse, with tumult and bullets and sometimes shells in the air around; then D Company, led by Burgess, had the bad luck to be ordered back into support positions. I see the handsome cynicism of Ellis, their second officer, as he waved his walking-stick to us on the way back. The other companies and headquarters took shelter in a sandy trench, and we waited. The enemy wondered what we were waiting for. A steady bombardment with big shells began, and luckily most of them fell a few yards short, but the mental torture, especially when, after one had been carefully listened to in flight and explosion, another and another instantly followed as though from nowhere, was severe. The trench around me was slowly choked and caved in by hits just outside. Our regimental sergeant-major, who used to swing his arm up and down at emotional moments like a flail, lifted it with such judgment that he was wounded in the hand. We were not too much destroyed to enjoy this jest of chance. Maycock came up in the early dusk with a train of mules carrying Royal Engineers' material and tins of water to a point near Bodmin Copse, a star turn for which he earned the General's stern reproof on account of his not obtaining a receipt for the deliveries. He had his revenge. He went back, obtained a receipt, insisted on having the General roused, and with deliberate silence, delivered the paper.

The eastern sky that evening was all too brilliant with British rockets, appealing for artillery assistance. Westward, over blue hills, the sunset was all seraphim and cherubim.

xxiv

1917 in Fading Light

Towards midnight we were withdrawn – a small and dazed contingent – as gas-shells began to take charge of Bodmin Copse, and guided by some instinct rather than conscious sense, we assembled at Bus House, Saint Eloi, before morning. Once this had been a storm-centre of the British Front Line. Lorries arrived, we saw the chilly light of daybreak on the still shapely buildings and cottage shutters of Kemmel, and at length went into tents in a farmyard and its home-fields near Mont Kokereele, a noble highland. There we stayed several days – baths, lectures, football, Divisional General, musketry, and 'Fancy You Fancying Me.' Worley and myself constructed a revolver range of which we were intensely proud, and it would have been still finer but for the weather, which was once more insistently cheerless and wet. A rifle range elsewhere kept us in training, and gave us occasional scenery of tall gilded trees and terraced valleys into the bargain; thence, what was the greatest moment of any rest in Flanders for some of us, a sudden break in the clouds one morning revealed as in some marvellous lens a vast extent of the country southwards, towered cities and silver rivers, master-highways, blue church-spires, a broad and calm plain, until pyramidal shapes in the extreme distance were identifiable as the great slag-heaps in the Lens and Béthune coalfield, and some thought the wisps of whiteness floating across them were the usual signs of bombardment. Our minds receded with actual joy to the 1916 war, and particularly that season when we were within the kindly influence of Béthune. When had we heard the words 'a bon time' since? How few there were left even to understand what hopes had then borne the battalion on singing towards the Somme! When we left this camp of disastered 1917, to be merged again in the slow amputation of Passchendaele, there was no singing. I think there were tears on some cheeks.

It was even a pleasure here to see Williams, the Divisional Gas Officer, and his same old sergeant, at their kindly, deadly work again. I forget what type of gas it was that Williams discharged upon us, leaving it to us to get our helmets on or pass out. However, I believe it was not at full strength, for some hens poking about in the stubble did not suffer. Perhaps God tempers the gas to the Ypres hen.

At this camp Colonel Millward told me that he had recommended my promotion to a captaincy, but the General would not hear of it, declaring that I was too young. My offences against propriety of speech and demeanour were in any case sufficient to spoil my chances. Yet the next time that the battalion went into the trenches, I was in charge of B Company. Before that I had had a special duty to do. It was to act as 'Tunnel Major' in Hedge Street Tunnels – to regulate the very limited and fiercely coveted accommodation there, and the traffic in and out. This appointment took me back to the accursed area again, and even while I made my way there the evil nature of the place displayed itself – apart from the instant exchange of farms in autumn for a dead sea of mud. Going up by way of Zillebeke, I was obliged to stop. I sat down in a trench corner near our old terror, Valley Cottages. An 'area shoot,' a solid German bombardment lasting an hour on a measured space, was flattening several battery positions. This shelling was so concentrated and geometrical that, leaning against

the side of our old trench just beyond its limit, we were in safety. But
the area covered was treated as with a titanic roller and harrow. About
half an hour after this shoot began, from the very middle of the
furnace two artillerymen suddenly emerged, running like demons,
but unwounded.

At the door of the large dugout which I was to supervise, a quarter-
master-sergeant's body was lying. Men were afraid to pause even a
few seconds at this point, and bodies were not quickly buried. A
battalion of pioneers, the dear Divisional pioneers, were attempting
to lay down wooden trolley-lines, but they could scarcely outpace the
destruction of their work by shells. I found the tunnels crammed with
soldiers on business and otherwise. The Colonel and Adjutant of the
RF's, who had taken our place in the Tower Hamlets sector a fortnight
or so before, were here, occupying a new and half-finished dugout;
they used me very hospitably. The Colonel remarked, pouring me out
a drink, 'We no longer exist.' I asked how; he explained that their
casualties had been over 400. Our experience had been only the
prelude to their full symphony. We talked on, the subject changing;
presently it came to German character and morals, whereon the
Colonel spoke of a recently discovered letter in which the limit of
obscenity had apparently been reached by some enemy *paterfamilias.*
'Ah, well,' he said, throwing a crumpled paper at the adjutant, 'we'll
be off. There's a great hole on top, young man; I had it partly filled
up, but it's not the only one . . . *We no longer exist.*' He had it by heart,
he said it lightly, but I interpreted him. 'Good luck to you,' he said,
'let's look at the war, Charlie,' and he and the Adjutant, all neat and
soldierly, went out into the darkness.

For a week, I think, I patrolled this dirty but precious underworld,
and fancied I improved the conditions. Not the actual state of the
works. It was the business of the tunnellers to pump out the canals of
foul water which stand along the passages, the light of the electric
lamps falling on it doubtfully through the black lattice of flies which
hung to the warm bulbs, swarming and droning round the head of
the passer-by. The holes on top I did indeed cause to be filled. But I
was of more use in finding out who ought to be in the tunnel, who
not, and in acting accordingly. The space available became hourly

more important. Once a machine-gun Major threatened to destroy my labours, which had cleared a chamber or two for some officially incoming troops, by sending his men in and telling me to go to hell. I had to call for aid to General Hornby, who was in Canada Street Tunnels, and returned to eject my pirate with a signed paper proclaiming that 'In the Tunnels, the word of the Tunnel Major is law.' Whether this action or the paper gave me a certain notoriety in those dismal parts I don't know; but soon afterwards an artillery Major with a couple of gunners appeared and very mildly requested my sympathetic treatment, at the same time producing a bottle of burgundy and a poetry-book. I was sorry (but not more sorry than he was) when he departed. I did not hurry him.

The worst of the place was that one only had to go to the doorway to see at one view (between the crashes) as brutal a landscape as ever was, and a placid distance of grey-blue hills gently regretting that one more harvest was done.

Upon the arrival of the 11th Royal Sussex in the dungeons, I was inflicted upon B Company, and we were soon threading our way behind a dubious guide, through darkness crimsoning into unholy flames, towards the front line. We went with great apprehension, for the sector was a little distance from that of our last tenancy, but on the way up we did well, escaping casualties and keeping contact, despite the usual shoal of angry and maledictory Jocks coming down. The mounds and holes looked savage enough in the passing glare of German lights, the channel of the Bassevillebeek resembled a gulf of mud with four-inch planks across, but all went tolerably well; we entered Bass Wood, and manned a decently dry trench in sandy soil along a prominent ridge. I took over from Andrews, the remarkable young officer already referred to, and before he would leave the line he spent an hour or two with me creeping about on the left of 'our bit,' endeavouring to make sure where the nearest post of the next battalion was. But we could not place it, and the German lights seemed to be fired at some distance from us in that direction, though close enough ahead. These lights were in any case misleading, for they would be fired from a support or reserve position as well as the foremost shell holes.

We three company commanders and our subalterns occupied a concrete dugout in the little wood, called Bass Wood, three or four hundred yards back. The company sergeant-majors and others were in a trench at the rear of the place. They were not in truth worse off for being in the open; inside, the pillbox was nearly a foot deep in water, which was full of noxious and rancid matters, metamorphoses, God knows what – *scire nefas*. There were a table, floating boxes, and beds of the usual type. In this 'Hunwater Dugout' Vidler and Amon played cards and damned everybody, especially me in my nervous desire to arrive at an agreement on some urgent point. A 'lucky shell' (so our laconic fatalism termed a direct hit!) would have wiped out all the control of the line, for battalion headquarters in a pillbox behind could not show their noses outside in daylight. Their dugout was visited, we heard, by the new Divisional Commander, who stood on top of it, pointing out various 'features' with his stick; shortly after which indiscreet and even licentious action the place was barraged. An aeroplane even came to bomb it. I heard our artillery observation officer, presently, who had to attend during the episode, describing it in just language. 'I was pursuing my profession at the usual hour,' he began, 'when I was accosted by a Major-General' – but this book is for publication.

That formerly our coppice was regarded by the Germans as beyond danger, the shattered timber of wooden huts among the tree-stumps told us. Hunwater Dugout must have been a reserve headquarters, its weed-grown roof and the coppice branches rendering it quite secret. Now it was no secret! It was not shelled much while we were there – four days, generally quite calm. At dawn it was impossible to avoid a gnawing anxiety, but no trouble befell us. Among the oddments fired at our trench, there was one previously unknown to me – a gas container, which burst with a huge report, and scattered a sharp gust of poison on the damp shades. Millward went round the line at night, trying to make his long body less long; Vidler followed him, stopping because of short sight; and I came last, with other shadowy spectators, admiring these imitations of great age. Meanwhile, we had found our way over to the adjacent battalion ('establishing contact') and regularly met our neighbours with hearty esteem.

Vidler's old liking for No Man's Land now returned to him and we went out together to discover all we could on the night which brought our relief. It was black and heavy. A curious tree like a clumsy cross just gave us a direction. We nevertheless turned here and there quite nimbly, and identified a farm track and a flattened ruin. Here we picked up a ploughshare, which Vidler thought the Intelligence Staff should be thankful for. Regretting the dearth of incident, and skirting a pillbox crowded with corpses, we at length returned. The incoming battalion two or three hours later were troubled by a light machine-gun from that patch of ground where we had been, and, sending out one or two stout fellows, brought in two very youthful Germans, who said they had been there with their guns for many hours. This barbed news reached Vid. and myself all too soon, and considerably perplexed us, not to use our expressions of the time.

But as yet we are not relieved. The most dangerous moment of the tour is to come. Upon the arrival of the 'guides,' there was the usual process of sorting one another out near company headquarters, and some mistake led to a certain amount of noise. The moment was when my company was halting in the open, near Hunwater Dugout. At once the Germans fired so many illuminants that the ground with its pools was like a jeweller's shop; I shouted to my anxious men to stand fast, but one or two were new or nervous, and ducked or moved on; then the enemy's machine-guns played; the informing white lights multiplied, were repeated farther off; red lights bursting into two like cherries on a stalk went up by the dozen. There seemed now no doubt that a box barrage of the latest quality would come down on us, and my skin felt in the act of 'shrivelling like a parchèd scroll.' To our amazement, the German guns held their peace; the streaming bullets raced over a little longer – fifteen minutes in all – then slackened, and we went with sober minds on our way. It seemed a long way, as all night journeys in the Salient did, but we knew we had been lucky this time, and as we picked our way between the bellowing batteries and the greasy roadside wreckage, we rejoiced. Finally a phantom of short leafy trees in the mist showed that we were on the borders of life again; it was Voormezeele, and our camp was at hand – Boys Camp. A hot meal awaited all, and I suppose the surviving officers still reckon that night's roast pork particularly notable among Quartermaster Swain's many capital performances. 'The Daily Prevaricator,' said Swain, 'won't give you a Christmas dinner like this, my boy.' It made us forget the wind darting through the torn canvas of the marquee.

We lay in bivouacs, and found them poor comfort; there was water on the field floor of many of them, and it was late in the year for canvas in that district. To warm and freshen the men next day, and to give them a view of the vicinity of once famous Dickebusch, I took them for a route march, which was not popular. My quest for customs and antiquities did not mend the state of their feet. Yet there may have been one or two who noticed the many singular relics of earlier fighting from the Brasserie to Scottish Wood, and some were destined to fight and drop not many months later on that very ground. It was strange to pass freely beside buildings which had been familiar and dangerous to hundreds and thousands of our predecessors, and parts of which survived. It was also the pathetic evidence of a warfare which, in comparison with the present fury, was almost Arcadian. There are many degrees of mutilation. Here at least were the walls of a white château, the brickwork of a culvert, a well, the cellars and gate of a farm; the *Hic iacet* was just permitted, and some evidence of the individuality of the departed.

XXV

Coming of Age

A day or so later (my company being handed over to its ordinary commander), the battalion marched back several miles to another camp. The route lay through Kemmel, where we made a halt, wondering to see the comparatively sound state of the houses and particularly the château's ridiculous mediæval turrets in red brick. Its noble trees were a romance and poetry understood by all. The day was gloomy, but to be 'stepping westward' among common things of life made it light enough. Gently the chestnut and aspen leaves were drifting down with the weight of the day's dampness. We passed over hills still green, and by mossy cottages, with onions drying under the eaves. It was as though war forgot some corners of Flanders. (Next year, war remembered that corner with a vengeance.) Our camp by Westoutre at length appeared, through a drifting rain, in the bottom of a valley, undisguised slabby clay; the houses hereabouts were mean, and no entertainment for the troops could be anticipated, except a hot bath in an enormous brewery. Indeed, the merest physical needs were unanswered by the tattered canvas of this wretched open field, formerly horse-lines. Protests were 'forwarded,' and we were moved to a hutment camp in a wood, called Chippewa, as fine as the other was miserable. Here 'training' was immediately threatened, but a large allowance of leave began.

From this refuge I was soon called away to the line, in order to make preparations for a piece of trench digging to be done by the battalion. Worley went with me – it would have taken considerable force to keep him away. Lately he had begun to – I would say 'amuse' himself by drawing pictures, but the word does not comprehend his intense patience and effort. In his Army notebook with its squared leaves his slow pencil (trained chiefly in a butcher's round) worked out the reminiscence of places at which the old battalion had been, and he was evidently determined that no single brick, no wheelbarrow, no sandbag should be omitted. He showed these drawings to very few persons, to me most, for he believed I knew about such matters. I loved him for this new expression of a simple but profound trust. The bond between us had been swiftly struck at Cambrin a year and a half before. It holds, it holds to-day; though at the moment of writing I have no news of Worley, and once I heard a rumour that he was lost to the world. I thought his sudden series of drawings showed a queerness. But I wander from the track, which is taking us up to Larch Wood near Hill 60, through a sunny, but cold-fingered autumn day. The arrival is a little untimely, for we must pass vile Verbrandenmolen, a prominence crossed by wooden roads and littered with slimed breakages; and just now the Germans are annoyed with two heavy guns of ours, tilted under their paltry camouflage on this knoll. An engineer was walking just ahead of me. He had scarcely lifted his feet from a duckboard between us when a great shell plunged through the board – and did not burst. I found myself staring at the hole and the torn-up woodwork in dull astonishment. Then explosions and whizzings all round urged me to be going, with 'stopped ears.'

Larch Wood Tunnels were a magnificent work. The passages excelled in height and width and air supply. At this time they were principally in use as a medical headquarters, and once inside them it certainly seemed that safety and calm were assured. But outside, people were being killed from time to time. A strange scene was to be viewed from the southward outlets of this tunnel – the deep old railway cutting, passing Hill 60. It was a dark canal now, the banks of which were shattered and the timbers tossed aside by cataclysm. Hill 60 was not noticeable, having been transformed into a mine-crater, but a bridge beside it still spanned the railway cutting with a rough red-patched arch. Water dripped and slipped down the chaotic banks into the greasy flood beneath. The market train from Comines looked like being delayed for all eternity. Philip de Comines would not have known the place.

An engineer officer pointed out to us the position of the proposed trench; we walked up to it, through trees like black tusks, and brown clods of hillocks, blue shadows, weak sunlight, a naked poverty. John Nash has drawn this bad dream with exactitude. Just behind the tape already laid for the trench, a British aeroplane had fallen, its nose downward in the mud. We were about to examine it more closely, but the gunners opposite, who all this while had us under observation, resented this, and sent over some shrapnel and high explosive. This high explosive was fitted with the instantaneous fuse, and the speed and range of its jabbing fragments were formidable. Having outlived this little disturbance, we surveyed our business, and decided how best to bring up and distribute the battalion, when darkness fell. As we walked back to Larch Wood, a fragment from a shell bursting on my side happened to ricochet and freakishly wounded Worley in the leg. He regarded this as insult rather than injury, and hobbled on.

That night the battalion dug for hours and made the best part of a valuable trench; for once all were satisfied, and there were scarcely any casualties. Larch Wood Tunnels served as headquarters. Towards daybreak the companies left the line, and passing Zillebeke found the lorries awaiting them (like angels of mercy) near Shrapnel Corner. Our new doctor, Crassweller of Detroit, was on his way down with me, and we had at one time lost direction, when an intense though local shelling broke upon us. It was a mixture of gas and high explosive, and we thought our time had come; scurrying through the tumult we saw a dugout entrance, rushed for it, slithered into it, just as a couple of gas-shells burst in the opening. Below, miners were at work, and in spite of words about gas they would not put on their masks. Before we went, two or three of these obstinate men were gassed, and fell exhausted. I suddenly remembered, here, that midnight had passed, and this was my twenty-first birthday. At last the noise on top ceased, and with clipped noses we hurried through the vaporous darkness, down by Manor Farm's meaningless location, on to Shrapnel Corner and seats in a lorry, a vehicle than which at the right hour and in the right road the chariots of Israel are not more glorious.

As we went the misty daylight came, the wayside trunks of trees and rags of roofs glimmered, the old threadbare, galvanized-iron and tin-can area of batteries and battalions in support exposed itself like the ashes of a tramp's fire to the tired eye. I may have remarked as we passed on the dragging length of war, for Crassweller in the kindness of his heart told me that he thought I was going to be free of it for several weeks. A signalling course. I hoped that this might be wrong, but he was strong on it, and sure enough that day at Chippewa Camp, while I was hurrying round with pencil and book enlisting performers for a concert in the large hut there, orders came for my departure. It was wonderful to be promised an *exeat* from war for weeks, but I saw once again the distasteful process of separation from the battalion, and felt as usual the injustice of my own temporary escape while others who had seen and suffered more went on in the mud and muck.

xxvi

School, not at Wittenberg

My horse ambled on through the caressing haze over the hills and past the windmills, in the direction of Mont-des-Cats. The signalling school was two miles from that monastery, on high ground, whence in the best light Ypres was easily seen. A young and inexperienced Scots officer was in command of the place, which everybody present seemed to resent, although it was in accordance with a common active-service maxim. Training and lecturing soon began, but they were tasteless to me, and I think I had the slightest aptitude for understanding the principles of electricity, the mechanism of the 'fullerphone' or 'power buzzer,' the nature of the wireless apparatus (then so apt to squeal nonsense of its own) that ever man or woman had. Hitherto I had been concerned with signalling chiefly as a regimental organization, combining other duties with it, and I had to some degree acquired what working knowledge I needed; but now, confronted with an exhaustive academic training, I revolted silently. So long as I could send and receive messages by flag or disc or buzzer, and had the practice of communication at my fingers' ends, I had been satisfied; now I was to become a student. The professors were not perfect, I suspect, in those theories to which they drew our attention by the hour, but at any rate they were excellent operators, and useful throaty vocalists at the concert hut in the evenings.

Probably the underlying cause of the numberless 'schools' in the BEF at this time was as much the desire to give officers and men a rest as to instruct them. Rest and recreation undoubtedly occupied our minds in this camp, situated about midway between Poperinghe and Bailleul, of which the latter was the general choice, though I recall that I once directed, with some difficulty, a party of grinning Chinese to 'Poplinge.' Even when we heard some vicious long-range shell racing across Belgium into Bailleul, it did not deter or detain us on our way to the still unshattered civic illusion, with its little market place behind the church always filled with waiting horses, its long

Grande Place of cleanly shops, the packed Officers' Club, with its air of Victorian tradition and much good company. But the journey there and back was itself a pleasure and reward, being entirely bucolic and antique in its effect. The military occupation was always moving and altering, the old farms and farmers and their property did not change, nor, essentially, did they move. Old furrowed faces, blue caps, velvet trousers, wooden slippers were always visible one way or another among those hop-holes, under those onion-tasselled eaves, by the dusty shrines. It was thought that they hated the soldiers, and on one of our signalling 'schemes' a peasant levelled his gun at a section who had posted themselves in a corner of his midden yard. This was in a place whence the skeleton of Ypres could often be seen in the sunlight.

That was the skeleton of our holiday. To see that distorted whiteness even in calm was a sharp cut; to look that way when the rain was slanting down and blotting out distinctions and filling the ruts and gullies at the camp gate was worse, for at this period attacks were still being launched (an appropriate equivocation) against Passchendaele. Three months of sacrificial misery had not been enough to pay for that village height, and so in the distance we heard through the ruining autumn many mornings of gunfire, stubborn and constant, and knew that wounded men were drowning and the unwounded being driven mad before the concrete forts. It was said that the Canadians took Passchendaele, and finding it utterly untenable, of their own accord came back to their old posts. It was said that the Australians themselves had taken an hour to advance one hundred yards. It was said that certain divisional headquarters, themselves a dozen miles behind the front, judging merely by the state of the ground round themselves, challenged GHQ about the madness of a proposed attack; but without result. What might be happening to my battalion? It was a relief when at length I heard that they had been employed in digging and in carrying, not in these attacks.

To us the news of the Cambrai drama, which suddenly arrived now, was exciting, in part, because it suggested that the Ypres aberration was at a close. The secret of Cambrai was guessed by none of us before the event, neither did anyone anticipate the sequel, which intensified the gloom of endlessness cloaking all genuine optimism. The German wireless beat out the remorseless truth for us. I began to be careless whether I was in the line or out of it; nothing seemed to signify except the day's meals, and those were still substantial despite the lean supplies of the people at home. The price of all luxuries in the shops was rising fast, but still one could manage it; why trouble about getting back to the battalion? This was the general spirit, and we did not lament when the course was lengthened and the year ended with us waving flags in unison in the snow, or attempting the heliograph, or rapping out ludicrous messages to the instructors' satisfaction, or listening to muddled addresses on alternating current.

At the moment of midnight, December 31, 1917, I stood with some acquaintances in a camp finely overlooking the whole Ypres battlefield. It was bitterly cold, and the deep snow all round lay frozen. We drank healths, and stared out across the snowy miles to the line of casual flares, still rising and floating and dropping. Their writing on the night was as the earliest scribbling of children, meaningless; they answered none of the questions with which a watcher's eyes were painfully wide. Midnight; successions of coloured lights from one point, of white pendants from another, bullying salutes of guns in brief bombardment, echoes racing into space, crackling of machine-guns small on the tingling air; but the sole answer to unspoken but importunate questions was the line of lights in the same relation to Flanders and our lives as at midnight a year before. All agreed that 1917 had been a sad offender. All observed that 1918 did not look promising at its birth, or commissioned 'to solve this dark enigma scrawled in blood.'

The thaw came, just as our 'examination' took place, and soon I rejoined the battalion in a bleak camp north-east of Ypres. They had been holding a position at Westroosebeke, where their main enemy was the weather, flooding them out of all shelter, and sending up the figures of 'trench feet,' an ailment now treated as a military crime! It was their last tour in the Salient for the present. A reckless, disunited spirit seemed to be working among them. I found to my anger that the battalion was in the temporary command of one of our old companies, not the most cordial, who had been attached to the staff for some time, and whose industry and self-esteem had grown altogether in excess of his tact and sincerity. I also found that my turn for leave had come round again. The new commander called for me with assumed and patronizing jocularity and 'young-fellowed' me over this coincidence. But now I had my revenge. I said I would not give up the leave if I could help it; it had been against my own desire that I had been sent to the signal school for two months, and so on. So away from St Jean with its new railway siding and its prodigious new crater, caused by some unlucky private dropping a fuse beside a dump, away from a battalion headquarters of sycophancy (so I thought) I went next evening. Before going, Olive and I walked round our old assembly positions of July 31, now clustered with round-roofed Nissen huts, and traversed with elaborately drained roads. We could not recapture ourselves at all! We also went to a lecture by a war correspondent, who invited questions, whereon a swarthy old colonel rose and said, 'The other day I was obliged to take part in a battle. I afterwards read a war correspondent's account of the battle, which proved to me that I hadn't been there at all. Will the lecturer explain that, please?'

xxvii

My Luck

During my leave the battalion went south, and as I got on the return train at Boulogne I knew that I was in for a prodigiously long and cold journey. It ended after an icy age at Péronne, with the famous Somme's frost-blue streams hurrying by, and old round towers standing firm; but perhaps the extraordinary German strongholds built in concrete under the station and elsewhere looked firmer. There were warning notice-boards outside these, and German bombs and boxes of explosives were still lying about in the entrances of some. Civilian life was as yet inactive in Péronne, nor could I find an estaminet open. This city had been in the same state, perhaps, after Waterloo. From here I went on to Mont St Quentin, and found some of the battalion shivering in bare linen-windowed huts on a bleak hill.

The next month was principally passed in the trenches just south of Gouzeaucourt. At first the whole area was deathly still, as though no war ever happened here. The civilians had not yet attempted to resume their properties and all the farms for miles were only shells of brick. It was truly a devastated area, apart from all question of the cutting down of orchards and the dynamiting of churches or cross-roads. Upon our arrival (in open trucks on a light railway) a heavy hoar-frost was loading the trees and telegraph wires and all projections and points with beards of greyish crystal – a singular sight, and the air's near whiteness thickened into the impenetrable at a few yards' distance. Dry weeds stood without a quiver on the fallows wherever one went. This solemn muteness and slumber of nature was not the only cause why the trenches were peaceful here, at our incoming; there was a great space between our line and the Germans, and besides it appeared that both sides were garrisoning their defences with the fewest possible men. The British Army was in process of reorganization and extension southward, and that accounted for the scarcity of immediate reserves. The men in the line were to all appearances the only troops, save for supply and so forth, between the Germans and the Atlantic. But the Americans were coming, and were beginning to be talked of in millions.

Our position was extensive, and included two 'strong points,' called Quentin Redoubt and Gauche Wood. The actual front trench east of these was a straggling ill-sited concern. West of them stretched a valley and a railway, parallel with the front, and a ridge, again parallel; under the ridge, in a cutting, battalion headquarters and supporting companies lived; thence, overland, one walked by the duckboards or the tramway back to a group of buildings commanding the support battalion's positions, called Revelon. The grassy tableland was incised with trenches, some achieved, more inchoate – too many intentions of trenches, perhaps. A little wire made the 'system' slightly stronger. This area was all to be involved in the battle of March 21, of which some rumours were already adrift among us, and the battalion was used not only to hold the position but also, simultaneously, to fortify it in every detail. Some argued that there was to be an attack by the British, us, and therefore all the labour, all the working-parties came to pass; but that did not console some others. There is no pleasing your ancient infantryman. Attack him, or cause him to attack, he seems equally disobliging.

Mutual molestation, at first unnoticed, gradually increased, until the ground was liberally shelled in routine. At first battalion head-quarters under the ridge lived and laughed in a light hut above ground, but presently they divided their time judiciously between it and a tunnel deep down. Shells clanged down in the sunk lane, and the valley and railway between us and the firing line were transformed into a savage place. There was no trench across; and waterlogged hollows compelled the use of regular tracks, besides which a system of wiring existed only permitting those tracks. At the gaps in the wire one found oneself suddenly in the middle of a bursting salvo, but the ground was luckily soft. A minefield, rumoured to exist at this point, might add a picturesque effect to one's last appearance.

Here several duties were assigned to me, but especially the control of the signallers and observers. Our observers could see well behind the German lines, but it was surprising how little effective evidence could be picked up. Indeed, daylight movement on the other side was now a rarity. Asked to give the gunners a target, the best that Corporal Sands, Clifford's old assistant and now, by the hand of death, his successor, could do was to recommend for punishment some harmless sentry smoking his china pipe in a quarry, who promptly went inside as the British shell went some furlongs over. The silence and inertia in the German trenches were a puzzle, and the old remark about 'holding the line with a man and a boy' was passed round among us. One might candidly sit, as I did, upon our parapet, and spend several minutes looking at the opposite line and the ruins and expensive cemetery of Villers Guislain, without any disaster. One night, the whole battalion, 'together with 14th Hants, 13th R. Sussex, Gloucesters and RE's,' was ordered to put out wire in No Man's Land, and although such an order created the usual terrible imaginings, the reality was almost like a practical joke. Conversation went on among the men, the wire was uncoiled with all possible noise, the jangling tin crosses on the ends of the reels were allowed full voice, company commanders bawled for sergeant-majors – No Man's Land became (to speak comparatively) a parade. Worley was the specialist in charge, and he ran about with his favourite gloves on, putting mistakes right here, and fancy touches on there, and telling me loudly the work was going on well – 'is the old General about, d'you know, sir?' At last a machine-gun was turned on us, but the wire was in place, and no harm was done.

The machine-gun seemed to play particularly on a corner of Gauche Wood called Gun Post, over a deep dugout used as battalion head-quarters for this extensive wiring operation. I was standing there, taking breath after a little exploration in front of the wire, when the General arrived, and pushed through the waiting men there to the fire-step, which he mounted, to look about. As the bullets had just struck the sandbags at that spot, I ventured to ask him to avoid it, which he did, calling me by name and with great gentleness, adding, 'I will go down to see Colonel Millward, Blunden.' This I record, for I think this was the last occasion on which this redoubtable, dry, often tormenting yet meritorious commander spoke to me, and it seemed to me that even in those simple words he expressed in his own quaint fashion a kindly appreciation of my now lengthy period under his command.

Strewn about this sector were relics of the Cambrai fight of the previous November, cavalry lances, guns with crumpled barrels, tanks burnt out, German machine-gun belts and carriers, and a few dead, preserved by the cold weather. The salvage artists had a little head-quarters in Heudicourt behind, to which with the aid of the light railway (operated by American engineers, men of splendid but risky ease of mind) they carried tons of miscellanies. Probably it was the principal side-show in the divisional area: for of amusement and the variety of ordinary billets there was nothing here. It was believed that presently there would be motor trips to Amiens. Meanwhile, days came and went, and every available man was holding the trenches, or working in them, or combining the warrior and the workman.

In the effort to provide alternative communications of all sorts, I one evening climbed a tall thin tree in Gauche Wood with a signalling lamp, which I fixed there; and then attempted a test, flashing a few words to battalion headquarters. By ill luck and stupidity the direction was wrong, the Germans opposite could detect the flashes, and a machine-gun began pecking at the wood. I made a lucky jump.

Everyone began to feel the strain of sleeplessness and a relief was expected. One weary private, having to express himself, chose the Brigade-Major on his morning round as the object of his satire: '*Look* at 'im,' he cried to his embarrassed neighbours. 'Milintary Cross an' all – look, chum.' The Brigade-Major was himself a humorist and saved the satirist from some grim expiation. While relief was still expected, I was shown a Brigade message referring to me, and applying to me the same treatment as had already taken Vidler and others from us – namely, six months' duty at a training centre in England. This order was, like all my recent movement orders, good and bad, too; but it seemed time I went. Not that my nerves were spent – I felt better than usual in that respect; but I was uneasy in my job, and could not bring myself into the proper relations with my seniors. Besides, the battalion altogether was now strange and disordered. Doctor Crassweller, whose wit and wisdom and Wilsonian aspect had been our delight since he came to the battalion, would hear no sentiment from me on this occasion. He gleamed satisfaction as if he were going into peace and not me; he passed on to me the kindest things he had ever heard said about me; and he warned me on no account to volunteer to return before my time, for by Nature's ordinance such an action was equal to suicide. I hated to mention to my old friends, such as Sergeant Ashford, that I was departing. I scarcely dared to face my servant Shearing, now wearing his Military Medal for admirable courage in last September's Menin Road massacre. Poor Ashford stood, delighted for my sake, but not glad that I should go; old hands were now very few; he looked between smiles and tears, tapped with his foot, took my hand, and I think he then divined that it must be his own fate to stay in Flanders. All congratulated me, but I felt I ought to have been in a position to congratulate them.

Some unanalysed notion led me to go round the battalion trenches thoroughly, the last day I was there, and the walk was lively, for most of the crucial points were being 'registered' by German guns; the railway valley was now in a poor state, and men did not loiter there.

One or two nights had been particularly anxious and bombarded ones, and the future here would evidently be much the same as that of Ypres. It was some comfort to be told that the battalion would be relieved in a night or two; in the belief, which was a delusion, I said good-bye, and went away. The long duckboard track to Revelon Farm was for the moment quiet, and I was thankful, for having made the severance from my surviving friends I was unashamedly eager to reach England. Had a shell come, I thought I should have exemplified in action the mild joke then current:

A. 'Did you hear that shell just now?'
B. 'I did. Twice. Once when it passed me, and again when I passed it.'

I passed a night with Maycock, ruddy-faced and buoyant as ever, at the transport lines. Old Swain was actually Adjutant now, grey-headed as he was, so I had already bidden him farewell. Then next day the mess cart took me and my valise to the nearest station; we nearly lost the train; my servant hurled the valise into the horse-truck just in time, and my trench career was over. Let me look out again from the train on the way to England. We travel humbly and happily over battlefields already become historic, bewildering solitudes over which the weeds are waving in the mild moon, houseless regions where still there are lengths of trenches twisting in and out, woods like confused ship-masts where amateur soldiers, so many of them, accepted death in lieu of war-time wages; at last we come to the old villages from which the battle of 1916 was begun, still rising in mutilation and in liberation. Then – not troubling overmuch about those droves of graceless tanks, exercising and racing on the hill-top – we view Albert, pretty well revived, its tall chimneys smoking, its rosy roofs renewed and shining, and all about it the fields tilled, and young crops greening. No need any longer for that old swaggering signboard, To BAPAUME ▶▶▶ . The mercy of nature advances. Is it true?

What, says someone, filling a pipe, *haven't you heard? the Haig Line, being dug by labour corps somewhere back here? About time, too*, another comments; *and I hope it's not the only one.* I wonder why they are concerned, for it is fifty miles behind the British line. A third: *Poor old France, hope I never see the damned place again.* I fear that I do not take these utterances very seriously, looking out on the tranquillized valley of the Ancre, wishing I might walk along as far as Hamel now and see if the apple trees (it cannot be that those, too, perished) are not still able to put forth their blossoms. But here is Buire-sur-Ancre, where we must change our train, and wait indefinitely for the next; and while we prowl inspectingly in the way of the fighting man round huts and possibly useful stores, the willows and waters in the hollow make up a picture so silvery and unsubstantial that one would spend a lifetime to paint it. Could any countryside be more sweetly at rest, more alluring to naiad and hamadryad, more incapable of dreaming a field-gun? Fortunate it was that at the moment I was filled with this simple joy. I might have known the war by this time, but I was still too young to know its depth of ironic cruelty. No conjecture that, in a few weeks, Buire-sur-Ancre would appear much the same as the cataclysmal railway cutting by Hill 60, came from that innocent greenwood. No destined anguish lifted its snaky head to poison a harmless young shepherd in a soldier's coat.

A Supplement of Poetical
Interpretations and Variations

A House in Festubert

With blind eyes meeting the mist and moon
And yet with blossoming trees robed round,
With gashes black, itself one wound,
Surprising still it stands its ground;
    Sad soul, here stay you.

It held, one time, such happy hours;
The tables shone with smiles and filled
The hungry – Home! their home is ours;
We house it here and laugh unkilled.
    Hoarse gun, now, pray you—.

It knew the hand and voice of Sleep,
Sleep was its friend and nightly came,
And still the bony laths would keep
One friendship, but poor Sleep's gone lame.
    O poisoner, Mahu!

A hermit might have built a cell
Among those evergreens, beside
That mellow wall: they serve as well
For four lean guns. Soft, hermits, hide,
    Lest pride display you.

It hived the bird's call, the bee's hum,
The sunbeams crossing the garden's shade –
So fond of summer! still they come,
But steel-born bees, birds, beams invade.
    – Could summer betray you?

The Guard's Mistake

The chapel at the crossways bore no scar,
There never a whining covey of shells yet pounced;
The calm saints in the chapel knew no war,
No meaning there the horizon's roars announced;
    We halted, and were glad; the country lay,
    After our marching, like a sabbath day.

Round the still quadrangle of the great farm
The company soon had settled their new home;
The cherry-clusters beckoned every arm,
The brook ran wrinkling by with playful foam,
       And when the guard was at the main gate set,
       Surrounding pastoral urged them to forget.

So out upon the road, gamekeeper-like,
The cowman now turned warrior measured out
His up-and-down *sans* fierce 'bundook and spike,'
Under his arm a cudgel brown and stout;
       With pace of comfort and kind ownership,
       And philosophic smile upon his lip.

It seemed a sin to soil the harmonious air
With the parade of weapons built to kill.
But now a flagged car came ill-omened there;
The crimson-mottled monarch, shocked and shrill,
       Sent our poor sentry scampering for his gun,
       Made him once more 'the terror of the Hun.'

Two Voices

'There's something in the air,' he said
  In the farm parlour cool and bare;
Plain words, which in his hearers bred
  A tumult, yet in silence there
All waited; wryly gay, he left the phrase,
Ordered the march, and bade us go our ways.

  'We're going South, man'; as he spoke
  The howitzer with huge ping-bang
Racked the light hut; as thus he broke
  The death-news, bright the skylarks sang;
He took his riding-crop and humming went
Among the apple-trees all bloom and scent.

  Now far withdraws the roaring night
  Which wrecked our flower after the first
Of those two voices; misty light
  Shrouds Thiepval Wood and all its worst;
But still 'There something in the air' I hear,
And still 'We're going South, man,' deadly near.

Illusions

Trenches in the moonlight, allayed with lulling moonlight,
Have had their loveliness; when dancing dewy grasses
Caressed us stumping along their earthy lanes;
When the crucifix hanging over was strangely illumined,
And one imagined music, one ever heard the brave bird
In the sighing orchards flute above the weedy well.
There are such moments; forgive me that I throne them,
Nor gloze that there comes soon the nemesis of beauty,

In the fluttering relics that at first glimmer awakened
Terror – the no-man's ditch suddenly forking:
There, the enemy's best with bombs and brains and courage!
– Soft, swift, at once be animal and angel –
But O no, no, they're Death's malkins dangling in the wire
     For the moon's interpretation.

Escape

A Colonel –
     There are four officers, this message says,
     Lying all dead at Mesnil.
     One shell pitched clean amongst 'em at the foot
     Of Jacob's Ladder. They're all Sussex men.
     I fear poor Flood and Warne were of that party.
     And the Brigade wants them identified . . .
A Mind –
     Now God befriend me,
     The next word not send me
     To view those ravished trunks
     And hips and blackened hunks.
A Colonel –
     No, not you, Bunny, you've just now come down.
     I've something else for you.
               Orderly!
                     (*Sir!*)

Find Mr Wrestman.

Preparations for Victory

My soul, dread not the pestilence that hags
The valley; flinch not you, my body young,
At these great shouting smokes and snarling jags
Of fiery iron; as yet may not be flung
The dice that claims you. Manly move among
These ruins, and what you must do, do well;
Look, here are gardens, there mossed boughs are hung
With apples whose bright cheeks none might excel,
And there's a house as yet unshattered by a shell.

'I'll do my best,' the soul makes sad reply,
'And I will mark the yet unmurdered tree,
The tokens of dear homes that court the eye,
And yet I see them not as I would see.
Hovering between, a ghostly enemy.
Sickens the light, and poisoned, withered, wan,
The least defiled turns desperate to me.
The body, poor unpitied Caliban,
Parches and sweats and grunts to win the name of Man.

Days or eternities like swelling waves
Surge on, and still we drudge in this dark maze;
The bombs and coils and cans by strings of slaves
Are borne to serve the coming day of days;
Pale sleep in slimy cellars scarce allays
With its brief blank the burden. Look, we lose;
The sky is gone, the lightless, drenching haze
Of rainstorm chills the bone; earth, air are foes,
The black fiend leaps brick-red as life's last picture goes.

Come On, My Lucky Lads

O rosy red, O torrent splendour
   Staining all the Orient gloom,
O celestial work of wonder –
   A million mornings in one bloom!

What, does the artist of creation
   Try some new plethora of flame,
For his eye's fresh fascination?
   Has the old cosmic fire grown tame?

In what subnatural strange awaking
   Is this body, which seems mine?
These feet towards that blood-burst making,
   These ears which thunder, these hands which twine

On grotesque iron? Icy-clear
   The air of a mortal day shocks sense,
My shaking men pant after me here.
   The acid vapours hovering dense,

The fury whizzing in dozens down,
   The clattering rafters, clods calcined,
The blood in the flints and the trackway brown –
   I see I am clothed and in my right mind;

The dawn but hangs behind the goal,
   What is that artist's joy to me?
Here limps poor Jock with a gash in the poll,
   His red blood now is the red I see,

The swooning white of him, and that red!
   These bombs in boxes, the craunch of shells,
The second-hand flitting round; ahead!
   It's plain we were born for this, naught else.

At Senlis Once

O how comely it was and how reviving
When with clay and with death no longer striving
    Down firm roads we came to houses
    With women chattering and green grass thriving.

Now though rains in a cataract descended,
We could glow, with our tribulation ended –
    Count not days, the present only
    Was thought of, how could it ever be expended?

Clad so cleanly, this remnant of poor wretches
Picked up life like the hens in orchard ditches,
    Gazed on the mill sails, heard the church-bell,
    Found an honest glass all manner of riches.

How they crowded the barn with lusty laughter,
Hailed the pierrots and shook each shadowy rafter,
    Even could ridicule their own sufferings,
    Sang as though nothing but joy came after!

The Zonnebeke Road

Morning, if this late withered light can claim
Some kindred with that merry flame
Which the young day was wont to fling through space!
Agony stares from each grey face.
And yet the day is come; stand down! stand down!
Your hands unclasp from rifles while you can;
The frost has pierced them to the bended bone!
Why, see old Stevens there, that iron man,
Melting the ice to shave his grotesque chin!

Go ask him, shall we win?
I never liked this bay, some foolish fear
Caught me the first time that I came in here;
That dugout fallen in awakes, perhaps,
Some formless haunting of some corpse's chaps.
True, and wherever we have held the line,
There were such corners, seeming-saturnine
For no good cause.
      Now where Haymarket starts,
That is no place for soldiers with weak hearts;
The minenwerfers have it to the inch.
Look, how the snow-dust whisks along the road
Piteous and silly; the stones themselves must flinch
In this east wind; the low sky like a load
Hangs over, a dead-weight. But what a pain
Must gnaw where its clay cheek
Crushes the shell-chopped trees that fang the plain –
The ice-bound throat gulps out a gargoyle shriek.
That wretched wire before the village line
Rattles like rusty brambles or dead bine,
And there the daylight oozes into dun;
Black pillars, those are trees where roadways run.
Even Ypres now would warm our souls; fond fool,
Our tour's but one night old, seven more to cool!
O screaming dumbness, O dull clashing death,
Shreds of dead grass and willows, homes and men,
Watch as you will, men clench their chattering teeth
And freeze you back with that one hope, disdain.

Trench Raid near Hooge

At an hour before the rosy-fingered
    Morning should come
To wonder again what meant these sties,
These wailing shots, these glaring eyes,
    These moping mum,

Through the black reached strange long rosy fingers
    All at one aim
Pretending and bending: down they swept,
Succession of similars after leapt
    And bore red flame

To one small ground of the eastern distance,
    And thunderous touched;
East then and west false dawns fan-flashed
And shut, and gaped; false thunders clashed.
    Who stood and watched

Caught needled horror from the desperate pit
    Which with ten men
Was centre of this. The blood burnt, feeling
The fierce truth there and the last appealing,
    'Us? Us? Again?'

Nor rosy dawn at last appearing
    Through the icy shade
Might mark without trembling the new deforming
Of earth that had seemed past further storming.
    Her fingers played,

One thought, with something of human pity
    On six or seven
Whose looks were hard to understand,
But that they ceased to care what hand
    Lit earth and heaven.

Concert Party: Busseboom

The stage was set, the house was packed,
 The famous troop began;
Our laughter thundered, act by act;
 Time light as sunbeams ran.

Dance sprang and spun and neared and fled,
 Jest chirped at gayest pitch,
Rhythm dazzled, action sped
 Most comically rich.

With generals and lame privates both
 Such charms worked wonders, till
The show was over: lagging loth
 We faced the sunset chill;

And standing on the sandy way,
 With the cracked church peering past,
We heard another matinée,
 We heard the maniac blast

Of barrage south by Saint Eloi,
 And the red lights flaming there
Called madness: Come, my bonny boy,
 And dance to the latest air.

To this new concert, white we stood;
 Cold certainty held our breath;
While men in the tunnels below Larch Wood
Were kicking men to death.

Rural Economy
(1917)

There was winter in those woods
    And still it was July:
There were Thule solitudes
    With thousands huddling nigh;
There the fox had left his den,
The scraped holes hid not stoats but men.

To these woods the rumour teemed
    Of peace five miles away;
In sight, hills hovered, houses gleamed
    Where last perhaps we lay
Till the cockerels bawled bright morning and
The hours of life slipped the slack hand.

In sight, life's farm sent forth their gear,
    Here rakes and ploughs lay still,
Yet, save some curious clods, all here
    Was raked and ploughed with a will.
The sower was the ploughman too,
And iron seeds broadcast he threw.

What husbandry could outdo this?
    With flesh and blood he fed
The planted iron that nought amiss
    Grew thick and swift and red,
And in a night though ne'er so cold
Those acres bristled a hundredfold.

Why, even the wood as well as field
    This thoughtful farmer knew
Could be reduced to plough and tilled,
    And if he planned, he'd do;
The field and wood, all bone-fed loam,
Shot up a roaring harvest home.

E. W. T.: On the Death of his Betty

And she is gone, whom, dream or truth,
You lived for in this wreck of youth,
    And on your brow sits age,
    Who soon has won his siege.

My friend, you will not wish a word
Of striven help in this worst gird
    Of fortune as she gets
    From us our race's debts.

I see you with this subtlest blow
Like a stunned man softly go;
    Then you, love-baffled boy,
    Smile with a mournful joy.

Thereat I read, you plainly know
The time draws near when the fierce foe
    Shall your poor body tear
    And mix with mud and air.

Your smile is borne in that foredoom,
Beaten, you see your victory bloom,
    And fortune cheats her end,
    And death draws nigh, a friend.

Battalion in Rest

Some found an owl's nest in the hollow skull
Of the first pollard from the malthouse wall;
   Some hurried through the swarming sedge
   About the ballast-pond's green edge,
And flashed through sunny deeps like boys from school;
All was discovery, love and laughter all.

The girls along the dykes of those moist miles
Went on raft boats to take their cows afield,
   And eyes from many an English farm
   Saw and owned the mode had charm;
One might well mark the silence and the smiles;
With such sweet balms, our wounds must soon be healed.

The jovial sun sprang up as bright each day
As fancy's sun could be, and climbed, heaven's youth,
   To make the marching mornings cheat
   Still-hectoring Mars of his receipt –
Who cannot hear the songs that led the way,
See the trim companies with their eyes on truth?

At evening, by the lonely white-walled house,
Where 'Que-C'est-Drôle' and 'Mon Dieu' stole to glance,
   One bold platoon all turned to players
   With masquerade and strumming airs;
The short clown darted nimble as a mouse,
The tambourine tapped out the stiff-stepped dance.

A shadowed corner suddenly found voice
As in the dusk I passed; it bade me stay.
    The bottle to my lips was raised –
    God help us, Sergeant, I was mazed
By that sharp fire your wine – but I rejoice!
Could I but meet you again at the end o' the day!

Not seldom, soft by meadows deep in dew,
Another lit my soul with his calm shine.
    There were cadences and whispers
    In his ways that made my vespers –
A night-piece fitting well that temple blue
Where stars new trembled with delight's design.

Vlamertinghe:
Passing the Château, July, 1917

'And all her silken flanks with garlands drest' –
But we are coming to the sacrifice.
Must those have flowers who are not yet gone West?
May those have flowers who live with death and lice?
This must be the floweriest place
That earth allows; the queenly face
Of the proud mansion borrows grace for grace
Spite of those brute guns lowing at the skies.
Bold great daisies' golden lights,
Bubbling roses' pinks and whites –
Such a gay carpet! poppies by the million;
Such damask! such vermilion!
But if you ask me, mate, the choice of colour
Is scarcely right; this red should have been duller.

Third Ypres

Triumph! How strange, how strong had triumph come
On weary hate of foul and endless war
When from its grey gravecloths awoke anew
The summer day. Among the tumbled wreck
Of fascined lines and mounds the light was peering,
Half-smiling upon us, and our newfound pride;
The terror of the waiting night outlived,
The time too crowded for the heart to count
All the sharp cost in friends killed on the assault.
No hook of all the octopus had held us,
Here stood we trampling down the ancient tyrant.
So shouting dug we among the monstrous pits.
Amazing quiet fell upon the waste,
Quiet intolerable to those who felt
The hurrying batteries beyond the masking hills
For their new parley setting themselves in array
In crafty forms unmapped.

                    No, these, smiled Faith,
Are dumb for the reason of their overthrow.
They move not back, they lie among the crews
Twisted and choked, they'll never speak again.
Only the copse where once might stand a shrine
Still clacked and suddenly hissed its bullets by.
The War would end, the Line was on the move,
And at a bound the impassable was passed.
We lay and waited with extravagant joy.

Now dulls the day and chills; comes there no word
From those who swept through our new lines to flood
The lines beyond? but little comes, and so
Sure as a runner time himself's accosted.
And the slow moments shake their heavy heads,
And croak, 'They're done, they'll none of them get through.'

They're done, they've all died on the entanglements,
The wire stood up like an unplashed hedge and thorned
With giant spikes – and there they've paid the bill.'
Then comes the black assurance, then the sky's
Mute misery lapses into trickling rain,
That wreathes and swims and soon shuts in our world,
And those distorted guns, that lay past use,
Why – miracles not over! – all a-firing!
The rain's no cloak from their sharp eyes. And you,
Poor signaller, you I passed by this emplacement,
You whom I warned, poor daredevil, waving your flags,
Among this screeching I pass you again and shudder
At the lean green flies upon the red flesh madding.
Runner, stand by a second. Your message. – He's gone.
Falls on a knee, and his right hand uplifted
Claws his last message from his ghostly enemy,
Turns stone-like. Well I liked him, that young runner,
But there's no time for that. O now for the word
To order us flash from these drowning roaring traps
And even hurl upon that snarling wire?
Why are our guns so impotent?

        The grey rain,
Steady as the sand in an hourglass on this day,
Where through the window the red lilac looks,
And all's so still, the chair's odd click is noise –
The rain is all heaven's answer, and with hearts
Past reckoning we are carried into night
And even sleep is nodding here and there.
The second night steals through the shrouding rain.
We in our numb thought crouching long have lost
The mockery triumph, and in every runner
Have urged the mind's eye see the triumph to come
The sweet relief, the straggling out of hell
Into whatever burrows may be given
For life's recall. Then the fierce destiny speaks.
This was the calm, we shall look back for this.

The hour is come; come, move to the relief!
Dizzy we pass the mule-strewn track where once
The ploughman whistled as he loosed his team;
And where he turned home-hungry on the road,
The leaning pollard marks us hungrier turning.
We crawl to save the remnant who have torn
Back from the tentacled wire, those whom no shell
Has charred into black carcasses – Relief!
They grate their teeth until we take their room,
And through the churn of moonless night and mud
And flaming burst and sour gas we are huddled
Into the ditches where they bawl sense awake,
And in a frenzy that none could reason calm
(Whimpering some, and calling on the dead),
They turn away: as in a dream they find
Strength in their feet to bear back that strange whim
Their body.
                    At the noon of the dreadful day
Our trench and death's is on a sudden stormed
With huge and shattering salvoes, the clay dances
In founts of clods around the concrete sties,
Where still the brain devises some last armour
To live out the poor limbs.
                                      This wrath's oncoming
Found four of us together in a pillbox,
Skirting the abyss of madness with light phrases,
White and blinking, in false smiles grimacing.
The demon grins to see the game, a moment
Passes, and – still the drum-tap dongs my brain
To a whirring void – through the great breach above me
The light comes in with icy shock and the rain
Horribly drips. Doctor, talk, talk! if dead
Or stunned I know not; the stinking powdered concrete,
The lyddite turns me sick – my hair's all full
Of this smashed concrete. O, I'll drag you, friends,
Out of the sepulchre into the light of day,

For this is day, the pure and sacred day.
And while I squeak and gibber over you,
Look, from the wreck a score of field-mice nimble,
And tame and curious look about them; (these
Calmed me, on these depended my salvation).
There comes my sergeant, and by all the powers
The wire is holding to the right battalion,
And I can speak – but I myself first spoken
Hear a known voice now measured even to madness
Call me by name.
                              'For God's sake send and help us,
Here in a gunpit, all headquarters done for,
Forty or more, the nine-inch came right through,
All splashed with arms and legs, and I myself
The only one not killed nor even wounded.
You'll send – God bless you!' The more monstrous fate
Shadows our own, the mind swoons doubly burdened,
Taught how for miles our anguish groans and bleeds,
A whole sweet countryside amuck with murder;
Each moment puffed into a year with death
Still wept the rain, roared guns,
Still swooped into the swamps of flesh and blood,
All to the drabness of uncreation sunk,
And all thought dwindled to a moan, Relieve!
But who with what command can now relieve
The dead men from that chaos, or my soul?

Pillbox

Just see what's happening, Worley. – Worley rose
And round the angled doorway thrust his nose,
And Sergeant Hoad went too, to snuff the air.
Then war brought down his fist, and missed the pair!
Yet Hoad was scratched by a splinter, the blood came,

And out burst terrors that he'd striven to tame.
A good man, Hoad, for weeks. *I'm blown to bits.*
He groans, he screams. *Come, Bluffer, where's your wits?*
Says Worley. *Bluffer, you've a blighty, man!*
All in the pillbox urged him, here began
His freedom: *Think of Eastbourne and your dad.*
The poor man lay at length and brief and mad
Flung out his cry of doom; soon ebbed and dumb
He yielded. Worley with a tot of rum
And shouting in his face could not restore him.
The ship of Charon over channel bore him.
All marvelled even on that most deathly day
To see this life so spirited away.

The Welcome

He'd scarcely come from leave and London,
Still was carrying a leather case,
When he surprised headquarters pillbox
And sat down sweating in the filthy place.

He was a tall, lean, pale-looked creature,
With nerves that seldom ceased to wince;
Past war had long preyed on his nature,
And war had doubled in horror since.

There was a lull, the adjutant even
Came to my hole: You cheerful sinner,
If nothing happens till half-past seven,
Come over then, we're going to have dinner.

But he went with his fierce red head;
We were sourly canvassing his jauntiness, when
Something happened at headquarters pillbox.
'Don't go there,' cried one of my men.

The shell had struck right into the doorway,
The smoke lazily floated away;
There were six men in that concrete doorway,
Now a black muckheap blocked the way.

Inside, one who had scarcely shaken
The air of England out of his lungs
Was alive, and sane; it shall be spoken
While any of those who were there have tongues.

Gouzeaucourt:
The Deceitful Calm

How unpurposed, how inconsequential
Seemed those southern lines when in the pallor
        Of the dying winter
        First we went there!

Grass thin-waving in the wind approached them,
Red roofs in the near view feigned survival,
        Lovely mockers, when we
        There took over.

There war's holiday seemed, nor though at known times
Gusts of flame and jingling steel descended
        On the bare tracks, would you
        Picture death there.

Snow or rime-frost made a solemn silence,
Bluish darkness wrapped in dangerous safety;
      Old hands thought of tidy
      Living-trenches!

There it was, my dear, that I departed,
Scarce a simpler traitor ever! There, too,
      Many of you soon paid for
      That false mildness.

The Prophet

It is a country,
Says this old guide-book to the Netherlands,
– Written when Waterloo was hardly over,
And justified 'a warmer interest
In English travellers' – Flanders is a country
Which, boasting not 'so many natural beauties'
As others, yet has history enough.
I like the book; it flaunts the polished phrase
Which our forefathers practised equally
To bury admirals or sell beaver hats;
Let me go on, and note you here and there
Words with a difference to the likes of us.
The author 'will not dwell on the temptations
Which many parts of Belgium offer'; he
'Will not insist on the salubrity
Of the air.' I thank you, sir, for those few words.
With which we find ourselves in sympathy.
And here are others: 'here the unrivalled skill
Of British generals, and the British soldier's
Unconquerable valour . . .' no, not us.
Proceed.
'The necessary cautions on the road' . . .

Gas helmets at the alert, no daylight movement?
'But lately much attention has been paid
To the coal mines.' Amen, roars many a fosse
Down south, and slag-heap unto slag-heap calls.
'The Flemish farmers are likewise distinguished
For their attention to manure.' Perchance.
First make your mixen, then about it raise
Your tenements; let the house and sheds and sties
And arch triumphal opening on the street
Inclose that Mecca in a square. The fields,
Our witness saith, are for the most part small,
And 'leases are unfortunately short.'
In this again perceive veracity;
At Zillebeke the cultivator found
That it was so; and Fritz, who thought to settle
Down by Verbrandenmolen, came with spades,
And dropped his spades, and ran more dead than alive.
Nor, to disclose a secret, do I languish
For lack of a long lease on Pilkem Ridge.

While in these local hints, I cannot wait
But track the author on familiar ground.
He comes from Menin, names the village names
That since rang round the world, leaves Zillebeke,
Crosses a river (so he calls that blood-leat
Bassevillebeek), a hill (a hideous hill),
And reaches Ypres, 'pleasant, well-built town.'
My Belgian Traveller, did no threatening whisper
Sigh to you from the hid profound of fate
Ere you passed thence, and noted 'Poperinghe.
Traffic in serge and hops'? (The words might still
Convey sound fact.) Perhaps some doomster's envoy
Entered your spirit when at Furnes you wrote,
'The air is reckoned unhealthy here for strangers.'
I find your pen, as driven by irony's fingers,
Defends the incorrectness of your map

216

With this; it was not fitting to delay,
Though 'in a few weeks a new treaty of Paris
Would render it useless.' Good calm worthy man,
I leave you changing horses, and I wish you
Good food at Nieuport. – Truth did not disdain
This sometime seer, crass but Cassandra-like.

II Peter ii, 22
(1921)

Hark, the new year succeeds the dead,
The bells make haste, the news is spread;
    And day by day
    'Farther away,'
'Farther away' tolls through my head.

Here slinking Slyness rules the roost
And brags and pimps, as he was used
    Before the day,
    Now far away,
Saw him to's puny self reduced.

And Quarrel with her hissing tongue
And hen's eye gobbles gross along
    To snap that prey
    That marched away
To save her carcass, better hung.

Come, infant Hour, though much I fear
Thy bright will show more blackly clear
    How day by day
    Far fade away
The heights which crowned a deadlier year.

Recognition

Old friend, I know you line by line,
    The touch, the tone, the turn of phrase,
Old autumn day, beloved and mine,
    Returning after many days:
The ten years' journey since we bade farewell
No hinted change or loss in you would ever tell.

Your countenance still ripe and kind
    Gazes upon me, godlike day,
And finding you again I find
    The tricks of time all thrown away.
The recollected turns to here and now
Beneath the equipoising glory of your brow.

Now to your heaven the gossamers gleam,
    Still soaring in their trembling play;
Their rosy scarves are spied astream,
    Whence borne and blown no one could say –
All out and dancing in the blue profound,
The tranquil ultimation of the ages round.

And there's that narrow orchard grass,
    The last green luck for many a mile;
The patient lines of mules I pass,
    And then must stand and chaff awhile
With gallant Maycock, spurred and gaitered, glowing.
With this ripe sun, and red as any orchard growing,

This comrade, born to sow and stack,
    – A golden sheaf might seem his brother –
To-night will ride where the angry track
    Is death and ruin in a smother,
To-night I, too, must face the world's mad end –
But first we'll make this day, this godlike day our friend.

La Quinque Rue

O road in dizzy moonlight bleak and blue,
With forlorn effigies of farms besprawled,
With trees bitterly bare or snapped in two,
Why riddle me thus – attracted and appalled?
For surely now the grounds both left and right
Are tilled, and scarless houses undismayed
Glow in the lustrous mercy of sweet night,
And one may hear the flute or fiddle played.
Why lead me then
Through the foul-gorged, the cemeterial fen
To fear sharp sentries? Why do dreadful rags
Fur these bulged banks, and feebly move to the wind?
That battered drum, say why it clacks and brags?
Another and another! what's behind?
How is it that these flints flame out fire's tongue,
Shrivelling my thought? these collapsed skeletons,
What are they, and these iron hunks among?
Why clink those spades, why glare these startling suns
And topple to the wet and crawling grass,
Where the shrill briars in taloned hedges twine?
What need of that stopped tread, that countersign?
O road, I know those muttering groups you pass,
I know your art of turning blood to glass;
But, I am told, to-night you safely shine
To trim roofs and cropped fields; the error's mine.

The Ancre at Hamel: Afterwards

Where tongues were loud and hearts were light
    I heard the Ancre flow;
Waking oft at the mid of night
    I heard the Ancre flow.
I heard it crying, that sad rill,
    Below the painful ridge
By the burnt unraftered mill
    And the relic of a bridge.

And could this sighing river seem
    To call me far away,
And its pale word dismiss as dream
    The voices of to-day?
The voices in the bright room chilled
    And that mourned on alone;
The silence of the full moon filled
    With that brook's troubling tone.

The struggling Ancre had no part
    In these new hours of mine,
And yet its stream ran through my heart:
    I heard it grieve and pine,
As if its rainy tortured blood
    Had swirled into my own,
When by its battered bank I stood
    And shared its wounded moan.

'Trench Nomenclature'

Genius named them, as I live! What but genius could compress
In a title what man's humour said to man's supreme distress?
Jacob's Ladder ran reversed, from earth to a fiery pit extending
With not angels but poor Angles, those for the most part
    descending.
Thence *Brock's Benefit* commanded endless fireworks by two
    nations,
Yet some voices there were raised against the rival coruscations.
Picturedrome peeped out upon a dream, not Turner could surpass,
And presently the picture moved, and greyed with corpses and
    morass.
So down south; and if remembrance travel north, she marvels yet
At the sharp Shakespearean names, and with sad mirth her eyes are
    wet.
The Great Wall of China rose, a four-foot breastwork, fronting guns
That, when the word dropped, beat at once its silly ounces with
    brute tons;
Odd *Krab Krawl* on paper looks, and odd the foul-breathed alley
    twisted,
As one feared to twist there too, if *Minnie*, forward quean, insisted.
Where the Yser at *Dead End* floated on its bloody waters
Dead and rotten monstrous fish, note (east) *The Pike and Eel*
    headquarters.
Ah, such names and apparitions! name on name! What's in a name?
From the fabled vase the genie in his cloud of horror came.

A. G. A. V.

Rest you well among your race, you who cannot be dead;
Sleep lives in that country place, sleep now, pillow your head;
Time has been you could not sleep, would not if you could,
But the relief stands in the keep where you so nobly stood.

Ardour, valour, the ceaseless plan all agreed to be yours,
Wit with these familiar ran, when you went to the wars;
If one cause I have for pride, it is to have been your friend,
To have lain in shell-holes by your side, with you to have seen
    impend

The meteors of the hour of fire, to have talked where speech was
    love,
Where through fanged woods and maw-grey mire the rain and
    murder drove;
There unchanged and on your mark you laughed at some quaint clue,
And now, though time grows dull and dark, I hear, I bless you anew.

Sleep – bless you, that would not please you, gallantest dear.
Should I find you beneath yew trees? better to look for you here.
With those others whom well we know, who went so early away,
Will not rather gladden my view? on a dead, deathless day,

Riding into the ancient town, smiling scarcely aware,
Along the dale, over the down, into the drowsy square,
There to tarry in careless ways, in church, or shop, or inn,
Leisuring after fiery days; calm-shining, more than kin;

Though dim the guns of chaos roared upon the eastern gate,
Though every hour the clock-hand scored brought closer a
    desperate date –
Well shone you then, and I would will you freedom eternal there,
Vast trial past, and the proud sense still of vast to-morrows to dare.

Their Very Memory

Hear, O hear:
They were as the welling waters,
   Sound, swift, clear,
They were all the running waters'
   Music down the greenest valley.

   Might words tell
What an echo sang within me?
   What proud bell
Clangs the note that rang within me
   Then to be with those enlisted?

   When they smiled,
Earth's inferno changed and melted –
   Greenwood mild;
Every village where they halted
   Shone with them through square and alley.

   Now my mind
Faint and few records their showing,
   Brave, strong, kind –
I'd unlock you all their doings
   But the keys are lost and twisted.

   This still grows,
Through my land or dull or dazzling
   Their spring flows;
But to think of them's a fountain,
   Tears of joy and music's rally.

On Reading that the Rebuilding of Ypres approached Completion

I hear you now, I hear you, shy perpetual companion,
Whose deep whispers
Never wholly fail upon my twilight; but for months now
Too dimly quivered
About the crowded corridors of actions and the clamouring
Swarmed ingresses where like squinting cobblers and worse
    creatures
On a weary ship that moors in dock, with grimy hatches,
Cross-purpose jangles.

Those the master, with a sudden fountain anger, towering
By his mood a Cyclops,
Back has driven, back, and snivelling, cackling, down the ladder.
I, so springing,
Have lashed the buzzing bullies out, and in the freed air pause now,
Hearing you, whose face is ever one and ever million,
This dear dead one's, this dear living one's, no man's and all men's,
True map of Flanders.

Wordless language! well to me this moment making music,
Utmost union.
So, so, so we meet again; here we know our coexistence,
And your voice is
My self-utterance, while the region thus is hush and lonely,
Not a charlatan thought there left to gnaw my heart is skulking,
Nor one sunbeam sets the tingling atoms dancing by me
Like doubt's mad apings.

But my danger lies even here, even now worn weak and nerveless
I go drooping,
Heavy-headed, and would sleep thus lulled with your love's fulness.
Sharply awake me

With fierce words, cold as the fangs of bayonets in the frozen saps,
Simple as the fact that you must kill, or go for rations,
As clear as morning blue, as red and grotesque as the open mouths
Of winter corpses.

I hear you now: the voice, the voice of marching bowed battalions,
Of one strong soldier,
Now black-haired Daniels, now more saxon Clifford, now hale
    Worley –
O, speak. Our old tongue.
'I was thy neighbour once, thou rugged Pile, thou whiteness, Ypres,
How mighty in thy misery, how royal in thy ravishing,
With fingers brittle as ice, I champed and clattered by the convent
And shouted orders;

Which echoes scrambling on the snowy walls and eyeless bulwarks
Made haste to carry,
But they could not, for the curious air was overburdened
With ancient echoes.
Vaults below the convent, when they pitied and would shelter,
Scarce could lure me, counter-lured though eyelids pressed like
    roof-leads;
Nor such sights as the circling pigeons of poor St Martin held me
From my huge labours.

Blood-like swam the moon, the city's sable wounds lurked;
Still she cried out,
Be most constant! Thence with clumsy zeal and sacred cursing
Through the shrill grass,
Through the trapping thicket-thorns of death, that sudden planter,
While in the light of the moon and snow his blueness masked all faces,
Stern I went, the weaker kind most mercilessly heartening
To the shambles

All for her, that gat-toothed witch, that beauty at the butcher's,
To me intrusted;

Nor did I desert her, though without so much as a second's warning
Some harsh slash-hook
Slit my skull and poured out all the fountains of my senses;
Burst the blood-gates; still I came, and went and came to man her,
Left Posthoornstraat and Goldfish Château, joined with waxen
    hands the cleft trench,
Hating and loving.

She, with that, was sometime mild and from the spectre ruin
Herself seemed lifting;
Walking in some silent moments, to the glimmer of candles,
I smiled and marvelled
How the dusky houses in the rainy gloom with feigned renascence,
Stood for life, and surely from the opened doors would be duly
    coming
Women and lightfoot children, lover there in the lamplight grow to
    lover—
Death, stop that laughing!

Nor has ever been the man, not Milton with his angels,
Who found such chorus,
Such diapason and amazement in strange old oriental
Fantasy-places,
As I in gross and clod-like names of hamlets by the city;
The fame of Kemmel clanged, and Athens dulled: I listened
If one spoke of Zonnebeke with thronged imagination,
A dazing distance.

For words spoke at the *Mermaid*, I would not give the meanest
That I heard echoing
In some green-shuttered *Nachtegaal* or *Kasteel*, a brief evening,
While the panes were jumping;
Far less one of the sweet astounding jests and sallies
That dared contest with smoking salvoes the forlorn hope's attention,
That wreathed the burning steel that slew with man's eternal laurel
In that one city.

For her was much accomplished, and she will not forget me,
Whose name is Legion;
She will know who knew her best, and with his rough warm
     garment
Would have wrapt her;
Her midnight tears will ever well as greyly she remembers
The hillock's signifying tree, that choked and gouged and miry
Was like a cross, but such a cross that there no bleeding Figure
Might hang without tautology.

And mine she is; they now may build, sign and assign there,
Above bright doorways
Paint in gold their titles; shrine among their tufted gardens,
As did their elders,
The statues of their mild desire Arcadian: but I
Am in the soil and sap, and in the becks and conduits
My blood is flowing, and my sigh of consummation
Is the wind in the rampart trees.'

Another Journey from Béthune to Cuinchy

I see you walking
To a pale petalled sky,
And the green silent water
Is resting thereby;
It seems like bold madness
But that 'you' is I.

I long to interpret
That voice of a bell
So silver and simple,
Like a wood-dove-egg shell,
On the bank where you're walking –
It was I heard it well.

Undertones of War

At the lock the sly bubbles
Are dancing and dying,
Some the smallest of pearls,
Some moons, and all flying,
Returning, and melting –
You watched them, half-crying.

This is Marie-Louise,
You need not have told me –
I remember her eyes
And the Cognac she sold me –
It is you that are sipping it;
Even so she cajoled me.

Her roof and her windows
Were nothing too sound,
And here and there holes
Some forty feet round
(Antiquer than Homer)
Encipher the ground.

Do you jib at my tenses?
Who's who? you or I?
Do you own Béthune
And that grave eastward sky?
Béthune is miles off now,
'Ware wire and don't die.

The telegraph posts
Have revolted at last,
And old Perpendicular
Leans to the blast,
The rigging hangs ragging
From each plunging mast.

What else would you fancy,
For here it is war?
My thanks, you young upstart,
I've been here before –
I know this Division,
And hate this damned Corps.

'Kingsclere' hath its flowers,
And piano to boot;
The coolest of cellars,
– Your finest salute!
You fraudulent wretch –
You appalling recruit!

– O haste, for the darnel!
Hangs over the trench,
As yellow as the powder
Which kills with a stench!
Shall you go or I go?
Oh, I'll go – don't mench!

But both of us zigzag
Between the mossed banks,
And through thirsty chopped chalk
Where the red-hatted cranks
Have fixed a portcullis
With notice-board – thanks!

A mad world, my masters!
Whose masters? my lad,
If you are not I,
It is I who am mad;
Let's report to the company,
Your mess, egad.

Well, now, sir (though lime juice
Is nothing to aid)
This young fellow met me,
And kindly essayed
To guide me – but now it seems
I am betrayed.

He says he is I,
And that I am not he;
But the same omened sky
Led us both, we agree –
If we cannot commingle
Pray take him and me.

For where the numb listener
Lies in the dagged weed,
I'll see your word law,
And this youth has agreed
To let me use *his* name –
Take the will for the deed.

And what if the whistle
Of the far-away train
Come moan-like through mist
Over Coldstream Lane,
Come mocking old love
Into waking again?

And the thinkings of life,
Whether those of thy blood,
Or the manifold soul
Of field and of flood –
What if they come to you
Bombed in the mud?

Well, now as afore
I should wince so, no doubt,
And still to my star
I should cling, all about,
And muddy one midnight
We all will march out.

– Sir, this man may talk,
But he surely omits
That a crump any moment
May blow us to bits;
On this rock his identity-
Argument splits.

I see him walking
In a golden-green ground,
Where pinafored babies
And skylarks abound;
But that's his own business,
My time for trench round.

Flanders Now

There, where before no master action struck
The grim Fate in the face, and cried 'What now?'
Where gain and commonplace lay in their ruck,
And pulled the beetroots, milked the muddy cow,
Heard the world's rumours, wished themselves good luck,
And slept, and rose, and lived and died somehow –
A light is striking keen as angels' spears,
Brightness outwelling, cool as roses, there;
From every crossroad majesty appears,
Each cottage gleams like Athens on the air;
Ghosts by broad daylight, answered not by fears

But bliss unwordable, are walking there.
Who thirsts, or aches, or gropes as going blind?
Friend, drink with me at these fair-foliaged wells,
Or on the bruised life lay this unction kind,
Or mark this light that lives in lily-bells;
There rests and always shall the wandering mind,
Those clumsy farms to-day grow miracles:

Since past each wall and every common mark,
Field path and wooden bridge, there once went by
The flower of manhood, daring the huge dark,
The famished cold, the roaring in the sky.
They died in splendour, these who claimed no spark
Of glory save the light in a friend's eye.

Return of the Native

About the Ramparts, quiet as a mother
Leaving a child in dreams, the summer night
Cast a soft veil; the power beyond the stars
Was now intent upon the consonance
Of boughs and airs and earthy purities.

We stood, hard-watching in the eastward dark,
A glowing pyre and vapour by Hill Sixty,
And wondered who was mocking, Peace or War?
The last train answered with far-dying echoes,
And passed along the cutting; now the plain
Lay in its first sleep, all its dwellings slept

And called the night their own. The old law here
Had come again with peasant tread to claim
So full and unabated property.
That not one mark of a mad occupation

Might be conceived.
                We only, watching, seemed
The relics, if in truth we were not cheated
By dreaming ecstasies; could we have seen
The ordinance of eternity reversed,
And night disdained and dazzled into day
And day shot into gulfs of glaring gloom?
Man in our time, and with our help, became
A pale Familiar; here he struck the Sun,
And for a season turned the Sun to blood;
Many such nights as this his Witch and he
Unmasked their metal, and with poisonous blasts
Broke the fair sanctuary of this world's rest
And circumvented God. But now misrule
With all its burning rout had gone on the wind,
Leaving us with this south-west breeze to whisper
In bushes younger than the brows it cooled;
Foreheads still trenched with feverish wonderings
Of what was once Time's vast compulsion, now
Incapable to stir a weed or moth.
                          Ypres, 1929.

The Watchers

I heard the challenge 'Who goes there?'
Close-kept but mine through midnight air;
I answered and was recognized,
And passed, and kindly thus advised:
'There's someone crawling through the grass
By the red ruin, or there was,
And them machine-guns been a firin'
All the time the chaps was wirin',
So, sir, if you're goin' out
You'll keep your 'ead well down no doubt.'

When will the stern, fine 'Who goes there?'
Meet me again in midnight air?
And the gruff sentry's kindness, when
Will kindness have such power again?
It seems, as now I wake and brood,
And know my hour's decrepitude,
That on some dewy parapet
The sentry's spirit gazes yet,
Who will not speak with altered tone
When I at last am seen and known.

Made in the USA
Lexington, KY
19 February 2014